THE LONELY SKY

THE LONELY SKY

THE PERSONAL STORY OF AMERICA'S PIONEERING EXPERIMENTAL TEST PILOT

by William Bridgeman and Jacqueline Hazard

iUniverse, Inc.   New York   Bloomington

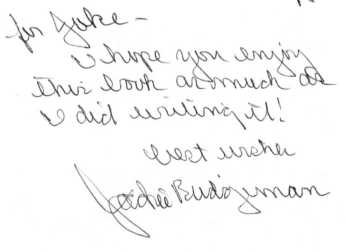

april 23, 010

for Jake –
I hope you enjoy
this book as much as
I did writing it!

best wishes

Jackie Bridgeman

The Lonely Sky
The personal story of America's pioneering experimental test pilot

iUniverse books may be ordered through booksellers or by contacting:

iUniverse
1663 Liberty Drive
Bloomington, IN 47403
www.iuniverse.com
1-800-Authors (1-800-288-4677)

Because of the dynamic nature of the Internet, any Web addresses or links contained in this book may have changed since publication and may no longer be valid.

ISBN: 978-1-4401-5870-4 (sc)
ISBN: 978-1-4401-5871-1 (dj)
ISBN: 978-1-4401-5872-8 (ebk)

Printed in the United States of America

iUniverse rev. date: 10/21/2009

Dedicated to the memory of

CAPTAIN NORMAN "BUZZ" MILLER, USN,

Commanding Officer of Bombing Squadron 109,
"The Reluctant Raiders"

PROLOGUE

This is the story of an experimental high-speed airplane and the test pilot who flew it.

The story of America's experimental airplanes, the supersonic pioneers, could begin in the dawn of a summer day above a German countryside. The year is 1942.

Out of the brightening sky an unarmed, stripped-down Mosquito, cameras whining, shot in low over the remote Nazi airstrip. The RAF officer again noticed the many peculiar-looking black streaks at the end of the runway; some as even as railroad tracks. Seconds later the little bomber disappeared into the west.

At Medmenham the developing laboratory of the RAF Photo Interpretation Unit verified the news once more. The Germans were busily experimenting with something radically different from anything the Allies had in the air—probably rockets and rocket-propelled aircraft. And there was little doubt, the even, parallel streaks were burned by the flames from a twin-jet fighter.

The United States had no such weapons. Upon our entry into the war a high-level decision was made. Only a fraction of our resources would be devoted to jet and rocket research. Time and men and money would be used to pour out and perfect more of what we had going already. The huge production machine would be uninterrupted while the conflict lasted.

But with the news from Medmenham, added to the top of the pile of intelligence reports from other sources, General Hap Arnold, chief of the Army Air Forces, appointed a special committee of scientists and engineers in the allied fields of aerodynamics to advise him on the future of aircraft and aircraft weapons. He particularly asked the committee to think about the aircraft not only of tomorrow but of 20 years from then. To head his advisory committee he chose, on the advice of his close friend Robert Millikan of the California Institute of Technology, a member of Millikan's staff, Dr. Theodore von Kármán.

As head of Arnold's Scientific Advisory Board, von Kármán, a long-time prober of supersonics and a strong advocate of applying its principles to the design of aircraft, began to explore the possibilities of a truly supersonic airplane.

At the same time the military services were demanding that manufacturers produce tactical aircraft capable of reaching speeds of 400 mph. The designers were handed the sizable task of molding a shell sleek and strong enough to reach this speed with the available, puny reciprocating engine.

It was true we had access to a jet engine. But it wasn't much more powerful than the engines we had already and it ate up twice the fuel. General Electric had put it together, at General Arnold's request, from plans of the British Whittle engine brought secretly into the country by Arnold in 1941. Arnold gave the job of wrapping a frame around the G.E. turbo-jet attempt to the young and enterprising Bell Company.

The result was America's first jet, the P-59. It flew valiantly enough late in 1942, but according to Arnold's own account of the experimental ship, its "legs weren't long enough" to successfully reach a target. The model never got into combat.

Arnold turned back to the "right-now" aircraft. He listened to the problems of the manufacturers who were successfully turning out the faster ships he had demanded. He talked to the combat pilots who flew the high-performing planes that were now coming off the line by the thousands.

"What can we do to improve performance?" he asked his fighter pilots.

"They're pretty hot right now, sir. If you make them any faster we won't be able to fly them. I dove my Mustang on an ME-109 last week . . . the controls froze up on me and she shook like a rivet handle. I couldn't pull her out of it. I was a fast thousand feet from the bottom before I could get the nose up."

A new problem. In the airplanes that reached the 400-mile-an-hour mark demanded by the military, pilots, diving in combat, were running into the raw edge of the speed of sound (Mach 1), into the air-monster, "compressibility," a phenomenon that eventually became more romantically known as the sound barrier.

The Germans and the Japs were not the only enemy that the fighter pilots had to face. There was the reef of the sound barrier, the dark area of speed where compressibility lurked to shake a plane to pieces or suck it out of control straight down into a hole in the ground.

An effect of high speed, compressibility was a phenomenon known to the aerodynamicists in theory for many years. Because of this phenomenon, it was generally agreed that flight at and beyond the speed of sound was impossible.

However, as a result of combat demands, aircraft had flown right into the monster and the scientists were caught with no answers. In order to get the answers, investigations into high speed were urgently needed. This need for all-out research into the unexplored area where compressibility lay was apparent to the aircraft industry, the Air Force, the Navy Bureau of Aeronautics, and the nation's aeronautical research establishment, the National Advisory Committee on Aeronautics.

It also became apparent that new tools to investigate the area were needed. Methods of reaching speeds where compressibility could be studied just didn't exist. Wind tunnels "choked" as speeds reached that of sound. Test pilots could dive into such transonic speeds, but it was too dangerous. There was only one answer: full-scale, high-speed experimental models, fitted with instrumentation recording devices, to fly in nature's big laboratory, the sky; airplanes that would do in level flight what had only been done in dives.

When things began to look pretty good in Europe, General Arnold became a champion of the "research-airplane" idea. By the end of 1943 the Navy, Air Force, and NACA held conferences at NACA headquarters in Washington to discuss the feasibility of such research airplanes.

Pursuing a slightly different course, Dr. von Kármán's Scientific Advisory Board had already stimulated the Air Force's interest in the long-range research approach to a supersonic airplane. General F. O. Carroll, in informal sessions with manufacturers, had brought up the idea of such an aircraft, not so much as an exploratory tool as an attempt toward a conventional-operating ship capable of supersonic speed in actual flight. Douglas Aircraft Company picked up the challenge and with their own resources assigned their then-small research-design group to come up with something. The project became known as X-3.

A year later, toward the last days of the war, Germany got her V-1 rockets and her jet-powered ME-262 and rocket-propelled ME-163B into the air. But they were too late. They were a futile attempt, a final bid; and their appearance caused more wonder than destruction.

The war in Europe was over. It was then that the final decision was made to go ahead with the hurry-up research-airplane program. Two projects were ordered: the Bell X-1, sponsored by the Air Force, and the Douglas D-558, sponsored by the Navy. Both projects were eventually to be tools that would enable NACA to find out all about high-speed flight.

The X-1, fitted with a rocket engine, was to fly briefly at transonic speed; while the D-558, using a turbo-jet engine, was designed to explore, for a longer period, in the high subsonic range.

On V-J Day a group of Navy, NACA, and Douglas engineers met in a conference room of the nearly deserted El Segundo plant to work out the details of the D-558. A year had passed since Ed Heineman's El Segundo staff had been offered the idea of the original experimental research plane. In that time advantages of the swept-back wing in cutting down compressibility were picked up from Germany after V-E Day.

The Navy project became two airplanes: the Phase I straight-winged D-558 and the Phase II D-558. The D-558-II utilized the swept wing and, in addition to the turbo-jet engine, it was equipped with a rocket engine similar to that in the Bell X-1. She was named Skyrocket.

Sometime later the Air Force signed a contract with Douglas to go on investigating with their X-3 project the possibilities of a true supersonic airplane. The X-3 was eventually ordered in 1949, to be added to the small stable of weird-shaped Navy- and Air Force-sponsored research airplanes, seven in all, including the Bell X-2, the Northrop X-4, and the Bell X-5.

While the airplanes that were to blast into the new frontier of flight were gradually pushing their way into existence, I was beginning my piloting career on Ford Island in the middle of Pearl Harbor. After a year of training at Pensacola, my first official duty at the Naval Air Station was Officer of the Day. The day was December 7, 1941.

CHAPTER I

The morning had begun gently, warm and fragrant, like most Honolulu mornings. Then, one hour after I had taken the duty on the week-end-deserted base, Sunday exploded. At once I was no longer a shiny new ensign; the old chiefs promoted me, within minutes after the first bomb dropped through Number 3 hangar, to an equal, a comrade pitching in against an awesome catastrophe.

Until this morning I had been an onlooker, respectfully staring up at the United States Navy; she answered my needs, she did the thinking. I had been taught very thoroughly to fly; the rest, the matter of decision, would wear off on me slowly as I grew into the organization.

It was disquieting to discover that the giant mother and father, the protector, needed me. If I felt any pride at being accepted, integrated all of a sudden, it was dampened by the unsettling awareness that I was the Navy.

And now in the welcome dark, I huddled around the radio with the rest of the PBY squadron in the shelter of Number 2 hangar. We discussed vacantly the day we had lived through, and we waited for the Japs to return. The weary drone of conversation was interrupted occasionally by the arrival of trucks that rolled up mysteriously to pass out food, coffee, and, finally, saw-horses and planks that were to be used for cots. All was done that could be done—carbines had been passed and trenches had been dug. The wounded had been found and carried down to the BOQ. There was nothing more to do.

From the little radio before which we attentively sat came the familiar voice of a Stateside news commentator. The sound of the voice at first was reassuring. It was the sound of home.

"We have lost the islands! We have backed up to the West Coast, where we will hold the enemy."

At home they had given us up. Now there was no doubt at all in my mind that we were trapped. The voice that dismissed us was a voice of authority. One I had heard since I was in high school. He was announcing our defeat to us. There was no recourse now but to wait. I slept.

The rough board under my back, the darkness of the now-enforced blackout, the image of a thousand screaming little Jap troops, bayonets pointed, climbing onto Ford Island didn't stop me from sleeping. Though I was now certain that Ford, a ship adrift headed for an iceberg, was helpless, I could escape into sleep.

0430 . . . it began. The ominous shrill of the sirens, 24 hours too late. The radar had picked up something—a squadron of Jap dive bombers or a seagull—and the sirens set off a warning.

Seven of us were ordered out into the predawn darkness from our wooden beds to look for the Japanese fleet. Out of 45 flying boats, only one PBY was capable of taking to the air.

I awoke as if a searchlight had flashed in my face. After a few hours' sleep my body was restored to the point where weariness no longer acted as a buffer against fear. I remembered yesterday and I was afraid.

One plane was going out to look for the enemy. Out there in the blackness every gun in the Japanese fleet was waiting for us. Where was my other sock?

The fat PBY wallows in the black water, ready for the crew. Her belly is sunk deep with the heavy load of fuel that is required to get us 700 miles out over the water, 100 miles across, and 700 miles back. A big piece of pie cut out of the Pacific.

She begins to taxi down the water runway; a boat before us sweeps the broken pieces of Navy out of our path as we move slowly through the graveyard that is Pearl. We lift heavily from the water, low out of the harbor, over the awkward, looming projections of battleship carcasses. The canefields pass beneath us and we head out into the "piece of pie."

Out of the wet darkness sliding by under us the sun is rising and the search begins. The searchers have little qualification for their mission. We are young, uninitiated, and bewildered. In a matter of hours, from an easy, unenterprising Navy life, we are dropped into the middle of war. We are to find the Jap fleet and report its position to the somewhat optimistic headquarters at Pearl

On our wings we carry bombs that we have been ordered to drop on the Japanese fleet. Two machine guns are warmed up every 30 minutes by gunners who will fire at the squadrons of Jap carrier planes that will fly out at us when we sight their nest.

To break the monotony, which is added to by the vibration of the ship, the noise from the engines, the constant attention on our particular duty, we make bets on the degree of drift. Although we make a joke of it, we are afraid of getting lost.

The sun is high now, burning a white path in the metallic ocean, blistering the eyes of the watch. We are all the way out. We change course and head out on the leg across the "piece of pie."

The constant flow of radio traffic is carefully decoded from a lead-bound decoding book. But the messages we break are not for us. Radio silence is kept with our home base—even that thin string of authority is cut from us. Back at Pearl they will send only to warn us of an attack.

We take a high-noon sight and the search is relieved by lunchtime. Coffee, turkey sandwiches, canned tomatoes; the meal unleashes nervous small talk.

Now we go back to our corners. We are on the way home. Just a half a day more of searching dutifully and finding nothing and maybe we will make it back, after all—that is, if we are still on course.

Radio silence is broken with a message to Pearl, a report on the patrol: NO HITS. NO RUNS. NO ERRORS.

Halfway back on the last 700 miles of the search the sun has lowered over the empty, darkening sea. The heat in the vibrating plane is lessened, the anxiety of the crew is lessened—we have not found the Jap fleet, we're going home. The enemy has evaporated.

It is night when we sight the unlighted harbor. Now all that remains between us and the small comforts that still remain on Ford is a landing. To separate the land from the water, we look for the blackest area—that is the harbor.

Hanging over the water at night, it is impossible to judge distance. The pilot must rely on instruments entirely.

In the faint light of the cockpit we attentively watch the calculating dials on the instrument panel. Speed is set at 77 knots and we begin our gradual descent of 200 feet per minute from a mile out. We drop gradually, holding at 77 knots. There it is! The short hissing, shish . . . shish . . . shish . . . shish of the small waves as the water feels the keel skim through it. Throttles off! The belly drops down into the water, rocks gently; we taxi up to the figures on the ramp waiting to pull us on shore.

No hits. No runs. No errors.

CHAPTER II

It had been almost two years since I had left Hawaii for uneventful, tedious duty in Australia, where I continued to search for the enemy in a PBY. And now, flying in from Sa Diego to Kaneohe on the windward side of Oahu, with the other members of the newly commissioned 109 Bombing Squadron, the island lay beneath me, healed up and bustling with the sure movements of offensive war. Under the roar of our starboard engines Pearl Harbor floated by, mended.

Things had altered since my last arrival, I had evolved from an obscure ensign into a lieutenant, j.g., and my fat, awkward flying boat had finally been replaced with a Goliath. Now I was the commander of the four-engine 4800-horsepower ship, something capable of going after the enemy.

Things had changed on the island too. At night it was ablaze with light. Over the field, beacon swords two miles high swept the sky. Honolulu wasn't hiding from anything.

We were expecting orders to join our sister squadron already in the Ellice Islands, and so each week was lived as if it would be the last that girls, liquor, and sleep would be available.

The war was "somewhere out there" as the first month lagged into two, then three, months. The sun was hot and the surfing was good at Waikiki. Our lumbering ex-Air Force bombers sat polished and painted, newly dressed in Navy blue and fitted with typical Navy engineering—an added gun there, extra armor plate, and the latest in long-range overwater navigation devices.

About 75 per cent of the crew that manned them were veterans, but everyone in the outfit was brand-new to Lieutenant Commander Norman "Buzz" Miller's first squadron. The duty that any of us had seen had been, for the most part, a pull-in-your-horns kind of duty, looking for the enemy, while hiding behind clouds.

But now the day of the negative search was over. The battle of Midway had been fought and won, the offensive war had begun, and we waited in Honolulu for the day we would be ordered out to join it.

While we waited, the Navy kept us busy flying—two hours in the morning, two hours in the afternoon. We were drilled with tedious repetition in tactical attack maneuvers.

In the late afternoons, when the "play-war" was finished for the day, we gathered on the beach to ride the surf; and as we lay stretched out in the warm sand the conversation dealt mainly with women and little with war or what was waiting in the string of islands, 2200 miles away. It could hardly be said we were enduring any hardship, our leisure interrupted only from time to time with a wave of anxiety. However, the amount of guilt suffered by any of us was quickly overcome by a night in Honolulu, and the war continued to remain a long way away.

The morning after a particularly hilarious evening, I was supporting myself with a cup of coffee in the squadron office when

Hal Bellew, a good-looking "live-it-up" character, stuck his head through the door in a rare state of excitement.

"Have you guys seen the plane in from Funafuti? God . . . " Coffee cups settled in saucers and we all clamored down to the field.

The ship stood with great authority on the runway, the paint peeled off in spots; careful, ugly patches marked her sides. There was no nonsense with the crew; everyone knew what to do. In the rear of the plane was a well-worn mattress and the emergency kits all had broken seals. The crew wore no ties; the sleeves of their grayed and faded khakies were frayed where they had been cut off above the elbows; side arms hung from their waists and their skin was leathered.

It wasn't any of the combat stories that the "old campaigners" told us, it was this used and weary B-24, landed triumphantly amid our manicured planes, that sobered us. The crew of the beat-up bomber watched with something close to amusement as we poked and peered at their ship. A bunch of eager boy scouts, respectfully asking questions about what "raiding" out of Funafuti was like. The black-burned crew had been out five months; they were old warriors.

The war had ceased to exist for me these last four months. But now, curiously, these men had flown out of it three days ago— Funafuti to Canton, across to Palmera and into Kaneohe. A bird out of a storm.

The visitor from our sister squadron set off a period of restlessness and rumor, resulting in heavier and longer drinking at night. The skipper occasionally joined the sessions at the officers' bar. After an hour or so he would disappear alone.

"Buzz" Miller was a quiet man with dark, Indian features and reddish-tan, smooth skin. He managed to accomplish what he wanted with a minimum of conversation; he had yet to lose his temper. The young skipper was friendly with his officers, but always there was that air of preoccupation about him. The enlisted men immediately respected Miller. He understood them; it was easy for him to see their point of view. He himself had entered Annapolis from the ranks.

Although none of us had ever seen the captain drunk, there wasn't one of his officers who could out drink him. I remember a morning in San Diego at the prim, other-era Coronado Hotel, before our Transpac. Bellew, who, second to the skipper, was the most respected drinker in the outfit, was feeling his way down the dark corridors of the old, Victorian building on his way down to the bar for a morning pickup. The old man was similarly indisposed and heading for his room. They passed each other and continued for several yards, then simultaneously they stopped, turned back to verify what they had just seen, and with obvious horror at the sight of each other painfully groaned in unison, "Good God!"

On duty, however, Miller never showed the effects of the night before. He stood stick-erect and because of his narrowness he appeared taller than the six feet he was. If he had nerves we never saw any evidence of them. Everything about Miller was hard and unyielding.

Then one morning the news appeared on the bulletin board with Miller's big signature under it:

> Attn all Personnel Bombing Sq. 109—As of December 3,
> 1943, the first echelon will leave for Apamama at 0900.
> Aircraft will stop over at Palmera and Canton en route.

Two days later we flew out to join the war. Apamama lay 75 miles southwest of Tarawa, the Jap fortress recently flattened and occupied by the Marines. It was a tiny atoll in the Jap-held Gilbert chain, part of the steppingstone path of islands used by the enemy to work their way deep into the southwest. Above the Gilberts were flung the Jap-mandated Marshall Islands and above them, north and west, lay the Mariannas and the Bonin Islands, leading like beads on a string to within 150 miles of Tokyo.

Admiral Halsey's surprise party had softened up the Marshalls the year before and now the big offensive was rumbling toward the Central Pacific.

The Navy Liberators were sent into Apamama beforehand to break down Jap resistance and stir things up generally through the Gilberts and the Marshalls, all the way up to Kwajalein at the top and Eniwetok in the neighboring Carolines. The two squadrons on Apamama were to act as raiders deep in enemy territory, keeping an eye open for the Jap fleet, laying mines in the dozens of atoll harbors, and hitting enemy installations where they could be found.

From the air Apamama was a solid thicket of green palm trees, sheared down the middle by a white runway. The main body of the atoll was no more than six miles long and a mile across, followed by a tail of loosely connected pieces of land that formed a crescent-shaped lagoon.

The lush green oasis in the sea was unbelievably lovely, almost absurdly picturesque. It stood as Robert Louis Stevenson had drawn it in Treasure Island—sun glinting off the white said, pillared with tall palms; clear emerald water and the thick growth of polished leaves and bright blossoms.

Those first few days on the island were jumpy ones; we were waiting to be called into actual strike procedure. We didn't have to wait long. Three nights after we arrived we were briefed on our first strike. After dinner the Old man pulled down the big map in the Operations hut. Every rock that breaks water in the Pacific was charted there . . . small reefs, lagoons, and water depths, all clearly marked.

"Tomorrow morning we will mine the harbor at Makin," he pointed to the island. "Three crews will go . . . I'll take Johnny and Bill."

My name burst over me. Across the blue map he traced our path into the lagoon and out.

"You can expect fire from these two positions. A submarine called Lifeguard will lay out at this point," he designated a spot in the sea. "In the event you are forced down, radio him your position."

The commander, still remote, a stranger, looked into the face of every man before him. It was to be Miller's first strike too. "This should be an easy one. We won't drop any bombs and we don't expect to meet any fighter opposition. We will drop our mines and get out. That's all. Take nothing with you. Is that clear? I don't think you'll have a bit of trouble."

The palm trees dripped yellow light from an enormous moon. A ridiculously poetic night to be thinking about the isolated, disconnected acts that make up war—it was a night for Long John

Silver to be searching the island for treasure.

On my cot in the oppressively hot tent I reassured myself that it was only a milk run, that I had been thoroughly trained for this business, and all I had to do was remember what I had been taught. I had supplied the crew with swim-fins as a personal precaution, a move that caused Bellew great delight. "What do you think you're going to do, swim all the way back?" Besides the fins, that I had ordered hung above every man's station on the plane, we carried extra rations, extra water, compasses, navigating equipment—enough stuff for a cruise back to the States.

At two-thirty the orderly leaned over my bed. The strike was called. The moon was down and the tent was black. For a moment I couldn't remember what I was dressing for; I was not quite awake. Then I remembered and it was as if I had been submerged in ice water: that morning I would fly 400 miles over the water and mine a Jap harbor. It was difficult to take an aggressive attitude when you were limp from the comfort of sleep. My body responded slowly. Mechanically, sitting on the edge of the flat cot, I pulled on a pair of khaki pants and shirt, the heavy marine boots. The rest of the tent was sleeping in the darkness and as I passed down the aisle between them, Bellew rolled over and dryly whispered, "Go get 'em, Tiger," as he dropped his face back into the pillow.

Down the line of tents here and there a flashlight moved—my companions for the early flight could be heard grumbling as they stumbled across tent ropes out into the starlit, still night.

The jeep pulled up. "The Old Man's already down on the field. Come on, let's get going . . . " We stopped where the flashlight beams shone bright dots here and there in front of the row of sleeping tents and picked up the men who would fly that morning.

Nobody spoke. We were empty, nervous, and ill-tempered; and the hard jolting of the jeep, as it made its way along the two miles of pitted road to the field, did little to improve our mood.

At the strip, flashlight beams cut across each other, falling on the planes, into my eyes, down the runway, back in my eyes. In the oval, empty, metallic cockpit I took command of my plane and began to give orders to the crew. The sound of my voice giving orders seemed unreal, almost comic to me. Who was I to be giving orders?

But soon the everyday tasks to be performed, the familiar details, gave me confidence.

Out over the field the first plane was warming up. Now it was necessary to forego the luxury of sensations—loneliness, hunger, irritability—and get the plane into the air. A bad piece of flying into the black hole over the water ahead of me could destroy my crew of 11 men as easily as a squadron of Zeros or a burst of ack-ack.

The skipper was up. He would fly out three minutes, make a 180-degree turn, pick us up, and lead the way into Makin.

Here we go. We are on instruments. She feels heavy with her load of mines; it seems a long time before she begins to climb . . . now she is going and behind us the twin beacons are raising a reassuring V from the field. Ahead the black hole spreads out into the sea 600 feet beneath our engines.

We have been out two hours and the sky has faded from black, to dark blue, to medium blue. Some of the crew are sleeping and my eyes sting from too little sleep. The hot coffee is comforting.

"Makin ahead." The Old Man's voice breaks the quiet. His ship drops within 50 feet of the water, we sweep down behind him. Now the sky is light. Makin Island sits serenely green around a lighter green lagoon where a white finger of sand reaches out into the surf. It is incongruous that there can be menace lying in that beauty. I search the ground for some movement, a sign of a weapon, but the island appears deserted.

Across the sand bar into the harbor, the captain's bomb-bay doors open, the black porcupine mines fall out and splash into the water. I call through the intercom to open our bomb bay, the ship lifts slightly, it grows lighter as the bay is emptied. Below now, figures scatter from small structures—the enemy scurrying out of a wood pile like a nest of confused mice. Plow-plow. The ack-ack finally gets going. It's way off and we are heading out to sea into the sun. The plane bounces. One guy on the end of the island knows his business, the burst was close.

We are out across the water and it is over with before the wave of fear catches up with me.

CHAPTER III

The milk runs were over. The squadron was initiated quickly. We joined the big league in two weeks' time, impudently ferreting out the enemy.

The B-24 became a sea-raider. Instead of appearing at 30,000 feet accompanied by 100 sister ships, she came in across the sea at 200 feet above the water, many times alone. It was an operation of surprise, hundreds of miles from any fighter cover, raids as the word implies.

The sea was our ally. Out of the empty ocean unexpectedly one, two, sometimes three of us wheeled in toward a Jap harbor. We flew low over the water under the Jap radar, straggling out of the sky toward their harbors and landing strips in an audacious clatter of propellers. The raids were quick, three or four minutes, and before the fighters got up, we were gone, absorbed by the sky, too far out for the Jap fighters to safely follow.

From 50 feet we drop down over the water, white caps licking against the ball turret as we come out of the sun toward the landing strip at Kwajalein. The strip guards the lagoon—and this trip it holds a destroyer, a tanker, a couple of sub tenders, and a submarine. We lift up to 200 feet and head over. The strip wakes up as the 40 and 20 millimeters bob sullenly. They have been waiting for us. Hal Bellew, flying at my wing, mimics the Old Man's voice. "Yes, gentlemen, the strike will be a complete surprise. I don't think you'll have a bit of trouble."

Here it comes.

"Hey, Hal, we'll take the can."

A big shot of adrenalin and something takes over to suppress the panic that begins to rise i me. Maybe if I do a very thorough job of this, they won't hit me; automatically I duck my head and pull in my shoulders. I head into the shells blooming rhythmically out of the strip.

"Get that guy on the right," I tell the tail gunner. My voice sounds thin. Another order: "Hold your bombs." Below, a gun flips back, pointing at the sky in an awkward moribund posture, its gunner sprawls at its base.

We are over, past the thorny nest and into the harbor heading toward the destroyer huddled inside. I make a diagonal pass over the ship. The blast of the bombs exploding on her midsection nudges the plane with a current of air. It feels good up here. A second to decide whether to turn back and let her have it again.

We make the turn. The destroyer's big guns have had a good chance to line us up as we come back. She is almost caught behind the yellow line, painted on my windshield—Miller's own improvised bombsight. Just a little closer.

Erratically we dip to the left as a giant fist slams into us; the prop runs away, whirring above the others with a sickening whine. I press the pickle. The bombs head out and drop beneath us astern of the midsection on the listing destroyer. The harbor is crossed and we are hurrying out to sea—sanctuary. Two lone planes in the big sky, with 600 miles of ocean to cross, start back home—one without an engine and, in the back, wrapped in a parachute, its navigator is bleeding to death.

A month and a half of this and the Navy was ready to move in on Kwajalein. We had done what could be done from Apamama. Eight days after the bombardment of the Jap stronghold began we were ordered up. A big jump, from one end of the Marshalls to the top of the chain.

The squadron flew out in two sections and instead of reaching the island at sunup as had been the case in our previous trips, we hit it at high noon. From a lonely piece of land floating in the Pacific, overnight the fortress had drawn a crowd.

Below us, cornered Kwajalein was the hub of 150 ships flung out across the sea. The transports, a spoke in the wheel of the Navy, moved in slowly with their equipment. Carriers, battleships, and destroyers lay out in layers on either side of the vulnerable work ships, protecting the tedious and important operation. My original awe for the might of the United States Navy was restored by the vast armada that filled, up to the horizon, what yesterday was a desert of water. And the center of all this activity, Kwajalein, the garden oasis we had visited a dozen times with our raiding parties, was a piece of naked ground; thin ribbons of smoke rose from the smoldering palm stumps, striping the sky. A big hand had wiped clean the surface of the island; from a secret, green place it had been leveled flat to black spikes, dirty yellows, and deep, wide, brown holes.

Kwajalein still smoked and the fighting continued in one corner of the island when we landed on the torn-up Jap runway. As we made our approach, my shoulders tightened and my head automatically lowered, a conditioned reflex by now. This time the Japs were silent. Fifteen hundred of them were piled in a communal graveyard, rotting, waiting for the Seabee bulldozers to mulch them into the ground.

Our immediate job on the little island, that now held 3000

American troops—two squadrons of bombers, a photographic squadron, and a Navy night-fighter crew—was to patrol for the Jap fleet until the huge task force that protected the transports, as they unloaded, could be dismissed.

Almost at once the climate of Miller's command began to alter from what it had been; on Apamama we were feeling our way. But now Miller had been exposed to the area and he began to emerge as the exceptional leader that he was.

The new base called for organization and Miller began to pull in the strings. He remained close to his tent, sitting on the beach in a pair of GI trunks, poring over dispatches.

We felt the change the moment we landed. Within two weeks the squadron was a taut ship, the skipper could point his finger at any one of us and get the right answer. There was no more lying on the beach in the afternoons; we all had jobs to do. Miller got what he wanted. There were very few mistakes made.

Back on Apamama, the Old Man went on twice as many strikes as any of us, but here on Kwajelein the fever of winning his own war really took hold.

A group of us were dragging ourselves through a hot night with a poker game when the Officer of the Day came in with a radio message from Miller who was out alone, hunting for a convoy.

"Look what old 'blood and guts' is up to now." He threw the message on the table. The skipper's terse communiqué read:

UNABLE TO MAKE CONTACT WITH ENEMY CONVOY. DIVERTING TO TRUK.

It might as well have read "Japan."

We got to our feet and headed for the communications tent, where we found his position on the map. We charted his progress to Truk. He would be there in two hours' time. We waited for further word but the Old Man sent none.

Truk was the Japanese naval bastion. Its mountainous terrain, broken into five parts, held go fighters and in its harbors lay the enemy's largest pool of carriers, destroyers, and battleships. Truk was 'way up in Japanese land and in two hours' time the Old Man, a noisy hornet in the sky, would be raiding this giant. Nobody left the tent. The clock read one—he would be over now. In 20 minutes the message came ticking out:

RETURNING TO BASE. ALL'S WELL.

It would be four o'clock before he would be in. We went to bed.

The next morning at breakfast we jumped on Miller for the story.

"We dropped on a can and strafed the runway. You know, I think we can get away with murder down there." We were full of pride and full of anxiety; Miller was the first man to raid Truk, but it would undoubtedly be a target from now on.

Miller never missed a strike on Truk; it became his personal enemy, and thinking of ways to outsmart the Japs became a consuming game.

With each ensuing strike, Miller emerged greater in stature. He was never wrong. He became infallible. Like Hannibal, Cochise, Alexander, Miller reached way out and won. And in reaching, he pulled us with him; from an average squadron Miller inspired us into an exceptional one. There was no other way under his command; he did not make mistakes and he would not tolerate ours. He was bold, but he was never careless.

Those days on Kwajalein our spirits ran high; we became tightly wound for war, like Miller himself. The fever had rubbed off. Isolated from the rest of the body that was the United States Navy, the war became our personal business. We had a purpose. The Jap fighters painted on our bombers grew in number and our best moments were reporting to the Old Man that a destroyer or part of a convoy had been sunk. Miller would nod his acceptance. Our reward.

The squadron soon knew the islands like their own base. Truk became so familiar that we could swoop down in the blackness between her five spiny segments, turn in and out of her harbors like it was the Pasadena Freeway. Each plane commander had his pet island, one he knew better than the rest, and he soon became an authority on its position and defense.

Strikes were almost always hatched far from the briefing tent.

They were born on the beach, at a poker session, after dinner in the mess hut over the twentieth cup of coffee. Very rarely was a formal order outlining a strike handed down from the admiral. It usually worked in reverse—the pilots themselves developed the details of a raid, then took the plan to the skipper for his blessing. Miller listened carefully to the proposed strike. Then he would ask for our alternate plan. "How you going to get your ass back in one piece if your plan doesn't work? What have you got to substitute in an emergency?" If we had no answer he would dismiss us. "Come back when you get it figured." Usually he would demand two alternates for the original strike Able—plan Baker, plan Charlie—before he would give his approval. From Miller's tent it went to the admiral for formal treatment. It was a new approach to war, the book hadn't been written yet—a chain of command running backward. The admiral depended on Miller to devise his own methods of attack; part of that method depended on the judgment of his men. As far as Miller saw it, the pilot who brought his crews in and out of the forward area knew the situation far better than anyone else, and he made it clear that any man worth his gold stripe could plan his own strikes better than some orderly intelligence officer, snug in a cement dugout 900 miles away.

When things started moving the way he wanted them, Miller himself grew less formal too. Strikes were so spaced that each crew had no more than three a week, and usually the day after a raid a group of us would pool our liquor and have a party.

The first time it happened we were surprised; during the early-morning merriment the skipper suddenly appeared. From then on, if the Old Man didn't see signs of a party he would pad down to his exec's tent and wake him up. After a few drinks with the yawning officer, the Old Man would send him after Hal Bellew and, as the mod struck him, more of the squadron. The parties usually lasted for two days at a stretch, and no matter how many times any of us helped the skipper to his feet, he remained captain. When the party was over he was as assured and dedicated as he ever was.

We were going into our fifth month of combat when the grind began to show effects. One whole crew had to be sent home before we moved up to Eniwetok; and most of the squadron, after three months more on that base, began wondering what was eating the captain—we were due for relief.

Just a little longer. Miller did not want to leave Eniwetok; he wanted to go on to Saipan. Orders came through for our replacement but Miller requested that the admiral delay them. The orders were delayed and we continued to fly out against Truk, Guam, and Wake.

Rolling down the night-black road toward the field, toward a strike, we were too weary now to be apprehensive. Looking at the men, their heads bobbing on their chests, arms hanging loosely, they appeared most reluctant—Miller's Reluctant Raiders. The squadron had a name.

Miller's Reluctant Raiders remained on Eniwetok for two more months, with Miller supplying most of the enthusiasm, his lean body more lean and his black eyes more prominent than ever as he outlined strike after strike. Often he would take his crew out alone with a solitary inspiration. We watched him with alarm now.

The usual party sprang up after a tough raid—we had lost a plane. The party was still going at the end of a day and a half when Miller was handed a dispatch from the admiral requesting that three planes from 109 move up to the recently taken Saipan for runs on Iwo Jima. Six of us saw the Old Man drop his head. His tight body began to tremble. It had finally caught up with him; he cried softly. We ceased to be in the room. The exec handed him a half a glass of Bourbon; he drank it slowly and slumped down in his chair.

Before the captain was awake the next morning, three of us took off for Saipan.

Saipan was a new field. From it we saw the war—the works. Eighteen carriers were blasting Iwo by day and we were supposed to keep it going at night. We were no longer a lone-bandit group, we were reduced to a segment of the most formidable fleet the seas had ever floated. Miller's surprise tactics had worked fine for seven months, but a surprise can only last so long. The Japs were wise to us. These islands, reaching close to Japan, were not like Wake and Eniwetok; they were mountainous and misty. The field required brand-new tactics and we were an old and tired squadron.

We had been on Saipan only 18 hours when Miller caught up

with us. No mention was made of the fact that we had left him sleeping on Eniwetok with the rest of 109. He assumed command and we followed his plan as always.

Two weeks of steady strikes every night, every morning, with no rest and we could see that even the Old Man realized that he had made a mistake.

Ten of us sat at breakfast. There was little conversation as we drank a last cup of coffee before take-off. Miller and I stayed behind after the others had gone down to the field. Silently he went over the weather the raid would meet—the radar spans. His face was long and lined from the Pacific and the months behind him. The strike before us was one we dreaded. As we left the table to go out to the field, Miller pushed his way into the washroom and vomited. He returned to the table and without looking at me he reached for a glass of water and drank it down. When we stepped out on the runway he was recovered and the waiting crews received their captain.

In the midst of all the action, the bombing, the raiding, the exploding ships, it was brought to an end as abruptly as it started. We were ordered back to the States, not tomorrow but that same afternoon. This day we did not have to replace our burned-out gun barrels and load our bombs for the night's raid; we had a reprieve; it was all over. There was no immediate joy, just a deep breath as the war was lifted off our shoulders.

We took off for Eniwetok to pick up the rest of the group and, on a strange easternly heading, pointed for Honolulu and the West Coast—home.

CHAPTER IV

Squadron 109's Liberators flew back to San Diego, 15 scarred old soldiers, returned for a long rest, maybe the junk pile. The planned reunions and parties were spottily attended and the thing that had held us together no longer existed—the war was over for most of us. Miller's Reluctant Raiders broke into pieces. The squadron, as a tightly knit unit, ceased to exist. A time for celebration became a time of reflection and, ironically, nostalgia for something lost that could never be regained. The war was over, the fear, the blood, the awful destruction—what was it that could bring nostalgia to the cessation of evil?

Fourteen months, and that was that. After a month of days with nothing to be done, days in which there was time to think, days of returning to familiar things, orders came assigning me to a ferry squadron for the Naval Air Transport Service.

We flew everything: fighters, attack bombers, heavy bombers—the aircraft that were finishing up the war for us. And we were moving—New York, Los Angeles, Honolulu, a need that had become almost a compulsion with me. During the six months with the ferry squadron I learned the difference in planes and fast; the exhilaration of rolling a fighter on the way back from the East Coast where you have just deposited a big, steady bomber.

The lat six months of the year I spent as an instructor in PB-4Y's on the West Coast: a tedious business requiring patience and understanding. The Air Corps at Santa Ana allowed us to use their almost-vacant field for our instruction. It was in the middle of August and it was hot, my student and I were circling the field going through take-offs and landings, when the communication tower called to us, "Shove off, Navy, the war's over." For me the war had been over a year ago.

I stayed with the peacetime Navy for two more years, flying transport out of Hawaii to Guam to San Francisco. A leisurely life, contrasted and varied by soft, warm, lazy Honolulu and crisp, dressy, busy San Francisco. The war became a dream I dreamed a long time ago. From time to time I would try to remember what it was like but it was like trying to recall pain. It is recalled as if it happened to a stranger.

Then one Monday morning, hung over, I picked up the Honolulu Enterprise and the Reluctant Raiders came back vividly. There in a right-hand column under a prominent headline ran the story:

"BUZZ" MILLER, MARSHALLS' HERO, DIES IN STATES

Capt. Norman "Buzz" Miller, leader of the famous and colorful Reluctant Raiders distinguished for their achievements in the Central Pacific campaign, died today in the San Diego Naval Hospital. Miller, 41, succumbed to a lung disorder that he had fought the past six months. The flyer's wartime record of 180,000 tons of enemy shipping sunk won his squadron a Presidential Unit Citation and himself the Navy Cross.

In seven months of combat Miller lost three planes out of the original 18 that had flown out of San Diego. They were not with him when they disappeared into the sea. Out of a squadron of 600 men, only 107 were dead or wounded.

Honolulu mourns the death of one of its most beloved personalities.

"Buzz" was stopped. He no longer existed except in my mind and in the minds of the men who were his squadron, now scattered throughout the country. The stature, the vitality, the flesh and blood that was Miller's, was swept away in time, and now it was time to go down to the field where the big transport waited with its list of Navy personnel passengers on their way to Guam.

I stayed on the islands after my release from the Navy flying the Trans-Pacific Air Lines' interisland schedule but after two years of it I became saturated with the uncomplicated, lukewarm life. The island became too small. There was nowhere to go, it was too easy. Flying airline back and forth around the islands over the untroublesome Pacific was a boring chore. The world was on the mainland and it was time that I joined it.

The world, those summer days in 1947, consisted of the Southwest Airlines, a small company situated in San Francisco, a line that carried passengers between Los Angeles and Medford, Oregon. Southwest's sky highways were menaced by the coastal mountain ranges and inconsistent weather—a change that was welcome after the passive flat Pacific.

The mountains and the weather offered a contest. I was busy the first six months with Southwest just getting my load of 20 passengers zigzagged safely through the coast range.

Holding a gently vibrating wheel in your hands at 10,000 feet there is escape for a while. You are suspended in a kind of peace. Below and ahead the sliding treadmill slides away neat little farms, squares of precision-furrowed land, remote little cities that sprout against a mountain base or on the coastline, even rows of concrete buildings and toy cars that crawl along carefully drawn, intersecting lines; the hustle and activity hidden there beneath the orderliness can't touch you for several more hours. Up here no one waits to see you; the telephone won't ring; the view from your window is not the back of a building with the heat bouncing off of it. It is the timeless sky, shifting patterns gradually and continually.

We race effortlessly toward the soft downiness of the white cloud-meadow that is spread across the sky to the horizon. The cockpit is warm with the sun that reflects back from the frothy, clean rolls, and the soporific drone of the two big engines boring through the clear air is soothing.

Beneath the protecting white blanket lies a black storm. Sixty miles away, beside the cold bay, the control tower at the San Francisco airport advises us that the ceiling there is 600 feet, visibility one-half mile.

"Southwest 452, you may come in on a Number 12 frequency at 6000 feet." Above the weathered city eight planes wait to land. They are stacked at assigned altitudes where they will circle in a race-track pattern waiting for the plane nearest the ground to receive clearance for its final approach onto the water-slick runway at the bottom of the storm. The stacked airplanes will then receive airways clearance to drop down through the next thousand feet of "soup" to the vacated level where they will continue to circle.

All right, down through the fleece, out of the sun, into the ice and wet of the weather. It is four-thirty in the afternoon but already under the roof of cloud-meadow it is dark. The blowing rain is a wave of water against the windshield and ice begins to grab at the wings. To the right now the mountains are no longer visible.

We descend gradually through the 2000 feet of "scud" and follow the thread of the radio beam.

According to the green light shining on the instrument panel, dimly lit before us, we are at 6000 feet coming in over the radio range a little south of the east-west runway. The storm envelops us as we begin to circle in a giant oval pattern, holding at 6000 feet above the city that we cannot see there below us.

Five silent minutes pass. "Southwest 452. You are cleared down to 5000. Notify us when you leave six and reach five."

Into the damp rubber mouthpiece I call, "Leaving 6000 at this time."

"Southwest 452 received: 5000 at four-fifty-three." The radio is quiet once more. Behind the cockpit door now the passengers will grow still; there will be the occasional cough and the clearing of a throat. The magazines are laid aside.

Fifteen more minutes pass and we are surgeons in the rose-glow of the cockpit light, watching the reactions and indications of the airplane we manipulate, descending 1000 feet at a time when we receive clearance from the tower hidden in the weather there below us, that we may do so.

"Southwest 452. You are cleared for your final approach."

Down to 3000 feet above the field, we head out over the city lost below us in order to return on the final approach leg. We make our turn. The copilot remains attentive to the instruments now. As we drop steadily lower, I search ahead through the watery windshield for the ceiling and visibility advertised by the tower.

There. A hole in the bottom, a piece of wet street, reflecting long yellow headlight beams, flashes by. We are breaking through. Six hundred feet below the now-widening holes, I can see the early evening lights signal on from warm, comforting kitchens where dinner is cooking.

"Okay I got it." I take over the controls on "contact" for the landing ahead. The copilot releases the controls but continues watching the instruments as if he were still flying by them. In the sudden event visual contact becomes obscured he is at once ready to take over again on instruments.

In the dusk cars turn into driveways. Men finishing their work for the day bend over to pick up the evening paper. They hurry through the rain into the warmth of a house.

Forty seconds and our work will be done. The next 40 seconds are the most important; if I miscalculate, the DC-3 will come home the hard way. Now we point down the glide path to the runway, the 20 passengers behind the door in back of us breathing down our necks. Ahead in the watery dark is a reassuring red glow. That's it! The row of neon lights marking the runway are clear before us now. Four hundred feet, 300 feet, 200 feet, 100 feet, 50 feet . . . 20 feet the wheels obediently meet the slippery runway. We are back once more.

Six months of airline flying and the weather, the ice, the mountains, the sticky landings, became enemies that I had learned to meet. The contest was out of balance, the victories were easy to win and they became routine. The restlessness that had been growing in me the past three years, since "Buzz" and I flew back into San Diego, began to take over once more.

While my days were spent on empty, monotonous flights back and forth from Los Angeles, wearing a rut in the sky, the big news was that a Captain "Chuck" Yeager had driven a rocket-propelled research plane, Bell Aircraft's X-1, through a thing they call the sound barrier. According to the newspapers he had reached the speed of sound and had brought his ship back safely to tell about it. Until Yeager had poked a hole in the "wall," the fastest thing going here was a jet, the Army F-80, at 400 miles per hour. Presumably, until this summer, anything flying at speeds between 450 and 700 miles per hour would smack into a wall of compressed air that would shake the plane apart or pull it completely out of control. Somebody did it. This research plane had proved it could be done. Yeager and the X-1 had gone through the speed of sound, 760 miles per hour at sea level—I was flying at a fast 160 mph.

One hundred and sixty miles an hour, weaving through the mountains in a cloudless sky. And eternity lying out my window has become commonplace; the mountains have been conquered. I can look at their dark, formidable lines with assurance; but still I don't turn my back on them. They enter into my reckoning, but automatically now.

Where do I go from here? This is as far as I go. Another year and another year after that and maybe ten more years of the same mountains, an occasional storm to fight, followed by empty, bright days like this. The DC-3 breathes its steady hum—she undoubtedly will carry us back and forth for ten more years; that is, as long as I follow the rules.

The rules for me, the ones I have sifted out of 9000 hours of flying over a period of seven years, since I left UCLA for Pensacola, are a mixture of physics and intuitional calculus.

I respect the plane I fly. Any ship you take off the ground represents a challenge always—but now I'm a little bored with her—I know her story. Allowing for the possibility that she might blow an engine or have some mechanical ailment, chances are she won't trip us up.

This particular challenge is getting too familiar. There goes Santa Barbara, set between the ocean and the mountains on the left of the valley we fly over. The fog is coming in over the sea and is beginning to quickly cover the flat village with its bright white houses tucked against the hills. Far below, the fog moves rapidly like sea water washing in from the ocean; already it is banked up by the mountains and is escaping over the top through the uneven comb of the ridge, spilling into the valley below us in smokelike rivulets. Ahead lies Point Conception, the coastline beacon that points the way to Monterey and Carmel. The fog probably is moving in all along the coast and will hit Carmel before we get there. San Francisco radios the weather.

Through the fog bottled between the sea and the mountains, the DC-3 finds her way once more back to the field beside the bay.

What is the next step? The need to "go" is taking over again. Obediently the DC-3 settles down on the runway at San Francisco Municipal and rolls up to the terminal—the end of the line. In a half-hour the crew for Oregon will come aboard. The passengers pour out, leaving behind them popcorn bags, candy wrappers, orange peels. The purser looks it over. "You had it a little rough over Carmel, I hear. God, you had a few sick ones. . . . I hope we can get this mess cleaned up before the Oregon flight."

Slouched down in the seat, I make up my mind. This is the night I quit. The Pan-American flight from Honolulu rolls up on my right and into the fog are emptied soft, relaxed businessmen in bright sport shirts, with tanned faces and pastel leis about their necks. They are accompanied by smiling middle-aged women.

The terminal is unlike any other port in the world. The cargo and people carried in over the water from the East bring with them the smell of the land they have just left a day ago. There is no long ocean voyage to drown the scent.

"See you, Phil." Brief case under my arm, I head through the foreign smells and the fog into the hangar and into the chief pilot's office.

The waking morning dreams I dreamed long ago in a small room—Walter Mitty kind of flying dreams—I am to dissolve. A boy's high school decision to make a career in the sky is to be revoked. All the years spent in equations at college that eased the way toward Pensacola where I never wanted anything so much in my life, where for nine months I studied at meals, on the week ends, and half the night, would no longer serve any purpose. Seven years I had known nothing but airplanes, and to give it up is to give up a way of life. It is like giving up a woman you wanted and were used to, but a woman you don't want to grow old with, a woman who would keep you in a pattern.

"Look, Will . . ." There was no use making a big production out of it. I told the chief pilot at once. "I'm sick to death of this thing. I need a breather, maybe go away someplace where they never heard of a wing of a propeller . . ."

My boss for the lat year was surprised by the sudden decision; after a second or two he said pleasantly, "Well I guess you've thought it over pretty carefully, Bill. If you ever want to come back, the gate's always open."

It was finished. I took the same winding Pacific Coast Highway that I had flown over the past year down to southern California. It was July and the ocean was warm and the surfing at Malibu Point, seven miles up from Santa Monica, was some of the best on the coast. Here I re-established contact with old school friends from UCLA and Pasadena Junior College and settled down to a lazy summer on the beach where I could leisurely think about where to go next. There was the rest of the summer to chart a new course.

Intermittently I thought about the future as the summer floated by me. What was I qualified to do? I knew nothing but airplanes; I had never done anything else but fly. In college I had taken odd part-time jobs, a little lifeguarding during the summer on the beach—that was it. Meager qualifications for an ex-lieutenant commander; and then there was my strong aversion to a stereotype, nine-to-five job that just brought home the bread and butter. There had to be something more than that.

Malibu softened the problem. It was impossible to worry much about tomorrow when right now the weather was perfect and the waves were swelling under your board. In back of the broad beach across the busy highway, hills abruptly rose, splitting into deep, lush-grown canyons with finger streams running along their floors where often in wide, flat meadows forests of white-trunked sycamore trees grew.

It was home to me. All of my summers as a kid had been spent three narrow canyons down the highway and four miles of dirt road up the one they call Las Tunas. It was impossible to feel insecure in the familiar, secure surroundings of home.

The smell of the sea and the sage returned me sharply to the boy I once was. An old house you haven't been in since the time when you were a child—you open the door and the scent is unchanged. You are back, for an instant, to where you once were.

"Billy Bridgeman, you're a dreamer." Her constant appraisal of me. A long time ago. It was a quiet life, there wasn't much to do but swim, hike, and dream. Our house, a square batten-board structure with a big black wood stove for a heart, was the only house in the canyon. My grandmother and I lived there alone with a collie who wandered in one night and who later came to distinguish himself by killing a rattlesnake almost daily as he led the way for me on our hikes deep into the canyon. By the end of the summer Sport had supplied me with a fine jar full of rattles that I proudly displayed to my grandmother's infrequent guests.

Mabel Bridgeman, dark and fragile, was an enormously determined woman. She brought me to California at the age of two from Ottumwa, Iowa, a sparse town that was headquarters for my father, William Bridgeman, whose career was piloting a rickety old World War I craft for a barnstorming flying circus. Soon after I was born he and my young mother were separated and grandmother steppe din to raise me.

Those summers in the canyon I grew up thinking my grandmother was my mother and the tall, lean flyer with the stories about airplane races and inside loops who came to see us every two or three years was my older brother.

Although I was all that existed in her world, Mabel Bridgeman was not overly protective. She gave me the best training she could, she saw I was well fed and clothed—then she opened the door—from there I was on my own. I knew the complete freedom of the ocean and the canyon. She never worried or if she did, it was never mentioned. Often during the winter months in Pasadena, 20 miles away, I would disappear back to the cabin in the canyon. She always knew where to find me and she would quietly scold me for the inconvenience of the trip across town that she had to make in order to bring me back.

The summers in the canyon ended when she died. I was in my second year at UCLA the winter it happened. I had been working week ends as a lifeguard and I made arrangements to move into the guard station on the Santa Monica Pier. My room was over a merry-go-round concession that had been there as long as I could remember.

The rest of my childhood disappeared when on one of my frequent walks back to the old house in the canyon I found a crew of men tearing it down to make way for a new road. A long time ago.

CHAPTER V

The summer was nearly gone when the telegram came. It was waiting for me under the door one late August morning when I came in out of the ocean after a long swim.

> PLEASE CONTACT US AT YOUR EARLIEST
> CONVENIENCE. TESTING DIVISION DOUGLAS
> AIRCRAFT CO. SANTA MONICA.

The Douglas bid was the result of some conversations earlier that year with an old Pasadena Junior College chum, Bob Brush, who was now chief test pilot for the Santa Monica company. I hadn't heard from Bob in a couple of months.

Perhaps the future was temporarily solved. I had given up flying, but testing was something I didn't know much about. It was a new field. Besides, it could support me until I found something else. The telegram lured me back to flying, and the prospect of getting into an airplane again was good. It would do no harm to go see what they had to offer.

That afternoon I took the coast highway along the ocean, past the canyons that open on to the beach, Las Flores, Las Tunas, Topanga; past Santa Ynez, where Sunset Boulevard ends at the sea from downtown Los Angeles; past Santa Monica Canyon, the wind-swept Greenwich Village of southern California where Santa Monica begins. A turn east through a low-rent district for five miles and there, unexpectedly, in the middle of the neat, flat, stucco neighborhood, lay Douglas Aircraft Company, sprawled over ten long residential blocks, one story taller than the houses around it.

The policeman on duty behind the desk in the small, bare main lobby okayed my appointment. I signed in, a visitor's badge was pinned on my coat, and I was escorted to the Testing Division, a block east through the plant and on the second floor.

Douglas is built like a maze split lengthwise. On one side is the assembly line cut into expansive sections by hangar walls; on the other side, narrow corridors with temporary walls reaching only halfway up to the ceiling, partitioning off tiny offices, go off from a dark central hall that leads through the plant and occasionally into large half-block-long pools of desks.

The hangar heights of the ceilings over the desk-pools are lowered nearly in half by the even striping of fluorescent tubing, the cold silver light that spread precise illumination in a room where no windows exist. These vast rooms, crowded with desks, are the Engineering and Designing departments, with their closed-off, stall-like cubicles for the higher echelons shoved against one wall.

As I came into each new department it was necessary to sign in with the policeman who checks those who go in and out. Through the Engineering Department into another cut-up and fenced-off hangar, on the left, as I passed by, was the sign: RESTRICTED AREA, PROJECT X-3. Top-secret stuff. The thin wooden wall around the project was twice as high as any of the other walls.

Up the stairs, another policeman at a desk, onto the second floor where again the temporary-looking partitions divide the small offices of the Testing Division. On my right was the door I was looking for: FLIGHT DEPT. A-853.

I presented myself to the secretary who was separated by a waist-high fence from the large room full of desks—the pilots' pit. She gave me a bright smile and indicated with a gesture of her head that I could go through the open door into a private office. The heavy-set, balding man at the desk got up. We shook hands. "Sit down, Bill, I'm Bill Morrisey, Bob's assistant. He's in Canada on vacation right now, but before he left he suggested that you would be a good man to help Brownie out over at the El Segundo plant."

"How is the old man?"

"Fine. You know Lois spent a week tracking you down before we could send you that telegram." Morrisey squinted at me, "What's your background?"

It took five minutes to go through 9000 hours in the air. The assistant chief test pilot made no comment.

"Let's go out and take a check flight," he suggested.

The field lies at the end of the long Douglas plant, where the last hangar in the row of glued-together buildings spews out from the end of the assembly line the finished four-engine transports. And up a steep flight of ladderlike stairs in the front corner of the hangar are the flight and the ready rooms.

A schoolboy once more. I had to recite the lesson for the teacher, who would listen carefully for the least hesitation. Suddenly a familiar function became something done with self-consciousness, like being stared at while you eat.

We climbed into a DC-3, an old friend.

"Take it up to 10,000. Feather an engine and bring it back."

At 10,000 we went through the emergency procedure: the pedestal of levers pushed and pulled in the right sequence comes from years of experience, it is done to the tune of the motor. A matter of timing.

"It was a nice ride." Morrisey was satisfied but unimpressed. His daily work was emergency; it's the way he sold airplanes. "Go over to El Segundo and meet Brownie, tell the old gent hello for me. He'll check you out in an AD. That's what you'll be flying. Bob'll give you a call when he gets back."

An AD is a single-engine attack plane and I am a four-engine pilot. It was hardly the kind of assignment I expected but I decided to follow the thing through.

El Segundo is ten miles from the Santa Monica plant and is pretty much the same sort of setup, except that the field, part of the Los Angeles International Airport, is removed from the plant and is shared by other companies who have their own individual hangars. The El Segundo plant fills orders for Navy fighters and dive bombers, while the sprawling Santa Monica plant puts out the big commercial stuff.

At the field I gave my name to the cop on the gate and was allowed to pass. Laverne Brown, the man I was to see, was sitting at a desk in a narrow little room labeled COUNTRY CLUB OFFICE. He was older than I thought he would be, around 40 maybe, tall, leanly built, and dark. His skin was brown and weathered. I introduced myself.

"Hey, I'm glad to see you." The way he lit up I thought he really meant it. He waved his arm in the direction of the field where the attack planes were lined up with their wings folded. "I could sure use some help around here, they've been piling up lately."

Despite all the newly-put-together, never-been-tried AD's crowding the field, production wasn't exactly booming at Douglas. The entire testing staff at El Segundo consisted of Laverne Brown and now me. And there weren't more than ten engineering pilots scattered throughout the other five Douglas plants. The manufacturing of airplanes wasn't one of the more "going" industries after the war.

Brownie showed me around, introduced me to Jerry Kodear, the dispatcher, and a couple of inspectors.

"Take a locker. We'll get you something to fit you tomorrow." He reached into his desk and pulled out a handbook on the AD. "Look this over . . . tomorrow we'll try it out."

It had been a long time since I had been in a single-engine ship, not since my days of ferrying fighters for the Navy, almost four years ago.

The next morning came up, a hot August day. By eight-thirty I was in the flight room having a cup of coffee and going over the AD manual once more when Brownie showed up.

"Think you can find all the knobs?" he asked.

"I think so. A few minutes in the cockpit will help."

"We'd better go over the starting procedure together. Those Wright engines can be rough if you've never been behind one before." Brownie had the assured air that a man who has been flying for over 20 years wears. He knew more about how to handle a plane than any pilot I had ever met. The AD before me was the first I had seen at close range but Brownie didn't take advantage of the fact. He left me pretty much alone.

The panel came as advertised in the handbook. Brownie leaned into the cockpit, ready to give me a hand getting her started. With a deftness that comes with a 100 hours in a ship, he brought the big engine to life. I watched the first sequence of his motions, trying to memorize them.

Over the clattering roar of the engine he shouted, "If anything goes wrong phone us. Take her up for a half-hour or so and get acquainted." He was through; the ship was mine. There was no fatherly advice. He jumped down and walked back toward the hangar.

Now I tried to remember everything I could about single-engine airplanes. Remember, with the power you've got here it's going to take a lot of rudder to hold this thing on the runway. What else was there to remember?

Brownie wasn't kidding, the engine sounded as if it was ready to come out of the mounts. I pulled into the run-up position, unfolded the wings, checked the mags. A quick look at the engine instruments and I was cleared for take-off. On two-five-right, the Los Angeles Airport companion runway, Southwest was starting her take-off roll. Friends from home. I made the senseless gesture of waving and then self-consciously pulled my hand down. Southwest ignored me as she lumbered by.

"She's got a high rate of climb," Brownie had warned me. I lifted her off and pointed up. A high rate of climb? The AD went upstairs like she was shot in the fanny.

At 18,000 I nose over, reduce power, and there is it again—the world, new, and again always the same burst of exhilaration on the first look down, like Monday-morning flight after a long week end. Here is a kind of freedom that I find nowhere else. You are on top of it, nothing can hide from you, an explorer in an empty sky. Up here you're big. You can move.

I turn the energy churning in front of me south toward Laguna. There are no passengers in back of me and there is no schedule, no place to be, just me and the AD and the coast of California edged by the mountains. The attack plane is more power than I have ever handled; it's a big engine, a small airplane. At Laguna I run out to the ocean, turn north, and jump the waves. The AD is a colt in a blue meadow.

Into a steep climb, the engine kicking up a storm, I pick up altitude and level off. It has been a couple of years since I have been on my back. I try a few rolls and some Immelmanns. I dish out of the rolls and the Immelmanns are sloppy. Some old fighter pilot down there is probably staring at the sky shaking his head.

The dispatcher calls, asking my position. I had neglected to call him and he is checking to see if his new boy is lost. I report my position. The half-hour is gone and on the way back to the field I check Channel 3 on the radio and the remaining two items that had been given me to test on this first flight.

My confidence is somewhat shaken by the sloppy way I have handled the ship in the rolls, and the landing before me I approach with caution. There is another audience, for sure, at the hangar. I keep a little more power on than usual and my approach is fast. I allow lots of room; this time I don't try and see how close I can come to the end of the runway at touchdown. A nice, easy landing. There is no one watching.

Brownie greeted me in the office. "How did it go?"

"Noisy Goddammed things, aren't they?"

Brownie snorted, "You'll think so when you get a rough one. You know the area fairly well, don't you, Bill? Now I suggest you memorize the radio frequencies of all military fields so you can warn them if you've got to set down in a hurry." He went on in a serious voice. "We make it a rule that everybody wears a Mae West and carries shark repellent." He caught the side look I gave him. "It's up to you, boy, we all wear it. And another thing. Try to call in every 20 minutes or so; Jerry likes to know where the planes are." Then Browned smiled. "With Jerry we like to kid a little. Pick out a spot on the map that nobody has ever heard of. It drives Jerry crazy trying to find it. Everybody does it to him." Then he continued, serious again.

"If you get in trouble, let me know. If I'm on the ground I'll try to help you out; if I'm in the air I'll join up and give you a hand. We'll let you take it easy these first couple of weeks until you get to know the ship."

My first two weeks as test pilot I was allowed to take up second and third flights, after Brownie had worked the planes over first. While I was furtively trying to execute a respectable roll in a hunk of vacant sky over orange-grove country 40 miles from the field, after I had completed my test items, Brownie was taking up "first flight" on six to seven planes a day. He would set one down, make out a squawk sheet, climb into the next one, go over the items to be tested, bring it back, write it up, stop for coffee, and off he would go again. It took him a little over a half an hour to run through the check items on each ship. He handled the AD like a kiddy car.

Brownie's Immelmanns and rolls were precise and unfaltering; I didn't mind confessing to him that I was having trouble with mine. And although Brownie wasn't one given to "hangar flying" he explained in great and careful detail how to keep from dishing out. After 20 years in the air Laverne Brown, who once portrayed the dashing "Tailspin Tommy" in a movie serial some years back, was a little bored with flying. He had long since outgrown the wild-blue-yonder stage, but he saw with amusement I still liked kicking it around. Flying continued to be a form of sport with me.

And now I liked what I was doing after the confining routine of the airlines—getting up there and breaking loose. In testing as in no other branch of flying you are on your own; no one is leaning over your shoulder. And even though, again, it seemed like a temporary job, with little possibilities for the future, I was happy.

At the end of two weeks Brownie gave me a never-been-off-the-ground AD to test. "These things have got a sensitive carburetor, Bill, on first 'go' you have to find out quick if its correctly set. Take it up to 30,000. It'll cut out and backfire if the setting is off. You'll probably get a warning before that—the engine gets rough." He handed me a stack of cards. They listed power-plant tests to be made: a stall-warning chart to be filled, an autopilot card with ten items to be noted and a bunch of miscellaneous checks. The next-to-last item on the last card included climb, dive, and banking maneuvers. Brownie knocks this stuff off in 40 minutes?

"Circle and stay close to the field so you can put 'er down quick if she cuts," Brownie finished.

A new plane smells like nothing else: a man-creation with its own odor-mixture of newly joined, polished parts. The AD was spotless and ready to be tried, the original model had been tested by the engineering pilots for design faults, for stability and control, to see if it would fly. It had been modified and passed and the El Segundo plant was stamping them out at a rate of two a day. Now all that remained was to see if each airplane, as it rolled on to the field, had its parts put together properly. A thousandth of an inch off and the screw would cause the ship to complain and protest.

Walking up to the ship—a plane that had never been in the air— her wings folded as if she were shrinking from her purpose, a bizarre thought occurred to me. Maybe this one won't fly at all, the parts won't mesh. No one has ever proved this one.

This time I knew Brownie had his eye on me. I read over the cards carefully. Each card had items to be checked at varying altitudes, knobs to be turned at different speeds, and items to be tested in between trim alterations. There would be no sight-seeing on this flight; this was going to be work.

Before I wind it up I enter the gauge readings and set the knobs for items to be checked at take-off. The big Wright engine rips up the morning and I taxi out on the runway. She moves . . . now let's see if she flies. The AD picks up over the field, points high. She flies! Things are working for the first time, the parts are circling, pumping, meshing, as they have been engineered to do. A minor miracle.

Climbing to 24,000 to 26,000, to 28,000 feet. I suck my air from a bottle of oxygen. The air is thin outside and the carburetor now must feed the engine its fuel—neither too lean nor too rich. It is set correctly. She doesn't get rough and I turn to the cards clipped to the board that is strapped to my knee. As I come to each new card with its series of tests, I drop or climb to the altitude that the item requires. The entire flight is a matter of reaching for knobs, pulling switches, checking the radio, climbing up, and diving all over the sky. Two hours later I return the ship to Brownie: almost four times as long as it takes him for the same operation.

My arms and legs ached from all the activity in the new attack ship and wearily I unfolded into a chair with coffee and the squawk sheet that remained to be filled out—the pilot's literary attempt at evaluating the ship, an aviation critique.

Brownie came in from a flight, a parachute dangling from his back. "How did it go?" He asked for the cards and my squawks. "You think she needs a little nose-down trim at cruise power, huh?"

"Another half-degree will do it. God, I'm knocked out. How many operations can a plane have . . . up and down, back and forth, pull this, pull that . . ."

He read the cards. "You'll get used to it. Next time, you'll coordinate your items as to altitude—it saves times."

He looked at his watch and went out on the field again. I finished my coffee and followed after him. From the hangar door I could see him taxiing down the field in Number 48, the ship I had just brought in with eight squawks against it. Forty minutes later he landed. I waited for some comment as he headed for the flight office. He walked slowly. It was past quitting time; when he passed me he didn't stop. Over his shoulder he said, "See you tomorrow, Bill." He smiled.

First flights became easier; I learned to group items under altitude headings. At 5000 I would get everything out of the way that had to be tested at that altitude, the same at 10,000, and all the way up. Brownie never checked another plane of mine until the day I brought one back with a clean bill of health. Nothing was wrong with it. "I'll buy it, Brownie. As far as I'm concerned she'd sold." Every airplane that is delivered bears the name of the pilot who "bought it," who okayed it as a satisfactory working unit. If it comes up with a defect, the Navy refers back to the man who tested it. The test pilot is responsible for the performance of the plane.

Later that day Brownie took my no-squawk plane up for a flight. He never said a word. The report stood. The plane was "sold." I was a test pilot and it was a nice pleasant way to earn a dollar.

After I got the procedure organized, I could handle four to five planes a day. On first flight I no longer hovered over the field. I flew down toward Laguna, inland over the square acres of dark green orange trees; an area not too heavily housed, close to a couple of military fields and not many miles from the field at El Segundo. It became my ground.

"KAK6 calling. I'm over Anaheim, Azusa, and Cucamonga."

"Ah, knock it off, Bridgeman," Jerry's voice comes into the cockpit.

The ship is "sold" on this flight. She had been in good shape to start with, only six items against her and in three flights they were worked out. I am bringing her back for delivery. It is Monday morning and it is clear and sparkling and exhilarating, like the first time up, the first time you solo. There is the boundariless sky-country to run in.

Grinding up the coast over Balboa admiring the blue and white sunlit day, I have no desire to be in the water below me. I'm water-soaked from the week end. It is good to be flying again. My glance sweeps past the sun; it picks up what appears to be a speck in the sky. The sun is too bright to investigate. A part of a moment later a flash of aluminum goes by and the bright blue Skyraider wallows in the passing prop wash. The sudden intrusion shakes me. I'm a little annoyed and I search the sky for my new playmate. Off to the right and below, the sun that hid him now gives him away as momentarily the reflection bounces off his wings. It's a Mustang pulling out of a dive, clawing for altitude. The energy he picked up in the dive will take him well above me. Race you to the corner . . . and the fight begins.

Instinctively, in one motion, I catch the throttle and prop controls and sweep them all the way forward. She groans a little, shakes herself, and leaps forward. I pull the nose up and hang it there. The big prop chews up air and throws it behind; Balboa falls back far below. Above me the Mustang turns and starts his second pass. I turn slightly away. He turns in and commits himself. I didn't expect him to bite that quick. This is the pass he'll use. I turn and point the blue nose straight for him. In a wild gyration he swings to avoid me. The maneuver equalizes our positions. We stand off at approximately the same altitude and speed, two great engines churning up the quiet morning over beach and ocean. The giant circle begins. The turn into it puts 3 G's on me. The stalking. Pulling the circle tighter and tighter. The tight turns pick up G fast; I pull to the edge of stall and hold it there. She shakes and tends to roll off on a wing, I ease off the G a bit. The force of the turns pulls the skin of my face down tight and grabs my mouth open. As the blood is drained out of my brain, I can feel the blackout coming on; the world turns a foggy gray. I shake my head and scream from my bowels to keep the blood from pooling there and in my legs. I am used to pulling G's in flight tests, I can stand up to six without a "suit." The gray fades away now and I look over at my friend to see how he is doing. He no longer is directly opposite me in the circle, my turn is a hair less the diameter of his. Degree by degree the Skyraider is closing in on him, gradually I am moving up behind him. Were this combat, the process of "slow death" would have begun. In a moment it would all be over. Now his futile evasive action begins. He flips into a violent split S and shrieks off in a long, steep dive for the water and beach below. I flip with him, right behind him for a short time, and then pull up wing to wing. The Air Force fighter pilot looks over, nods his head, and smiles. Very slowly he rolls his airplane. Clumsily, I try to follow. Here I am no match with a fighter pilot. I know, too, if the ships had been switched, I would have been no match in the big circle above.

"KAK6, this is 482, I'm over Yapica and I'm coming in."

"You're late for lunch, boy."

There were three more planes waiting for me after lunch. The last one was a first flight.

The engine sounds smooth enough until we get close to 20,000, then suddenly the regulator controlling the carburetor isn't doing the job. The ship begins to shake.

Well, here it is. This is the day, the day they are paying you for. I become alert as a man who has had a bullet go by his ear. I pull the throttle back, but not fast enough. W-hop! Bang! The ship trembles under the blast. Brownie's carburetor threat has arrived. The AD drops through 3000 feet. At the lower altitude, where the air is thicker, I optimistically apply power, the engine protests in violent grinding and shuddering. The ship is not going to make it back, the engine won't hold up and at once panic that is beginning to crowd in me stands still for a second—this is what I am hired to do. Get the plane back. My ego and a separate calm consciousness that sees the practical and thrifty side of the issue prevent the basic reaction to jump from taking hold. Panic will have to wait.

Make up your mind quickly. Which field is closest? El Toro, Long Beach, Alameda? It had better be the first decision; with the loss in power the ship is settling fast. Five minutes ago things were in their proper place, a slight change in adjustment and now the once-obedient machine is 12,000 pounds of trouble. Long Beach, El Toro, and Alameda, warm-sounding places, might as well be a million miles away—there isn't enough power left to get to a field. Painfully I repeat a four-letter word into the metal-cold box I sit in. The damn thing won't make it to a field. A spot to set her down. There. A wide place in the road—not big enough. It is swept under and behind me. Over there, that brown field. That has got to be it. The ground is moving up closer beneath me. The field is covered with tall weeds that hide level ground or maybe deep holes or a pile of rocks . . . idle speculation, because there is no choice. One last attempt at the throttle. The AD coughs a response and the power increases a hair. Enough to get to a field? To leave it here is awkward; it would have to be towed home. I will nurse it back on the power she has left; it is better to bring the ship home myself than to have the company tow it back down the highway. I can do it.

The engine protests; it does not want any more and it shudders in its mounts as if it were trying to tear loose and drop to the ground.

"KAK6 . . . 522 returning to field. This is an emergency. Over."

The reply is immediate: "Five-tow-two . . . do you want emergency equipment to stand by?" Jerry's voice is calm and precise.

"Yeah, I think you better." A game with the dispatcher—who can sound the most detached? Under me the even squares of houses are getting thicker with their back yards of fenced-in kids. Just a little longer, Goddamm it, a little bit longer. The houses close beneath are running away from the clattering, sick, blue plane that rushes over them. Come on, baby! I suck in my breath, begging her home. My position is low. The engine could give up any minute and there is no altitude to glide in from and no brown field below to head for.

"Five-two-two . . . what is your position now?" The voice intrudes.

"Never mind," I snap. They don't ask again. I haven't time to answer questions. With each poke of the throttle she rattles and moans. Oh, Christ, come on, come on!

"Five-two-two, we have you in sight. You are cleared to come in on any runway . . ."

And there it is, the field, I get one chance at it, I won't be able to come around again.

The gear touches the ground. Tranquil, serene, and utterly beautiful field. I lean back in the seat and sop up the delicious comfort of just sitting. The harassed airplane under me bleeds oil and pants smoke. Then two firemen are on the wings, pulling me out of the ship. I resent the intrusion.

"What's the matter? She won't go up," I shout at the men. They haul me out anyway and the ambulance attendants move quickly over to us. I wave them away. "There's nothing."

In the hangar I dumped my chute in my locker and headed for the shower, the collar of my overalls was wet with sweat.

"Holy God," somebody complained from the radio room, "I never would have tried to get the thing in. You would be nuts to try."

"It sure is a mess all right. Anything to be a hero, huh?"

I was dressed and writing out a report when a mechanic walked in.

"What does it look like?"

The mechanic looked at me in disbelief. "It looks like hell. You broke three push-rods, you seem to have swallowed a valve, and number-three jug is completely disintegrated."

"Well, it's home anyway."

"Yeah, it sure is."

This time I was wrong. I had brought it in but I had not won the contest. I had made an error in judgment. I was wrong for a second when I made up my mind to nurse it back. A block, any block of those small, square houses along my path, just escaped having an engine bowled through a living room or a fire that could have eaten away its whole lapful of homes.

Next time there will be no decision with an engine that rough. It will merely be a set of circumstances that has only one answer: set it down quick.

In ten nasty minutes, bringing the strangling AD home, the first three weeks of freedom were paid for.

CHAPTER VI

Monday morning Bob Brush was back from three weeks in Canada. Lois, his secretary and general house mother to the Santa Monica flight office, called to tell me that the boss wanted to see me.

"How's it going, Billy boy?" Brush greeted me in his office. "How do you like it? You've been here a couple or three weeks now, how do you like Brownie? He's a great guy, isn't he? One of the best in the business." He didn't mention the trouble I had Friday.

Brush's office was as sparse as the rest of the Douglas offices I had been in, maybe a little bigger. Over his desk hung an artist's drawing of a sleek, narrow, dead-white plane with a rapierlike nose.

Its wings were thin and swept back, clean and menacing as a bullet in flight. Nose high, she dragged a stream of flame as she went. "What is that?"

"That is the Skyrocket, a high-speed research plane we built for the Navy in cooperation with the National Advisory Committee for Aeronautics. She's got a rocket engine and a jet combined. It's one of a series of six or seven experimental airplanes ordered by the government after the war to investigate transonic and supersonic areas. Northrop and Bell, along with us, were invited to build airplanes for the NACA research program. Of course Bell got there first with their X-1, when Yeager went through the sound barrier last fall. Gene May's out at Muroc Dry Lake at the Air Force Flight Test Center right now doing the testing on her. I might have to go out and get checked in the thing myself."

The words transonic and supersonic were foreign and the Skyrocket, an austere other-world craft in her nose-up attitude, was a radical. She did not inspire longing within me. "What'll she do?"

"She was designed to hit Mach 1. With the rocket engine in, she ought to hit 1 any day now." He turned to look at the little ship. "Too bad Yeager went through first in Bell's ship. We've got big hopes for the Skyrocket."

"What is all this Mach-number stuff I keep hearing about anyway?"

"It's a way of measuring the plane's speed with the speed of sound. The speed of sound is called Mach 1. We go up or down from there with decimal points according to the speed of your flight. If you're flying at Mach 1 at sea level, you're doing 761 miles an hour. The speed of sound lessens in miles per hour the higher you get, so at different altitudes you have different miles per hour readings for Mach 1. Designating the speed of sound as Mach 1 saves time in figuring."

"Perfectly clear."

"You run into compressibility effects –shock waves, buffeting, a high-drag rise at Mach 1—that's the so-called wall Yeager knocked over."

I remembered the news stories early this summer about Captain Chuck Yeager and the "wall." "You can have it—the AD's enough for me at the moment. I saw a jet for the first time last week over at International. It looked bad enough."

The jet had come in four days ago and now it lost some of its fearsome qualities after a look at the Skyrocket over Bob's desk. It was a brand-new F-80, the Lockheed fighter, the only jet-propelled model we had. Somebody announced to the El Segundo flight room that an F-80 was on the field. We all rushed out to look.

I didn't like it. There it sat on the runway, denuded of a propeller, a big hole in its fanny. Its pilot was a young lieutenant, a kid of 23 or 24, telling everyone to "Stand back, pl-lease." None of us did. We stood close to watch the thing take off. The kid shrugged his shoulders and climbed in, appearing none too confident as he reviewed the panel before him. Again he warned his audience, "Please stand back—please." A kid. Then he proceeded to light it off.

The engine boomed like a cannon, a bomb going off at your side. Our little group rapidly dispersed and made for shelter, where we prudently stationed ourselves for the rest of the takeoff. There was more. Flames poured out the hole in the back and it was to me an unearthly, unreconcilable sight. I was convinced I did not want to change places with the foolhardy lieutenant instigating the flight of the unholy craft. It streaked a clean line across the field, lifted and shrieked off.

"My God, what was that?" I asked Brownie, who was standing next to me.

"That, my boy, is time moving on," he had ventured sagely. "Come on, Father, let's get some of these buggies cleared off here. They'll be lined up to Sepulveda before we get caught up."

Now the Skyrocket hanging on the wall above Brush's desk made the jet look obsolete.

The chief test pilot again faced me. "An airplane's an airplane—only this one will go through the speed of sound. It couldn't be too spooky, Yeager got away with it."

Another month with Brownie and the AD's, and testing was becoming work. And hard work, 40 hours a month of flying—taking them up and bringing them down. Up and down like Yo-yo's, just Brownie and I alone were trying to keep the field cleared. Between us in one day we ran through 17 planes. They kept pushing them off the line and out the door, and as fast as we could get them in the air, we checked them out. By five-thirty each evening all I had strength for was a few drinks, dinner, and bed by eight-thirty. Eventually, after a month of this pace some of the Santa Monica engineering pilots were sent over to give us a hand. The engineering pilots were the boys who had first crack at the Skyrocket or any new design or experimental ship, handling the testing of the model usually from first flight until it was ready to be put into full-scale production. If the ship was for military production Brownie and I would eventually get its hundreds of offspring spawned onto the El Segundo field.

One heavy Monday morning Brownie brightened my day with the news that an engineering pilot, George Jansen, was coming over to help pick things up for us. When Jansen appeared I was nearing the point where I never wanted to see another AD. I was tired.

George Jansen, a handsome, tall kid in his late twenties, was four years younger than I. He was quiet, sure of himself—an intelligent pilot who knew his job and went right on studying more about it. This was a new breed of pilot, the first I had met of the engineering variety.

Jansen walked into the flight offices soon after eight-thirty. "I hear you guys need some help around here."

"You kidding, George? You saw the pile when you came in. We're real good to see you, boy." Brownie got to his feet. "Want some coffee?" They walked down the short hall to the locker room and to the hot plate set up under a flight of stairs. In flying, coffee and gasoline are the fluids most necessary to operate a plane. Jansen took the cup of black coffee from Brownie's hand.

"It's been a long time since I sat in one of those things."

"The AD revisited, huh? It's a grand little ship," Brownie rolled the "r" in grand. "Incidentally, George, what's happening out at Muroc? How's Gene doing with the Skyrocket?"

"He's doing very well—he finally got a successful rocket takeoff the other day." George shook his head. "You can have all that Skyrocket you want. Not for me. I'll take my new little A2D. If you think I want to run around with my ass on fire, you're crazy."

Brownie gently blew the steam from the top of his coffee cup.

"My sentiments, too. You can get too old for that stuff . . . rocket engines! Who needs a trip to the moon? Bell's had three X-1's blow up under them already."

I joined the conversation. "Exactly what in hell's a rocket engine anyway?" If anybody ought to know Jansen should, from what I heard all he did was study.

"It's Fourth-of-July apparatus." He seemed pleased at the opportunity. "Divided into four tubes that burn pure alcohol and oxygen, when all four tubes go at once it looks like one big acetylene torch with a 25-foot-long flame and if old Gene makes rocky take-off that stuff will blow the plane all over the desert. You should see the preparation that goes into getting that thing ready for flight. They start the fueling at four in the morning and keep feeding the liquid oxygen till take-off time, the stuff boils at minus 297 degrees and steams off at a terrific rate."

He paused for a gulp of coffee. "I'll bet Gene doesn't know which is going to go up—him or the ship—when he hits the rocket switch. Believe me, he is doing one whale of a job with that baby. It was a very smooth first take-off."

The Skyrocket was never a popular airplane. It had been viewed skeptically by the Douglas engineering pilots ever since it had been announced two years ago that the experimental ship was ready for trial. The Skyrocket was designed to exceed Mach 1, and to most pilots, at that time, the speed of sound represented a brick wall.

The story goes that one spring morning word went up from the Engineering Department at El Segundo to the flight-testing offices at the Santa Monica plant, where the engineering pilots wait behind their desks for assignments, that the Skyrocket was ready for bids from the eligible suitors. It seems that nobody wanted her very badly. A conspiracy was formed. The engineering pilots talked it over and arrived at the most gentlemanly way out of the situation. They agreed to send in outrageously high bids for the D-558-II contract—that would delay things for a while. Every pilot in the Santa Monica flight room was in on the plot except Johnny Martin. Johnny was in Paris delivering a ship when Brush sent word that the D-558-II was ready to go and that Robert Hoskinson, chief of the Testing Division, was waiting for Martin's bid. Unaware of the plot at home, Martin innocently cabled a respectable offer. He won the prize that nobody wanted. The ship was his.

Johnny Martin is one of the best pilots in the company. He had to be to handle the Phase-II rocket airplane of the D-558 research program. At that time Gene May was flying the Phase I airplane, the red Skystreak—underpowered and jet-propelled. After the initial testing, Johnny Martin turned over the rest of his Skyrocket contract to Gene May, who was now putting the jet-and-rocket-powered, swept-wing plane through her paces out at Muroc Dry Lake.

The Skyrocket existed in my mind as a far-removed, nebulous creature, the core of great attention at the Air Force Test Center in the desert, a lady I would probably never meet.

When George had finished telling us about her we had drained the coffee pot. "Gentlemen," Brownie brightly suggested, "shall we have a got at it?" We moved to the lockers for our chutes and Mae Wests. The same old blue attack ships sat on the field waiting to go. Brownie gave us our cards and pointed out the AD's on the field.

George and I took off a couple of minutes apart; mine was a last flight that waited over the week end for me. It took less than a half an hour to "buy" it. George rolled in about ten minutes later complaining. "God, the breakout forces are a hell of a lot higher than they used to be. What are you guys trying to do—make a truck out of it?"

When George was back in the air I looked at his squawk sheet, an impressive document of technical engineeering hodgepodge. I could make out a few familiar references but that was all. Next to his squawk sheet mine looked like a fourth-grade arithmetic problem lying beside an Einstein equation.

"Brownie, translate for me, will you?" I handed him Jansen's sheet. He looked at it closely.

"I haven't seen this kind of stuff since I left engineering." Brownie had been a "slip-stick" pilot but gave it up to head the El Segundo Testing Division. He had no desire to go back to engineering.

Patiently, slowly, Brownie broke down the intricate squawk, translating symptoms I had never heard of. It was a thorough diagnosis of a pilot who understood the reason why, and stated in exact engineering terms, the ship reacted the way it did. After

Brownie's careful hour-long explanation of Jansen's report I became very much aware that I wasn't as informed as I thought I was. I was a freshman again.

I viewed George with respect and a certain amount of awe mixed with exasperation when later that day he brought back a first flight. He informed me, "The stick fixed and free static longitudinal stability seems to have changed since we ran this thing through Muroc. What have you clowns done, hooked a bungee into the system?"

What in hell was this guy talking about? What ever happened to simple, straightforward pilot talk?

He didn't pursue the problem any further. "You going to take this up next?" he asked. I said I was. "Well," he tossed it off, "the engine gets a little rough at 20,000." With that he walked out of the locker. The next day I took Jansen's overhauled "first flight" up.

The minute I turned her over a slight variation in the beat of the big engine alerted me. This one I would hold close to home. As I gained altitude in tight spirals, the engine trembled a little. She had no more power than a rubber band.

The lukewarm warning George gave me was in no way unusual. It is a universal attitude among pilots: you underplay the tough moments. No matter how "shook up" you are, if you bring the airplane back with no wings, it is a solitary experience not to be shared and not to be elaborated upon. The attitude most common is that the momentary terror you felt, the sickening helplessness that reduced you to a frightened animal never happened, that the little trouble you had was nothing at all.

The engine coughs only once and then in a shuddering spasm nearly rips itself from its mounts. The sudden failure of the powerful engine makes me feel sick, as if I had tripped and fallen on my face. Just in time I grab for the throttle. Large, dirty blobs of oil spatter against the windshield and behind me pours a river of smoke, hemorrhaging out of the crippled engine. The smoke draws a corkscrew trail of my involuntary descent as I head toward ground.

I call Jerry. "K6 this is 682. I've got a rough one. I'm bringing her in. Call the tower, tell them to keep two-five-left open for me. I'm going to ease on in from this position. Let 'em know I can only make one pass."

The dispatcher's voice is undisturbed. He plays his role. "Okay, Bill, you're cleared."

Jerry, the dispatcher—the man on the ground whose job it is to clear the way when it takes more than one to fly an airplane—is quiet and efficient.

High and steep, my approach is cautious. I open the dive brakes; most of the excess speed is absorbed. It is a little long. I manuever in a slight S turn over the highway; she lowers and thumps down on the long concrete strip. She is down and she will stay where she is on the runway, there is no power to taxi her off.

I am met by what must be every truck in the Douglas Company. I occupy myself with the instrument panel in front of me; I'm not ready to leave the AD just yet. In a few minutes I will be able to greet the mechanics with the right amount of detachment.

All right, the "fire" was out. I stepped out on the oil-dirtied blue wings and dropped heavily to the ground. A mechanic stopped me: "What happened, Bill?"

"You tell me. That's your department." I walked past him. The walk back to the hangar helped to steady me. In the flight room George and Brownie waited with somewhat self-conscious grins.

"Jerry told us you were having a little trouble up there. What's the story?" Brownie asked.

I looked at George standing beside him. A little rough! "Not much. At 10,000 she got rough . . . that's about it. Is the coffee hot?"

"I'll get you a cup," George offered.

"God, it sure made a mess of the runway. Were you able to get any power out of her at all on the approach?" Brownie looked out the window at the oil-drenched strip.

"I was in a pretty good spot to let her fall in. I didn't need to get any power out of her."

George came back with the coffee. "What kind of shape is she in?" "I don't know, the boys are carrying her off the runway now. She just sat down."

"Did you get black smoke or white before it let go?"

I began to write out my report. "It got a little white." The locker was filling up with mechanics. They all had something to say. It was difficult to fill in the report in all the confusion. George continued his questioning.

"Did you try to richen her up?"

I put down my pencil wearily. "No, it let go before I could get on the mixture."

"Hmmmm, white smoke and low blower!"

The guy should have been a lawyer, not a pilot. I went back to my report and left Jansen to figure out the answer, which he undoubtedly would come up with before the day was over.

The next week I began to study. Between flights there was a little more time with George and now Bob Rahn, another engineering pilot, helping us out. When the flight room was empty, I read books and papers that were lying in the bottom of Brownie's desk or shoved in the back of some of the engineering pilots' lockers— Aerodynamics of the Airplane; Principals of Aerodynamics; Navy flight engineering manuals; and papers on stability and control by the Douglas engineers and aerodynamicists. At first the technical terminology of the material was difficult to unravel, but the more I read the easier it became. When I was somewhat familiar with a subject, enough to ask sensible questions, I went to Brownie. Brownie was not averse to being called upon; he liked to expound theory, often long after I had grasped the meaning. He would sometimes carry the dissertation into a half-hour if you would sit still for it. I did. He was the boss. But Brownie's methods of redundancy firmly implanted valuable technical knowledge in my mind.

With the temporary addition of Bob Rahn to the slim El Segundo staff the technical talk really took off, but it was getting to the point where I could hang on.

Test pilots are chosen for two reasons: experience or education, preferably both. But the two requisites are rarely found in one pilot. A prospective test pilot usually shines in one department or the other, and the time spent in testing planes tends to equalize his abilities. In most cases, but not always, the more experienced pilot in self-defense will study on his own to keep up with the M.I.T. and Cal-Tech graduates. My major in college had been geology and fortunately it included physics and calculus. Both subjects were a big help in understanding the aerodynamic equations that came up in the books that I was now getting from the Douglas engineering library.

With a certain amount of assurance I could now lay a problem before Bob, Brownie, and George. This invariably set off a heated discussion that often lasted an hour. The AD's would have to wait while the problem was viewed from all angles. Often the conference would end with all of us heading back to various authorities for confirmation or refutation of a point that had been pushed by one of the three veteran test pilots.

A discussion about manuevering stability began one afternoon when Bob Rahn came into the locker from a flight.

"Have you people made any change on the original chord of the ailerons since we had the plane at Patuxent two years ago?"

Brownie answered him. "We made a slight change in the seal but the chord is the same as original."

"The adverse yaw seems a little worse than on the ship we had at the 'river.' Certainly doesn't seem to meet the spec now."

Jansen joined the circle. "I know what you mean. I had one the other day that was very marginal."

I couldn't let the opportunity slip by without giving an opinion. I broke in: "Now I wouldn't want to say you guys fudged any in the original demonstration—not that I would put it past you—but you know damned well the Navy would catch it anyway. If you'll think back, I'll bet you were very cagey in the rate of full-throw displacement you used. When you play around with it some more, especially in this airplane, I think you'll find the 'rate' is very important."

With a carefully considered look on his face Rahn said, "You know, I think you're right."

Brownie seemed startled; he nudged Jansen. "The kids' been reading or something, huh, George?"

I was making progress. The boys picked up their cards and headed out to the field for their flights. Brownie went back to his office and I settled down in the flight room on the beige synthetic leather couch with my coffee and a copy of Principles of Aerodynamics, feeling I could cope with about anything now. I was 20 minutes deep into "compressibility phenomena" when Brownie called me down to his office.

He wasn't alone. There were two men in business suits with him. "Bill, this is Ed Peterson and Cliff Masters, they're insurance adjusters and they would like to ask you about that rough engine you had a couple of weeks ago."

"Mr. Bridgeman, were you as far south as Imperial Highway on October 18," the smaller man spoke.

Here it comes. "Yeah, I think so. Yes, I was." That was the day I came limping over the highway spewing oil.

"Well, I guess that does it all right," he turned to his partner then back to me accusingly. "You know that 300 paint jobs on 300 cars parked along your path that day were completely ruined by the oil from your airplane, don't you?"

"I knew I was losing oil but you guys are lucky I didn't tear the tops off those 300 cars." I took the offensive. It had finally come out. I knew from the looks of my own oil-stained car that day that I had done some damage but I had kept quiet, waiting to see what would happen. It happened. I smiled weakly at Brownie. He wore a pained look.

"It'll cost the company around 300 new paint jobs," the adjuster told us.

He meant 299 claims. I didn't have guts enough to turn in one for my car.

CHAPTER VII

My piecemeal engineering education was beginning. These were times of study. A year had gone by since I had joined the Douglas Company, and flight testing had become routine. Again it seemed too easy. There was an occasional jolt of adrenalin when an engine kicked up—enough to reinstate the proper respect for the little carrier-launched ship designed for the deadly mission of attacking enemy fleets, but the long stretches in between emergencies were hard, tedious work. Like last year with Southwest, the confining schedules, and the sky rut back and forth between coastal cities, production testing became an endless and monotonous task.

Now, more than ever, I studied engineering testing problems.

In production testing it isn't necessary to weigh and figure flights. The preoccupied air worn by George Jansen, Bob Rahn, and Russ Thaw when testing a new design was not shared by the production test pilot. When the endless lines of identical blue planes were not being moved there was no compulsion to think about next flight. There was little to challenge your inventiveness or aerodynamic knowledge in this sort of check flying; it had already been done by the expert engineering pilots in the original evaluation. So time spent between planes at the El Segundo field in the small ready room, with the warning military safety posters tacked about its walls, was spent in tracking down a foreign remark, a phrase dropped by one of the Santa Monica pilots. To make the search more difficult, the overheard diagnosis of a new design's performance was most often in patois, the pilot's modification of exact engineering terms. Occasionally, while plodding through one of my borrowed volumes, I would run across the precise explanation of a point made in one of the sessions. "This must be what George was describing"—the key to a locked door.

Another accidental way in which I found myself making progress was to read a subject first and then be able to recognize its idiomatic pilot version in discussions later. It was like learning a foreign tongue and its dialects all at once in unrelated bits and pieces and then fitting them together. The dictionary I used at present was a book stolen from the bottom drawer of Bob Rahn's desk: Stability and Control. I had it photostated so that I could have my own copy.

The men I gleaned my new education from, the engineering pilots, operate from the flight-test office upstairs at the Santa Monica plant. It is a business office, like a small insurance company's office. Rows of big desks covered with papers, textbooks, and the inevitable slide rule. The ten men who sat behind the desks were dressed in business suits and, for the most part, conservative ties. They were between the ages of 30 and 45 and the one distinguishing feature shared by them was their color. They all, with the exception of Russ Thaw, the most erudite and dapper pilot in the group, were suntanned. Engineering pilots do a lot of waiting. And sometimes they wait on the beach or in a patio. They wait for planes to which they have been assigned to be completed, and while they wait they study the blue handbooks that a hundred engineers and designers have compiled to tell them how their ship is engineered and what it is supposed to do. They wait for the bugs, discovered in the testing of the new designs they currently fly, to be worked out. They wait for a part to be added to the modified design that they will prove. From a few violent moments, pulling 7 G's in an uninitiated fighter, the blood drawn into their legs and out of their faces, the force grabbing at their lower jaw, the pilots are given days of waiting, of comparing notes with their comrades, picking up bits of knowledge that will protect them next time they are in a tight spot.

Test pilots are security-conscious. When they are not figuring ways to protect their lives, they are figuring ways to assure their futures. You can test only so long; the oldest man in the business is Gene May, who is an exception at 50. So part of the time spent in the flight room deals with investment talk, the money gained from contracts must be put somewhere where it will bring in a return when they are too old for the strenuous dives.

Russ Thaw could usually be found studying the stock-market quotations. Even to another test pilot Russ was somewhat of a surprise, he most resembled a young English professor at Yale in his usual costume of a vent-backed coat, dark gray slacks, the button-down shirt, and Cordovan shoes. his manner was deliberate and slow and it was generally Russ who managed to have the last work in the technical sessions. He was known to the other pilots as "Father."

The photostated copy of Rahn's Stability and Control helped me to understand Russ' "last words" more than anything I had managed to find on the subject so far. It was a bible of testing; every aspect of flight engineering was thoroughly dealt with—every aspect, that is, except high-speed or supersonic flight. Not a line on it. The cupboard was bare. And I remembered what George had said last week when he told us that Gene May wasn't interested in going on with the second phase of the Skyrocket program. May had quit. George had said, "There isn't anything to write about sonic flight so far, because nobody knows." Gene May and Pete Everest and Chuck Yeager were up at Muroc bringing back the data in their flying laboratories, the X-1 and the Skyrocket. And now that the Skyrocket was once more without a pilot, the flight-room discussions touched briefly on the situation.

None of us knew anything about supersonic flight; the only pilots in the world who knew were Yeager, May, and Everest. Everest was an Air Force test pilot who has been checked out in the famous X-1. I couldn't help but share with the engineering pilots the feeling that the design people were pushing too fast. But the data gathered by the research aircraft were desperately needed. The assigned aerodynamicists and engineers were devoted to the task of developing research tools in the form of radical planes, to establish by diligent investigation the scientific principles and laws governing high-speed flight.

The X-3, hidden behind the high wooden partitions at the Santa Monica plant for the past three years, was one of the new tools. And the X-1 and the Skyrocket were already furnishing these engineers with the data they needed to design the supersonic planes of the future. Only a few pilots had seen the X-3, a highly restricted project that required a special clearance to pass its guarded doors. It was rumored that the X-3 would hit a Mach number of 2, twice the speed of sound, in level flight. Twice the speed of sound and right now only a small group of pilots in the entire country had been checked out in a jet, Lockheed's F-80, a ship with a top speed of 550.

After a gradual ascent in speed and performance over the past 46 years since the Wright brothers got a craft to fly 120 feet, now in 1949 the line was leaping clear off the chart—a sudden development that had made the cautious test pilots even more cautious. Years of experience had taught them suspicion. "Don't let them push you too far. They are not always right," was a common phrase among the men who were assigned to prove the engineer's and designer's theories. Intuition and practical application against equations—the ghost conflict between the engineers and the pilots.

And now once more the giant-sized experimental model, the Skyrocket, fitted with 625 pounds of recording instrumentation, waited for a pilot, and again the pilots were not very anxious.

It was a late summer morning, dry with the offshore wind blowing out across the unrelieved, flat land that stretches south of Los Angeles to the field where I tested the AD's. There wasn't a tree for miles to stop the hot breeze as it blew out to the sea; closer to Beverly Hills and Santa Monica where the hills and mountains began to slant up, the trees gradually became thicker. These mountains and low hills to the north form part of one of the chain circling the shallow bowl that holds the El Segundo field, where on the west boundary the Pacific lies. And today in from the desert the wind blew hot on its way to the ocean.

I sat in the windowless, stuffy ready room in the hangar with the big photostated copy of Stability and Control opened across my lap, waiting to be called from the radio room for my flight. On the couch opposite me George sat reading the Times.

"Hey, here's a piece about the Skyrocket." He read the item to me: "'The rocket-and-jet-powered research airplane D-558-II Skyrocket has repeatedly exceeded the speed of sound in level flight it was announced today by the Navy Department's Bureau of Aeronautics . . .'" I looked up and shook my head.

George found something else. "'More advanced high-speed research phases of the flight testing are being conducted at Muroc, California.'" He groaned.

The dispatcher's voice came into the room from the squawk box over the door: "Bridgeman, Brownie wants to see you in his office."

The last time Brownie requested a formal meeting in his office was six months ago when the insurance men came out to investigate the repainting of the 229 cars I had damaged. I tried to recall any recent incident that would warrant the formal summons.

The red door to Brownie's cubicle was open. Inside, Bert Foulds was sitting in the big leather chair. Foulds is assistant chief to Johnny Martin who had been elevated to head test pilot last year.

"Bill, Bert is over this morning looking for more engineering pilots. He'd like to talk to you about it," Brownie explained from behind his desk.

Foulds spoke then. "I was telling Brownie that things are beginning to pick up rapidly in the testing division. Everything is coming at us at once—the high-speed research programs are demanding pilots checked out in experimental work and, that, plus the A-2D, the F-3D, and the new AD and F-4D, and X-3 coming out soon puts terrific pressure on our engineering pilots." The assistant chief looked squarely at me. "You probably know by now that May isn't interested in the third phase of the Skyrocket . . . we'd like to see you get interested in it, Bill."

The Skyrocket! Bert's proposal dropped in my lap like a grenade. Surely he was not serious. I had no valid experience in engineering; I'd never even handled a jet engine. The Skyrocket combined both jet and rocket engines. I had to convince this man of my inadequacies for such an assignment. I tried to toss it off. "Bert, I appreciate your confidence but I don't know anything about supersonic flight, I . . ."

He interrupted: "Nobody does. I don't, Brownie doesn't, nobody here does, except Gene. That's the whole point . . . jump in and get your feet wet, at least go out to Muroc and have a look at her. I've got a new guy coming into help Brownie. Why don't you go up and talk to Gene. It's a good opportunity for you."

My hesitation caused me embarrassment. Bert seemed convinced. I had the feeling that the matter was settled, it was done. No matter what was said from that point on. It was done.

"You see, Bill, most of the engineer pilots are busy now with other projects and we need somebody to work with Gene right away. . . . It's an expensive program and we can't afford to waste time." He reassured me. "I know you're thinking we could get an outside man, one with more experience, but Johnny would rather have one of our own guys; we like to bring them up our way."

There it was. A new frontier laid before me. A frontier nobody knew much about. Pioneer days with no time for speculation, jump aboard. Fly it! Get in and find out, mistakes would be made, but find out! In this case I was as uninitiated as the rest of the pilots, we were all on equal footing. The problem broke upon us overnight— supersonic flight. The designers and the engineers were more confident than the pilots, they had had eight years or so to consider the problem, to advance formulas—they were fairly certain of what to expect. All their theories were not proved yet, however . . . it would be flight that would prove them.

And here in Brownie's office listening to Bert talk, although I was apprehensive, unsure of myself, I knew I would fly the experimental plane. The arguments my mind set forth against the idea was lost to the more powerful instinct of curiosity, challenge, and the restlessness that I couldn't define.

After all, I could always call a halt if I reconsidered, no one was forcing me to accept this project . . . the loophole acted as a buffer against my apprehension. At least go up and take a look at it, you could always change your mind. A game played with myself, the bit of preparation needed to face the reality at hand, the Skyrocket.

The following day I took the road through the northern hills, into the San Fernando Valley where the road serpentines through the green canyons on the other side. The road that leads to Muroc.

The deep canyon I drove through, Mint Canyon, was cool and fragrant, the sun was shaded by large old oak trees that hung over my path, leaving a dappled pattern on the black pavement. It is only a matter of 100 years since bandits waited around the rocky bends, and with the exception of the asphalt highway and a few Coca-Cola signs the trail is unchanged. At the end of this road, deep out in the desert, was the Skyrocket. Out of the valley of little farms into the Mojave Desert, a sea of varying brown waves, I thought of the plane at the end of the journey an hour away.

Here was a chance at freedom. I was freed from the monotony of El Segundo. A sudden departure—like the announcement on the board at Kaneohe five years ago that we were to join the war after the months of repetitious preparation. All overnight. The unknown met abruptly.

The desert streamed by and I tried to recall what I had heard about the Skyrocket; bits of conversation about her heard with detachment during the last year took on vitality.

Yesterday, after Bert had left the office, Brownie had offered advice for the first time.

"You do what you want to, Bill, but you're biting off a real mouthful. Don't let anybody push you, stop and find out what it is . . ." Well, I was about to find out.

The apprehension I felt was caused not so much by the ship in the desert but by doubt of my own ability. Brownie was right, I was asking for it good. I am a great believer in "luck" and my luck had held up—but the self-doubt still came over me like waves of nausea when I considered that I was about to take on. That austere, finely pointed mass of energy, which I had chosen to control at speeds I never dreamed possible, was scheduled to travel nearly Mach 1.5, over 1000 miles an hour in level flight, a feat no other plane in the world was capable of accomplishing. Who did I think I was? I had no experience to draw from in approaching this machine, it was foreign to me. I consoled myself with the recollection of what the assistant chief test pilot said yesterday in Brownie's office: "Gene knew nothing about it when he took over, nor did Johnny when he took first flight in it." There is no experience on which to draw when a new frontier is to be crossed, you just go out and cross it—there is no slight armor of the familiar.

And so I was on my way to meet the awesome lady. On the highway ahead stood a sign pointing off into the desert: AIR FORCE FLIGHT TEST CENTER. This was the road, a long black line cutting the rolling, undulating desert in two. Across the empty flatness long shadows wee pulled from the heavy, straight yuccas by the lowering sun. Even with the lowering sun it was no cooler, the air was furnace-hot and the miles and miles of desert lay motionless beneath it; not a bird or a house or a car but my own. Tranquility in heavy greens, yellows, and browns.

A dip in the road, a gradual rise, and there in immediate relief to the flatness were twin hangars, sphinxlike, looming out of the desert.

The terrain now was so flat that inside the car it was like looking up at the base from a shallow hole. Ahead was the dirt road that leads to the main gate, five miles away. The twin sphinx loomed nearer.

I presented my papers at the gate office to the colored corporal in charge. He gave me a sticker for my car, a base pass, and directions to the Douglas hangar located in the restricted area. My first visit to a military post in a long, long time. The usual whitewashed stones marked the streets and the sun-bleached wooden one-story buildings lined up evenly along the way. There wasn't a sign of green, the earth was parched, and the beige sand puffed by in the furnace air like powder. There was little movement on the base, an occasional truck or car; but no one appeared to leave or enter the air-conditioned wooden structures. Two F-80's thundered overhead.

Muroc, the run-down frontier base where the frontiers of

supersonic speed are probed, is a unique military post. It combines aircraft-proving activities of the Air Force, 18 aircraft contractors, and four governmental agencies. The major aircraft manufacturers maintain hangars on the field, where their military-ordered projects are stabled and tested, the test center provides facilities for the contractors and agencies in the development and testing of their projects. The desert base is one of eight Air Force Research, Development, and Test centers spotted across the country comprising the command that is assigned the task of keeping U. S. Air Force planes and equipment equal to or better than any enemy force. Normally a prototype model is flown 20 to 50 hours by the aircraft contractor to demonstrate its handling characteristics, and to prove it will fly, before the military test crews step in to make their evaluation in what is known as Phase-II testing. If the aircraft is accepted and is put into production, the first series of production planes are put through extensive tests by the military pilots. Performance data from this testing phase are used by the Flight Data Branch at Wright Air Development Center in Dayton, Ohio, for checking manufacturer's figures advertised in Pilot Operation Handbooks. The next phase of military testing is to determine the ship's endurance and maintenance requirements under combat conditions. All defects discovered are relayed to the manufacturer for correction or further study.

Next to the Douglas hangar sits the governmental agency assigned to investigate high-speed flight, the National Advisory Committee for Aeronautics. When the Skyrocket had been proven by Douglas, when Gene May and now maybe I had taken it up to his boundaries, the ship would be turned over to this scientific board for extensive inquiry into the realm of supersonics. Duplicate models of the Skyrocket would be made and NACA research test pilots would proceed to fill in the minute points of data within the boundaries deemed safe by the original Douglas test program.

I pulled my car up beside the Douglas hangar where I was to find Al Carder, project coordinator of the Skyrocket program. A sign on the hangar door read THIS PROJECT IS CONFIDENTIAL. DO NOT ENTER. Inside the big hangar the Air Force sergeant stationed at a desk, a 45 at his side, looked at my pass. The hangar was dark after the yellow afternoon light of the desert. I asked the sergeant where I could find Carder; he pointed toward the line of offices along the side of the hangar.

"That's his office, but you'll probably find him somewhere in the hangar."

My eyes adjusted to the shadowy hangar, I could see past the sergeant now. Deep in the immense, bare cavern sat a surgically white plane, swarming with mechanics. There she was! Al Carder was forgotten. There was the animal I was going to fly, dead-white and shiny, with a sort of purity about her. Her gear down, breaking the immaculate line of her body, she lost a great deal of the alien look she wore in the picture above Brush's desk. I moved down to her. The rocket ship looked like an airplane. Caught with her hair down, the lines spilling out of the open hatches, the mechanics crawling over her, she was like any ordinary ship in overhaul. Black smudged tools lay on her thin, highly polished swept-back wings and two mechanics sat on the fuselage leaning into the openings. Impudent probers. The slender wings were the only interruption in the straight, smooth line that began at the bayonet-pointed nose and gradually thickened over the cockpit; the small, faired-in windows formed a slight curve that melted back into the tapered body out of which flowed, high and back, the graceful tail. There appeared no way to get into the cockpit, no handles, nothing projecting, clean and finely pointed as a spitzer bullet.

I had never seen so many mechanics around a plane; usually there were two, maybe three. The Skyrocket had a crowd of 12. It ws difficult to get a close look at her, trying to squeeze in between the attendants who no doubt wondered who the hell I was anyway. They shouldered me out of their way. The cockpit looked pretty small for my lanky frame . . . the instrument panel was a surprise. From what I could see of it, it was much simpler than I thought it would be. Aft of the 45-foot-long ship were the rocket tubes, a large cylinder in the fanny, holding four empty cones. Catching her dressing like this made her far less awesome. Any fear that I had was lessened. This is the most beautiful airplane that I had ever seen.

This was something I had to do now. It was no longer a question of merely wanting to fly the Skyrocket—I had to fly it. Here sat a form of freedom. A chance to go. It was a chance that I could not turn down—even though there was the great possibility that I might not live to realize what ever it was that this plane promised.

"Where can I find Al Carder?" I asked one of the attendants. He looked impatiently at me and mumbled that Carder was down by the coffee-vending machine: "The one in the tan shirt talking to the engineers."

I tapped the heavy-set man in the tan shirt on the shoulder and introduced myself.

"Bill Bridgeman? Oh, yeah, yeah. You're the fellow who's supposed to take over the ship. Just a minute and we'll go into my office." Carder was pale and preoccupied. His hair was sandy, a shade darker than his face. He excused himself from the coffee conference and led the way into his office.

"Okay now." Unsmilingly he asked, "What have you been flying?"

I ran through my career briefly, winding up with the AD's. Carder remained expressionless, waiting for me to continue. A pause. He cleared his throat. "Yes. Well, I suppose you had better get some jet time in pretty quick if you're thinking of taking this thing over in a couple of months. We haven't got a lot of time." He added as he got up from his desk, "We've got a great deal of work to do; each day that this project is delayed costs the company thousands of dollars."

I had not impressed Al Carder, the man whose job it was to safeguard the exquisite and highly expensive experimental airplane and see that the program centered around it moved as smoothly and quickly as practicable.

"I guess you had better talk to Gene. He should be around here somewhere." He opened the door into the hangar and called down to the sergeant, "Gus, have you seen Gene May around? Send him in if you find him."

Five minutes later Gene May walked in. Gene May, the man I had heard about the last year in the flight offices at Douglas, was around 50, with at least 30 years of flying in back of him. A leathered old veteran of the sky, he probably had more years in a cockpit than George Jansen, Russ Thaw, and I put together. The Skyrocket's master was a wiry, small, dark man with an expressive, lit-up boyish face; both hands were pushed deep into his pants pockets and he jangled his change as he talked.

"Glad to meet you, Bridgeman." He looked at me and away again, around the little office, jangling his coins. Again I repeated my meager qualifications. "Okay," May bobbed his head. Carder went over some papers, withdrawn from the conversation. "You haven't had any jet time either, huh? Let's get that out of the way first. You'll have lots of questions to ask after you've been in an F-80."

May viewed me with a certain amount of uncertainty, the way Carder had; and with what appeared to be resignation, it was arranged that I was to take up one of the Air Force's F-80's as soon as a clearance could be had. I was given a handbook on the workings of the jet plane and assigned a room in the BOQ, several base blocks from the Douglas hangar.

The interview was over. In the hangar, outside Carder's office, the Skyrocket stood temporarily deserted. The four-o'clock crew of mechanics was drifting in at the other end of the building where the sergeant stood guard at the door.

She sat alone in the shadowy, big hangar; there was no ladder nor steps into her cockpit, instead a portable platform ladder stood at her side, several inches away from the polished white surface. I swung myself into the cockpit, slid my legs straight forward, straddling the control stick. The cockpit fitted like a mold; I sat on a flat cushion against a backrest, directly in the nose, behind the swordlike projectile pointing out into the dark hangar in front of me. Along either side of my upper legs were control-panel extensions. It was the most confining cockpit I had ever sat in. It was like a tight box.

On the deep control panel were spread the neat lines of alien instruments, only a few were familiar. Among the glinting foreign round dials were tailpipe temperature meters, a row of rocket-pressure gauges.

Out of the center of the panel looked the most arresting eye of them all: the Machmeter! Here is the dial that tells you how fast you are flying in relationship to the speed of sound, Mach 1. In a month or so I would watch the needle rise from .0, where it now rested, up to .7, .8, .9, .95, and then 1. This ambitious airplane had a

Machmeter that read up to Mach 2, twice the speed of sound.

And on my left the imposing lever with a cold metal knob that fitted my palm, dominated the cockpit. This was the rocket level. I felt it in my hand but it seemed unreal, the sound of it was unreal—rocket lever! Below it in a neatly spaced line were four innocuous little switches, number-one rocket barrel, number-two, number-three, number-four; four small pins that set off four thundering explosions. An enormous amount of engineering and arranging has resulted in these knobs, levers, and switches that only need be moved a little this way, a little that, to send this still plane into supersonic flight.

A member of the four-o'clock shift appeared beside the plane. He was startled to find someone in the cockpit. Security was too well enforced in the hangar for the mechanic to question my presence.

I called down to him, "How do you get out of it in a hurry?"

He looked up and wryly explained, "Nothing to it." He walked up to the nose. "You see that glassed-in handle on your right down by your leg? Open the door and just pull the handle."

"Yeah, then what happens? You ejected out of the seat?"

"Not exactly. In this ship the whole nose drops off. The pilot rides the pod down to a safe speed and altitude and then—see that other level there, next to your right elbow?—well, you pull that and the bulkhead drops away; then the pilot falls out of the back and parachutes the rest of the way down. So far nobody's tried it."

It was nostalgic to be on a military base once more and not be a part of it, not to sign the officer's roster that was posted in the hall of the BOQ, to be in a sport shirt. The hot climate, the hangars, the fine dust carried in off the desert floor, the field full of planes. Like the South Pacific, the service once more. Outside the young flyers in faded khaki hurried by, escaping indoors into the air-conditioned offices. The young men going through days of a life I once went through, the growing up under the watchful authority of the military.

My room at the BOQ, ironically named The Shamrock after the plush Texas hotel, had the aspect of a cell, narrow and stark with an air-conditioning unit hung outside the only window. There was a good mattress on the bed, no rug on the floor, and as if to compensate for its starkness the room was dominated by a large white refrigerator. A large, incongruous note of luxury. This would be home for the next year or so; and at least for the next two or three months there wouldn't be many trips to my beach shack in Los Angeles. There wouldn't be much free time to allow myself, not if I were to handle the ship that sat over in the huge Douglas hangar. It would be studying and asking, finding out all I could glean from the man who knew her best. Following May around was not going to be an easy job from the looks of him. He didn't sit still very long.

There was the F-80 first anyway, the preliminaries. The F-80 guide book and the workings of the jet engine occupied me in the tiny room until my eyes were dry and sore and reading was becoming a labor. It was well after two when I pulled the light out over my bed. The dead-white plane, the color of the refrigerator gleaming against the wall, occupied my thoughts for a while before I slept.

CHAPTER VIII

W hile I waited for an army clearance to "check out" in the F-80, I stood in the shadows of Al Carder's well-greased Skyrocket organization. The expensive research tool and each phase of its preparation for flight, then the flight itself, was as carefully controlled as the detonation of an atom bomb. The staff that devoted itself to this planning was not small. The hangar that housed the Skyrocket also housed its staff of 12 mechanics, project coordinator, eight engineers, one male secretary, and two technicians, representing the rocket-engine manufacturer, Reaction Motors, Inc., and the company that built the J-34 jet engine, Westinghouse.

Each flight plan was formulated by the engineers a week before the take-off was scheduled. The area of flight they wanted explored was measured precisely by approximately 625 pounds of especially designed instrumentation carried throughout the body of the white ship. When the air ripped over the Skyrocket in high Mach-number flights, the rapid impulses of this rigged-up nervous system were automatically recorded by an oscillograph and a manometer.

The eight flight-test engineers who deciphered the data brought back from flight devoted all of their talents to the Skyrocket. However, they were individually concerned with various functions and parts of the airplane. Howell Commons and "Long John" Peat coped with the electrical end of the ship, the power plant was overseen by two power-plant engineers, Bob Osborne and Harvey Sorenson, and the two manufacturers' representatives, Johnny Conlon from Reaction Motors, Inc., and Westinghouse's Gil Peers. Stability characteristics of the research plane were the province of Orv Paulsen and George Mabry, aerodynamicists: the boys who held priority over the rest of the group in the matter of what tests were to be made. Project engineer over the entire program was Bob Donovan. His assistants were Charles Kennedy and Tommy Briggs, who acted as liaisons between El Segundo and Muroc. Bob was rarely seen but his influence was felt. Most of Donovan's time was spent at El Segundo rounding up obscure parts or conferring with Ed Heineman, El Segundo's chief engineer and the man directly responsible for the design of the Skyrocket.

Here at the test center it was Al Carder's job as Douglas' project coordinator to keep things moving and to keep harmony among the stable of intent engineers—and the mechanics, the physical keepers of the hybrid plane. There was no time allowed for temperament in the project, a strong will among the specialists would delay the program by days—there was compromise.

And so a flight had been scheduled. It was an involved process that began in the hangar and led up to a formal request, almost the same way strikes in the Pacific were born on the beaches and returned, formalized, from the admiralty to the originators. Here the aerodynamicist had an off handed chat with the lead man of the mechanic crew—the ship was in shape to go again—she had been worked over for maybe a week, the bugs from last flight ferreted out, the important alterations executed—her surface coat repainted and polished in order that she might offset for a minute longer the clawing and hammering of the air that waited at supersonic speed for the audacious intruder.

With the hangar news that she was almost set to go again, Orv Paulsen found Al Carder in his office and verbally submitted a flight request for 35,000 feet. Carder then checked with the lead man—the ship was okay. Once assured, Carder informed the aerodynamicist that he might submit a formal request. Often Carder would find some minute fault with the condition of the Skyrocket and deny the request until the necessary alteration had been made.

Then the eight engineers, each interested in tests concerning his portion of the ship, got together and formulated a compromise flight plan touching on all phases of the ship's performance. This involved a series of maneuvers they wanted the pilot to perform in order to get confirmation of their wind-tunnel data.

The formal flight plan was presented to Carder for approval. If it was workable and in no radical way endangered the ship, he would okay the proposed flight plan, but usually he would make deletions and alterations. Often Carder would find the flight inconceivable because of the ship's capacities—not enough flight time available to perform all the requested items, or further study was needed on the forces and strains that new items would put on the ship before it was safe to include them in a flight.

The first Skyrocket flight I was to see was called for sunup on Friday morning. It was called for sunup so that the tricky takeoff would be blessed by the cold, stable air found over the desert only in the early-morning hours, a slight advantage for the exacting flight.

On Thursday afternoon the final preparation began. Gene May, whom I managed to keep step with, staying beside him whenever possible, read the flight plan and hit the top of the hangar over a couple of items that had slipped by Carder which May thought were—to put it quietly—ill-advised. The engineer-pilot conflict again. Gene wasn't about to risk his neck unnecessarily just for the convenience and expedition of the program. "If you think I'm going to pull a buffet check at 4000 feet, you're all out of your minds," he roared. "To hell with that stuff . . ." Carder deftly handled the situation, even to the extent of removing some of the offending items. It would probably delay the program, but obviously Gene wasn't going to buy all of the items and no matter how you cut it, the pilot had the last word: he flew the plane. I was in no position to take sides, not having a clear idea of what the thorn in Gene's side was, although intuitively I leaned toward Gene's camp—the pilot's inbred distrust of engineers.

After winning his point, Gene hurried out of the hangar door and disappeared onto the base. I had turned briefly to watch the stiletto-nosed ship being primed for flight and he was gone. It wasn't easy to stay with the pilot; he moved fast, never sat in a chair for more than a minute at a time. Often he would leave me in the middle of a conversation about some peculiar Skyrocket characteristic as if he suddenly remembered something more important. It was as if he never quite told me all there was to know about one of the ship's nasty habits. I had the feeling a lot was left unsaid.

There was little point in trying to find him now. I watched the mechanics prime the Skyrocket for flight. Tomorrow he would take her up once more and the mechanics were swarming about in last-minute attendance. Outside the sun burned low over the empty miles of desert, glinting off the silver skins of the weird, still flock of experimental planes that sat along field. Shallow waves of heat hung above the white runway, and beyond that lay the baked mud of the dry lake where the Skyrocket would scream into flight tomorrow morning.

Then she was rolled from the hangar, restrained; the enormous power required to send her 15,000-pound, sleek hull into the transonic region lay dormant . . . a gigantic animal in a somnambulent state, drowsy and docile.

Slowly, gently, the 12 trained attendants rolled the Skyrocket up a ramp onto a 13-foot-long "mother" trailer. When the ship's propellants were once aboard, hoses from pressurized tanks on the trailer continuously would feed nitrogen through the rocket engine until the exact moment of flight, to prevent an accidental accumulation of propellants in the combustion chamber, which could result in a highly explosive start. The ship was aboard the trailer; a canopy overhead would protect the Skyrocket and her entourage from the searing morning sun; another form of protection was in one corner, a shower in the event the volatile liquids accidentally sprayed one of the crew members. To safeguard the plane with its explosive load of propellant (a drop of raw hydrogen peroxide is enough to burn a hole in a concrete floor) an intricate system of fire hoses using fog and straight stream was supplied from a 700-gallon water tank, just part of the crowd of equipment utilizing every inch of the huge conveyance. She was ready for the important and dangerous job of fueling that would begin early the following morning.

"What time are we due back here?" one of the mechanics asked.

Carder appeared beside the trailer. The project coordinator answered, "I think we can make it at two o'clock this time, boys. Sunup is getting later with the fall coming on. That'll give us enough time. Dawn is scheduled for five-forty-five tomorrow."

Some of the crew members moaned. "That's a break, another hour's sleep."

"Well, as they warned us in Santa Monica, join a research program for adventure. Live a little." The mechanic slapped his complaining companion on the back. "You're making history, boy."

The lead man announced, "We'll come in at two and top off the tanks." The group dispersed into the coming darkness. The Skyrocket was left deserted in its awkward position, clamped to the bed of the trailer.

Surely I couldn't have been sleeping more than an hour when the thin, steady, high whistling began. It was as if a strong stream of wind were trapped somewhere, trying to escape. I sat up in the darkness, my mind groping to respond to whatever alarm it might be, and as I came in focus I could hear no other sound. Obviously no emergency. I fell asleep once more but with the steady, shrill whistle still wailing over the field.

The alarm jarred me awake, the signal that the flight procedure would begin. It was dark and once more I heard the chilling whistle floating over the base, unbroken and piercing.

I made my way toward the Douglas hangar through the empty streets of the sleeping base, the whistle became louder as I drew near the Skyrocket. The eerie scream comes out of the weird plane! Tightened, tensed—the explosive fuels oozing slowly into her sides, it was the Skyrocket that emitted the frightened, tortured whine. The men who had been feeding the Skyrocket her fuel at precision rate for the last three hours wore hoods with glass face-plates, specially made plastic coveralls, and heavy gloves to protect their bodies from the volatile fuels as they tended the white, frosted lines and hoses connecting the mother trailer to the embryo ship.

Into the under belly of the airplane the minus-297-degree-below-zero liquid oxygen was introduced into one of the large twin tanks that sit two inches apart from each other. If the liquid oxygen should be contaminated, it would blow the plane, trailer, crew, and spectators off the desert floor. It had to be fed carefully. Once in the tank, the liquid oxygen boiled off continuously at one pound a minute, forming gases that escaped through small orifices in the top of the fuselage. As the stuff steamed off it caused the sustained, early-hour whistling, the weird shriek I heard early this morning. Once the oxygen was at the precise level in the tanks it had to be kept there—as it boiled off the top the exact amount of oxygen was replenished through the hose connected to the supply tank on the trailer. Thus the necessity of the mother vehicle, in order that the lines tending the rocket propellant would remain functioning and undisturbed while the plane was being transported across the eight-mile dry lake to the position where it was to be released for flight. All the while the gauges reading pressures in the various operations were watched as cautiously as those in a surgery. Less pains-takingly, the other hooded members of the crew moved quickly and quietly around the still bird, filling the other big tank with alcohol. The liquid oxygen and alcohol were stored side by side in the twin tanks separated from each other by a thin aluminum vapor seal. A rubberlike compound is used as caulking to prevent any leakage between the compartments.

When the Skyrocket was ready to go, a small pump similar to the one used in the V-2 rocket, obtaining its power from decomposed hydrogen peroxide, pumped the subzero liquid oxygen and alcohol aft to the tiny rocket engine. When the two fluids burned in the engine, the resultant expanding gases provided the gigantic thrust that blasted the heavy load off the ground into flight.

Once the very nervous hydrogen peroxide was in the Skyrocket a speck of dirt in the hydrogen peroxide tank or in any of the myriad tubes and lines, and the little research ship would be blown to dust. Two models of the Air Force's X-1, our rival, the only other rocket airplane in the country—using identical fueling—had blown up in launching last year.

Al Carder took no chances with the Skyrocket. The pressurizing gases—helium and nitrogen—were sieved through Kotex to make certain no insidious segment of dust was carried in with the explosive fluids, an operation that explained why I had seen cartons of the incongruous supplies stacked in the hangar.

Carder had confidence in his men, they were trained well, yet he watched the serious business alertly, ready to intercede in case of an error. In his mind lay the whole flight plan; each of his assistants had been assigned various functions of the whole. While he watched the immediate operation, he was thinking ahead, anticipating what could go wrong and the consequent steps to be taken toward prevention. He was figuring how to save five minutes' time in the expensive flight plan—methods of further insuring its margin of safety.

Headlights flashed onto the field out of the darkness. The cars carrying the engineers, the technicians, and the pilot converged near the front of the hangar, ready to join the caravan that would begin its way slowly across the runway onto the parched, mosaically cracked clay lake.

Preceding the funeral-paced procession was the huge trailer carrying the Skyrocket, active as an atomic bomb, locked securely to its bed. Carder, a general leading a column of tanks, headed the fleet in a radio car. Through the mist that floated in long veils across the dead lake, the white plane was carried, with its entourage of green Douglas cars, a fire truck, and an ambulance, into the early-morning light.

The red beacon at the end of the runway flashed green and we began to creep toward the point where the plane was to be unloaded, five miles ahead.

I sat beside Gene May in the back seat of the radio car. In the seat in front of us Carder was issuing last-minute orders over the hand mike: "Metro One, this is Metero Six . . . from now until take-off transmit the wind direction, velocity, and temperature every five minutes." Metro One, a truck with a big square, searching theodolite on its roof, had been stationed by Carder midway along the path of flight.

The truck answered, "Metro Six, this is Metro One . . . wind, velocity, and temperature every five minutes, right." Carder was absorbed in the important details of the flight, preoccupied as though he were straining to remember something.

Straight ahead the faraway mountains were hidden by the mist—the edge of the huge lake on all sides was lost by the vapor drifts. The ground we moved over was sterile as concrete, no weed, no green—it was difficult to maintain a sense of direction, we seemed to be a ship on a flat sea sliding across an empty clearing bordered by fog. As if by radar, the dreary, little parade moved unfalteringly toward the end of the lake.

Another order from Carder: "Metro Two, this is Metro Six . . . we will be ready for the fire trucks in 30 minutes." And at the hangar Metro Two called into the moving car.

"We'll have fire trucks alerted in 30 minutes." If a program requires the use of more than one fire truck, the extra equipment is only sent at the time it is needed. Fire trucks on a test base are kept busy and their standby time is allotted.

Between radio calls the project coordinator turned around in his seat to Gene May. "Would you like a chase plane to take off and check the turbulence at your dive altitude?"

May rapidly shook his head, "No, the 'school' will have their planes up this morning, we can check with them." The matter was no longer Al Carder's responsibility; May had lifted this concern from Carder's pile of important details.

Again Al Carder spoke into the radio, "George," he called Mabry in one of the fleet of cars, "will you check the north-south runway for any debris?" The Skyrocket would eat up three miles of lake before she lifted off, a scrap of driftwood blown in off the desert onto her path would be enough to throw her off balance with her belly fat with explosives.

The ground wind came up cold now, clearing the mist away as

we pulled to a stop. The deep blue of the sky was fading as the light of the morning brightened. At the exact moment of sunup the plane was to leave the ground. The cars parked around the trailer a safe distance from the take-off point—the noise from the rocket engine would be loud enough to pop eardrums. Doors opened, the mechanics jumped to the ground and the Skyrocket was laboriously unloaded. Grotesquely the trailer "knelt" at the rear wheels so that the ship could be rolled off with its umbilical cords still intact. Above the desert the only noise was the putt-putt-putt of the motors on the trailer and the incessant whistle escaping from the plane. Carder's orders were spoken quietly, the mechanics spoke softly to one another, as if to keep from startling the restrained energy they worked around.

Every other minute the men who read the pressure gauges, intently as submarine captains, called out the pressures in the nitrogen tanks: "2000 pounds" was called and verbally relayed to Carder—"2000" . . . "2000" . . . and down the line . . . "2000."

"Hold it at 2000," the other echoed back. By sunrise the white plane sat into the wind, still fed by its cords, not yet free. Now the pilot was called; he emerged from the radio car. A gladiator heading for the pit, he swaggered with confidence; the wind whipped his flight jacket around his tightly laced G suit The size of his head was accentuated by the melon-shaped, heavy crash helmet. It was a costume weird enough for the role he played, the narrowness of his body, in the form-fitting, olive drab covering was congruent with the uncluttered, narrow bullet waiting for him, steaming and puffing on the ground.

Gene May gave his orders, climbed the portable ladder into the tiny cockpit and yelled, "Okay, let's wind this thing up." The jet engine, assisted in take-off with two of the four rocket tubes, was started whirling by the electric motor plugged into the side of the plane. A gentle, thin whee-eee-eee from the engine as the compressor started going and then the loud explosion that spit the flames out the tailpipe like red adder's tongues. The hurricane blowing out the fanny dug a long rut in the lake bed in back of the Skyrocket. She shrieked like a pig in a slaughterhouse. Sign language was used now; the noise from the plane smothered all other sound. Above, an

F-80 shot over—the "chase" plane was in the air. He would follow the rocket ship, looking for trouble to report to its pilot. He was an eyewitness in case the ship didn't come back. May made a sign, the canopy was closed. A loud-speaker was used now to communicate to the ground crew from the sealed cockpit in the Skyrocket. Carder sat with his assistant in the radio car holding the speaker that connected him directly to the pilot in the cockpit. He watched intently the last-minute activity around the plane—his runner would quickly deliver orders to the hustling men if he saw trouble.

From the cockpit radio Gene announced, "I'm pressurizing." The news was repeated down the line: "he's pressurizing" . . . "he's pressurizing" . . . "he's pressurizing." Again from the howling plane came the magnified and unnatural-sounding voice, "Al, I'm ready to prime." This announcement increased the tension in Al Carder; he leaned forward. Quickly the mechanics removed the lines and hoses from the Skyrocket and for the first time this morning she was unleashed with her load. She steamed heavily—read to go.

"What's holding things up?" May's sharp, rapid words fell.

Into the mike one of Carder's men advised promptly, "Okay, Gene, you've got a good prime."

The jet engine, assisted by the two rocket tubes in take-off, would climb independent of the rockets, once into the air, until 40,000 feet; then May would fire all four tubes to make his high-speed run. He was ready for take-off; he gestured, the crew stood back, and the engineers and technicians ran for the cars standing by. They started the motors so they could follow alongside the plane during take-off, watching the tail for a successful rocket "light."

A roar and she rolled rapidly, picking up speed. The green cars barreled along side her at close to 100 miles an hour for over a mile of the lake bed. Into Carder's car the pilot called, "Okay, I'm lighting one." A 20-foot streak of orange bled into the air.

Carder called back, "One is good."

And immediately: "Here goes two."

A second orange streak shot out, Carder saw it and said close into the mike, "Two is good." The blast from the rockets jolted the moving cars and the plane was still eating up the lake bed, far ahead of us now. Another quarter of a mile and the Skyrocket began to shed the ground; hanging heavily over the desert she reluctantly rolled a bit, the gear went up. I tensed with the pilot in the ship; if anything went wrong at this moment—that would be all! The seconds went by and she gathered speed, rocked obediently over, and began the steady climb up. The sky held, only for a few more seconds, the two bright spots with the chase pilot diving to catch up . . . and then the planes were absorbed into the distance.

The converging cars slowed down and stopped. In his lap Carder held the flight plan that the pilot was to follow, he would follow it as closely as if he were in the ship with Gene. The radio was silent.

That was the "beast" I would ride! In a short time I would be in the role of pilot, the core of all this preparation and tension. Next month it would be my responsibility to handle her well. The engineers and the men involved in the Skyrocket program viewed the plane with some kind of undefinable emotion; they not only took their work seriously—they lived it. Every murmur from the ship was cause for their undivided attention and interest. It was a form of dedication I have rarely seen—a devotion to work that was almost akin to love; and to feel this devotion unconsciously tapped an intuitive understanding within me. It intensified the ever-growing feeling of responsibility not only toward myself and the ship in this matter, but also toward the men this day I suddenly seemed to know.

CHAPTER IX

The Skyrocket was through for the week; she was carried back
to the large empty hangar where for the hundredth time the
mechanics set upon her—again she was stripped down and reworked.
And once more the engineers retired to their desks with the reams
of oscillograph charts and manometer readings and the attentively
marked notes from their postflight conference with Gene May, who
would try to recall and sometimes diagnose the subtle signs, or, as the
case might be, the violent performance of the experimental airplane.
The investigators viewed with acute interest the motion picture film
that read the instrument panel, that vast array of dials and gauges
that it would be impossible for the pilot to record or remember while

in the throes of controlling the enormous amount of energy he rides. While Al Carder's smoothly coordinated Skyrocket staff digested the data brought back from the last flight and formulated what investigations they wanted performed next, when the mechanics had put her back in shape—the pilot would wait. When everything was primed up again, ready to go, they would call him.

It was difficult to feel that I was a part of this well-integrated, going concern, that soon I would step into the role where all the preparation eventually focused. . . .

Okay, there it is. We have labored pains-takingly; every possibility to safeguard the ship has been thoroughly explored; our aerodynamic-trained minds have plotted out a pattern of investigation into the realm of supersonic flight. We want the information brought back. The instrument that we use to bring back this knowledge cost 4,000,000 dollars, drew the talent and attention of 150 designers, engineers, and draftsmen for a period of three years . . . now it's your turn.

My turn would come in a month's time. If I wanted to stay alive and keep this assignment I had to get to know this craft and as fast as possible. Days spent watching the mechanics work over the little ship in the big, vacant Douglas hangar supplied me with practical knowledge of the rocket plant and the intricate instrumentation. The nervous system, the bloodline, of the Skyrocket, was laid before me, a cadaver dissected in a laboratory.

The Skyrocket was similar in structure to her predecessor, the bright red D-558-I Skystreak, with the exception of the sweptback wings and the needle nose. The Skystreak was powered with a turbo-jet engine, but it was soon apparent in the Skyrocket that in order to realize the full advantages of the sweptback wing at high speeds a supplementary rocket power plant would have to be used. Even the largest jet engine available wasn't powerful enough to produce the necessary thrust or speed to thoroughly test the new wing. And now with added rocket power, the Skyrocket was proving the swept-back wing at supersonic speed. But in gaining stability advantages at high speed, the wing created problems at low speeds. The Rocket lacked the lift of the conventional straight-winged airplane. To get rid of some of these disadvantages at the low speeds necessary in landings, the wings had been provided with leading-edge automatic slats and wing fences that delay separation of air, providing greater lift.

The turbo-jet J-34 Westinghouse engine was originally supposed to get the plane off the ground, into flight, and in for a landing under its own power; the Reaction Motors, Inc., rocket plant was intended to be used only for high-speed test purposes. But with 250 gallons of aviation gasoline, the 625 pounds of instrumentation, the 3000 pounds of rocket fuel added to the weight of the airplane, and the low-speed lift characteristics of the swept-back wing, Carder's organization found it necessary to fire two of the four rocket rubes to kick the ship into flight.

The high-powered research craft was constructed as light as possible in order to reach more easily the extreme altitudes where the think air allowed for greater speed, and correspondingly she was built as strong as possible to withstand the rigors of this high speed. Her wind and tail surface construction was of high-strength 75 ST aluminum alloy, the bomb-shaped fuselage was mostly magnesium.

Every inch of space under her thick skin was cannily used, with only the minimum amount of space allowed for the cockpit. Just enough room, as if the cockpit were tailored around him, was left for the pilot. For high-altitude operation the cockpit was pressurized and equipped with a heating plant; for extreme high speeds, when the friction of the air passing over the ship can bring the temperature inside the cockpit to a cozy 240 degrees, refrigeration had been provided.

The Skyrocket was not designed to fight. Her pay load was the 625 pounds of telemetering equipment, pressure-measuring devices, and load-recording machines developed over a period of years in the instrument shops at the Langley Laboratory, the NACA Aeronautical Research Center in Virginia. The manometers, by means of three miles of pressure tubing that crawled throughout the wing and tail sections of the ship, measured and recorded at 400 tiny points pressures of the air as it passed over the airfoils. The oscillograph, using over four miles of wiring, measured, by means of 904 electric strain gauges, control forces and stresses in the structure as it met shock waves at supersonic speeds, and recorded the impulses.

In the placement of the power plants and fuel systems, extreme care had been taken to distribute the fuel evenly about the airplane's center of gravity so that there was no acute trim change as the plane gulped her fuel. With all four rockets going at once in a high-speed level run, she would gobble up a ton and a half of the liquid oxygen and alcohol in one and one-half minutes—the fuel it took three hours to nurse into her before each flight. If the fuel tanks were not balanced over the ship, the abrupt loss of weight would cause a violent change in control effectiveness—enough to make control extremely difficult, if not impossible.

There was a lot to be learned about the Skyrocket before I would be absorbed into the precision organization. I studied the huge manual on the experimental ship and the F-80 handbook. When I couldn't digest any more of the technical wanderings and diagrams at a sitting, I would go down to the hangar and watch the mechanics work her over. Or, if I was lucky, I could find Gene May, the man who knew her better than anyone, who could give me the real "how to cope with her" answers.

The first few weeks I was on the base the Skyrocket's pilot was pretty elusive. "You get checked out in the 80 first, and then you'll have a lot more questions," he would say, disappearing into the hangar. His answers to immediate questions were brief, concise. If I hesitated to mull over what he had said, he would abruptly excuse himself and walk off.

And so my first knowledge of the Skyrocket was gathered independently. There was so little time. I couldn't afford to lose an hour. The rocket engine. In case of a fire do I jettison propellant or try to put it out? The questions rang like alarms persistently in my head. It was hard to escape from them.

The only immediate escapes from the heat and the Skyrocket were the officers' bar and Pancho's. Pancho's is a combination bar and fly-in motel lost in the vacant desert, somewhere to go when you want to get off the base; a rambling wooden structure that is the occasional destination of aircraft company contractors, military personnel, engineers, pilots, and mechanics away from home. The usually crowded barroom, with its rickety wooden tables, looked as if someone had left the door open and the desert had blown in. Proprietor of this rustic airman's haunt is "Pancho" Barnes, a woman of middle years and an ex-flyer. Pancho is dark, small, and exceedingly homely, an ardent champion and friend of the Air Force. Even with ten years of Navy behind me I have never heard anyone who could swear with the complete abandonment and dexterity of Pancho Barnes, the flyers' pal.

I spent most of my drinking hours, however, at the officers' bar on the base, only journeying out to Pancho's when I was driven by restlessness and boredom.

In the evenings at the air-conditioned, smoky base bar I sat among the young pilots. They talked flying and they talked about Chuck Yeager and Gene May and the two rival research programs. I hadn't met Chuck Yeager yet, nor had I seen him around the base although occasionally he flew chase for Gene. Obviously, from the animated conversations of my fellow escapees, he was Number-one boy on the base. Since he became the first man to fly faster than the speed of sound a couple of years ago in the Air Force's rocket plane, he had worn his crown securely.

The young pilots told a story about Yeager and May that happened before I joined the program. It seems Gene wanted very badly to be the first man to take off on rocket power alone. And while the Skyrocket was being prepared for the big flight, Gene jubilantly announced the coming feat in the bar one night. Yeager heard about it and immediately alerted Washington to the Navy Skyrocket's plans. At once Washington sent orders to get the X-1 rigged up fast for a similar take-off. The Air Force's plans were kept very quiet; Yeager never opened his mouth; and all the while the X-1 crew at the Air Force hangar down the runway were working day and half the night readying the ship.

One burned summer day before May's big flight, Yeager appeared out on the lake to perform an all-rocket take-off, and once more the X-1 was first. Gene never got over the treachery.

Then there was the time Yeager and "Pete" Everest were flying chase for the Skyrocket while Gene was going through a series of tower passes. The Skyrocket was never known for her ability at low altitude on her jet engine alone and as Gene sluggishly attacked the towers at four hundred and seventy-five miles per hour, Yeager and Everest, at Yeager's prompting, came in on either side of the experimental plane in their F-86's and peeled off in flawless slow rolls, 50 feet off the deck. When asked later by Yeager's commanding officer if he would like to prefer charges against the pair, Gene gracefully declined.

Nevertheless the Skyrocket was still viewed with a certain awe by the mixture of Air Force and civilian test pilots at the bar. When they got around to asking me what I was there to test, they were impressed and I was treated with new respect and sudden silence.

On Friday the Air Force clearance came through: an F-80 would be available to me Monday morning. And although the F-80 wasn't the Skyrocket, it was something new—a plane without a propeller. It was a plane I hadn't coped with and it was cause for some apprehension. The first step toward the big moment.

The night before the flight, through 30 minutes of shadowy early-evening desert, I drove out to Pancho's. A jukebox glowed red and blue in the corner and the glasses on the bar looked unclean. Gene May sat on the stool nearest the door, jiggling the ice in his drink. I took the stool beside him. For the first time since I had met him he seemed relaxed, and before I could bring up the matter he volunteered some advice about my first "go" in a jet. He gave me the signs to look for.

Hunched over sideways on the stool, Gene told me, "It's slow getting its power; even though it's a fighter, it's slow. Like a transport . . . you know as well as I do a transport takes a while to accelerate. Now on your approach this is important . . . you have to make your decision ahead of time. You can't let it get slow and then suddenly apply power to drag yourself over the 'fence.' You need that speed to keep it going. Once a jet slows down, that's it. You've got to have your approach all figured ahead of time." He swallowed the rest of his drink. "Try and keep away from rapid throttle manipulation . . . other than that, it's an airplane, pure and simple."

Over the bar among the hundreds of pictures of Air Force planes ardently hung by Pancho was a photograph of the F-80, the one I would be checked out in on Monday. The Air Force reserved this ship, the second jet ever built, for the sole purpose of checking out visiting flying dignitaries and test pilots like myself. It was one of 12 jets on the field. Scrawled over the picture were the signatures of the pilots who had taken their first jet ride in her; most of the names were well known.

After my flight tomorrow perhaps I would be allowed to add my signature.

The Air Force hangar was a short five blocks west down the runway from the Douglas operation and purposely, so that I could take a leisurely look over the F-80 I was to fly, I arrived 30 minutes before my appointment with Captain Roth, who had volunteered to show me around the jet cockpit.

On the edge of the glaring white flight apron I left my car and headed through the wall of heat toward the flight line, the parachute twisting heavily on my back.

The apron appeared deserted and quiet in the morning heat, the metallic sun glinted from the wings of the uncluttered, propellerless new jets that sat poised in a sleek row. One stood out a veteran, thin of paint, well used, and visibly worn, Number 08777, the "check-out" ship. That was mine. No one came out to meet me, all of the line personnel who could had found excuses to be occupied in the dark hangar, the only escape from the relentless sun. Already from the short walk up to the F-80 my overalls were damp with sweat; at altitude they'd freeze to my body. A refreshing prospect. Here and there on the line I saw a few unlucky souls hiding from the sun in the slim shadow spots cast by the airplane wings.

No one stirred or spoke as I unloaded the parachute on the wing of 08777, but halfheartedly they looked somewhat curiously my way. My odd overalls and unmatching assortment of flight gear were alien to the military field where the mechanics were accustomed to the correct and matching blue of the Air Force.

Perhaps if I appeared to be about to fly this thing someone would come out and give me a hand. I walked around the jet, checking the items her instruction book said should be noted; still no one was concerned. I was wet clear through from the exertion of the walk around the plane. The broiler-hot metal of the ladder alongside the little ship burned my fingers as I crawled up to the cockpit. I was about to climb in when a sergeant rolled from beneath the wing. "Buddy, you going to fly this thing?"

"Yeah, in about 30 minutes."

"Do they know about it upstairs?"

"Yes." But the sergeant was not convinced.

From a nearby ship another mechanic yelled over, "It's probably all right . . . the civvies fly that old bucket every now and then; the old man okays it."

When I mentioned that Captain Roth was coming down to give me a cockpit check soon, the doubting sergeant was reassured. He proceeded to make a check of the ship himself.

Like the Skyrocket, this ship had a cramped cockpit; there was just enough room for my legs stretched out in front of me directly into the nose. The control panel was a surprise; even though I'd been studying the F-80 handbook for the past four weeks, I was not prepared for the simplicity of the little fighter. She was far less complicated-looking than the AD except for her plumbing—an excess of switches, lights, and indicators. What had at first been a purely automatic system to aid the harassed fighter pilot had degenerated into a plumbing chaos. But the rest of the controls looked easy. No complicated quadrant with the three handles—prop, throttle, and mixture—here was just one big, easy-to-find, easy-to-move throttle . . . the stick, the rudder, and the instrument panel! The alien round instrument eyes that I would use for the first time today slept on the panel before me—the turbine outlet temperature indicator, the Machmeter, and fuel-flow indicator.

Where was the emergency hydraulic valve? I groped around the cockpit. The valve was small and hard to actuate. I was leaning over grumbling about this when a shadow dropped into the cockpit.

"What's the matter; lose something?" Captain Rusty Roth appeared on the ladder, an affable, friendly, red-haired Air Force pilot. The easy joke helped to relieve somewhat the awkward feeling of facing a strange instrument panel, a new airplane. I was at a disadvantage with this plane; my only defense against her sudden whims was the advice given to me by Gene May and the clinical description of her behavior in the blue handbook.

Roth leaned in and, beginning on the left-hand side, we went around the cockpit; all instruments corresponded pretty well with what the handbook had described. Rusty added a little trick here, an added hint there, or maybe a warning. All of this would help me approach the airplane more deftly, but in a first flight you need something more: you need luck. No matter how well you have been alerted to the warning signs, the chances of recognizing them in actual flight are small. To the uninitiated the bad engine would never be recognized; the subtle signs and little queer sounds escape unheeded—to a stranger in a jungle, the sounds are indicative of nothing until one day a violent experience teaches the danger they announce. A sudden whine or loss of thrust or a faulty instrument and that could be it; you hear it, feel it, without alarm and first flight is your last flight no matter how skilled a pilot you are. First flight requires luck. I relied on mine in the F-80.

"The critical Mach number of this ship is .8, as you probably already know, Bill. You won't be getting close to that speed anyway . . ."

Satisfied that he had briefed me to the best of his knowledge, Roth advised, "Let's start her up. I'll stand by for the first time. You know you can blow one of these 'pipes' clear down to the rocket-test stands if you don't regulate your fuel just right."

Rapidly Roth ran through the starting sequence in a practice drill for me, pointing to the switches involved. He caught the alerted mechanic's eye and rotated his hand; the mechanic nodded—now we were three people allied in trying to avert an explosion. I remembered the kid in the jet down at International last summer.

As quickly as I possibly could I moved the valves, switches, and the throttle in the proper order. It was not fast enough. My inexperience showed badly; in some steps Rusty was compelled to jump ahead of me.

"You've got to be quick, son." He was patient but firmly he took over the switches for me. "Get a little fuel in there and then starve it out, or you'll melt down a turbine or the whole damned air base, one of the two, sure as hell." Now the fuel was introduced and the gentle whirring of the compressor was interrupted with a big noise, a bomb going off below me, and she was nudged slightly forward. The whine of the motor built into a crescendo and Roth couldn't hear my reply.

"Have a good one." I could barely make it out as he slipped down and walked away to the hangar. He didn't stand by to see me take off. The ladder was lifted down and it was all mine.

There was a short delay while I waited for a response to my tower call. The jet hummed evenly as an electric fan, smooth, with little vibration; already the fuel counter was clicking away the jet's propellant. She burned her fuel rapidly on the ground. How quietly she performed!

I was invited to join the party. "Air Force 777, you are cleared to runway two-four . . . wind out of the west, 13 knots, altimeter 29:91 . . ." The call from the tower was a familiar one—it was reassuring.

The high, refined wail of the engine increased as I inched the throttle forward . . . up, up, up, up—nothing happened! She didn't respond. I tried the brakes; they were off. Why didn't this thing move? More throttle, up, up, and up, now with the engine wound up to a shriek she began to roll slowly. A kiddy-car—a nose-wheel fighter—I swung her around and we glided down the taxi way, the Shooting Star and her uncertain jockey bouncing along the glaring cement taxi way past planes and pilots starting up or shutting down. An old transport pilot, I felt undignified and misplaced sitting high in the nose of the hot little fighter. I was about to join the club of young jet pilots. The prospect was at once ridiculous and exciting. I had better get used to the idea fast! There was a lot hotter one than this coming up. Let's get down to business.

Hatch closed, flaps set, one last look around and I was ready to take the runway. Now abruptly the picture changed. The tower cleared me to line up. I could not afford to be a novice any longer, a kid with a new and fearsome toy. The F-80 was part of the traffic; her appearance on the end of the runway immediately affected the lives and flight behavior of pilots 100 miles away. Already the sky held three planes circling in the landing pattern impatiently waiting to set down their used-up mounts—any indecision I allowed myself here forced them to remain in the air. What was a well-planned flight could change into an emergency. Once she appeared on the end of the long, vacant runway the F-80 was a navigational problem, an obstacle in the middle of a rapidly moving stream. She sat on space that had to quickly become available to the next landing jet. Any minute on a test base there might be an emergency-landing request; the planes had to keep moving. Overhead now the planes were waiting for me to take off.

"What are you waiting for, Charlie? It's your move."

"Air Force 777, you are cleared for take-off," the tower announced.

One last recheck—hydraulic pressure, turbine out temperature, fuel pressure, oil . . .

"What are you going to do down there, stake out a claim?"

Ahead, the hard path stretches away from me, a clean, broad highway through the desert. Oh hell, let's go. Full rpm, full temperature . . . I release the brakes and I am sitting in the middle of a God-awful shriek coming out of the slowest-moving airplane in the world. come on . . . where is that lunging fighter getaway, that leap down the runway, that sudden shift of direction as the great winding torque twists through the airplane? Instead, the big, restrained bundle of energy rolls sublimely forward as if she is being shoved firmly by a giant hand. The roaring clatter of the grasping, digging propeller is eerily missing; where is the noise that lets you know you have hold of something? When an engine is ready to go you can hear it, feel it . . . but not with this baby; she deceptively whirs and whines with a phantom power that is ostensively five times greater than any fighter I've ever handled. It is hard to remember that she needs speed, air velocity, to attain this power and I am amazed at how slowly she moves.

She picks up speed now evenly, a kiddy cart heading down a steep hill, and as she does her shrieking cry becomes more urgent. I am alerted, listening and now knowing what I listen for, rolling down the runway in the fast-coasting kiddy cart. Past the canopy the sage slips by. In an ordinary fighter the sage jumps by. Already I've used up half of the strip—an AD would be 1000 feet in the air at this point, but I wait, rolling, rocking, jolting along. Good God, I am halfway to Los Angeles and still she isn't ready. The end of the runway is coming up fast and this has to be it, the speed is up to 90

. . . 100 . . . the end of the runway flows into the desert as I lift the nose, pull slightly, and at once the rumbling path melts into velvet. The sleek little jet, delicately supported by the heavy, hot summer air, sheds the desert and rushes on deeper into the invisible air sea.

She cleans up nicely, settles, and then, a colt with the bit in her teeth, she cuts out across the desert dragging her whining cry. It is disturbingly quiet, without vibration, like soaring; a yawl with a good wind, she slides out across the desert floor, growing stronger as she goes. Low over the Joshuas and sage she is till picking up speed, gathering momentum. The airspeed indicator reads a startling 230 knots, building fast, 240 . . . 250 . . . 260. Hey, where've you been, baby, this is more like it! Two hundred and sixty—this is it, the best speed for climb according to the label. The nose tilts nicely upward and she climbs, not with a nose-high, clawing grind to altitude, but with an easy angle; she sails up and the desert falls away and rapidly sinks beneath me. God, this is good! The normal exhilaration of flying is greatly intensified by the effortless performance of the little fighter and the discovery of something totally new. This is the way to fly. What a doll this plane is. What a living doll.

Already I have reached the mountains that border the Mojave on the eastern side. I bank easily and the desert drops further away beneath me—the mountains slide down and we climb up. She rocks slightly, reminding me that my job is one of evaluation: control centering, breakout forces, spiral instability. Not now, this is too great, no interruptions now. There's time for that later.

Thirty thousand feet . . . 31,000, 32,000, 33,000, 34,000, and 35,000. It is cold now, the overalls, wet from the heat on the desert below, cling uncomfortably as leeches to my skin. Around me the crisp, think air is a deep sapphire color, and flung below is a quarter of the state of California. I squint against the extreme unfiltered brightness of the sun and there, ahead, the thin, small island of Catalina stands up clear in the dark blue Pacific Ocean 25 miles out from San Pedro; out of the fragment window on my right is Mount Whitney, its peak a crystal under the sun, 100 miles away. It's clean up here. Below nothing seems out of order. The earth is neatly divided into squares, rectangles, and curves. It's quiet. The stillness of the engine, the lack of vibration, the intensity of the moment, seem unreal, like a dream of flying. Like a daydream I had long ago in the warmth of a morning bed, the boy I was once escaping into some delicious danger or joy.

I feel the master of the ship I fly and the returned surge of ego is good.

A big sky to throw back your head in. A scope of freedom found nowhere else but in the sky-sea. How easily she rolls . . . Oops, she picks up G easily. Again . . . not bad. What a fighter pilot you would have made.

Okay, let's bring her up to stall and see what she does. Throttle back, brakes down, gear down, flaps down, slow . . . slow . . . slower. She shudders lightly at first, then more urgently. I wiggle the ailerons and she rocks obediently back. Good control! I horse back on the elevator and she shudders violently and then, all on her own, she pitches out, nose down . . . What could be sweeter than that? This could work into a love affair; what a great airplane, spirited, responsive, and, with a firm hand, restrainedly obedient.

Brakes in—flaps up—gear up. Okay, baby, let's really go. I push the throttle way up. The whine she trails behind rises a tone and the ship lunges down as her nose is lowered into a smooth roll. Pick up speed now, drop the nose more . . . yank it up high again and into a steep climb. Climb up and over into a half-loop, upright on top, Immelmann . . . Gad, what a fancy Dan am I! Once more a series of loops and rolls—round, smooth paths through the air with added refinements and frills. The finale. At the end of a long climb straight up, I roll the 80 over on her back and let my head hang down toward the state of California that lies flat and uninhabited-looking seven miles below.

How fast can you get back down? I point toward the desert in a split "S," roll her over, and pull her down. Down she slides in a long arc, the speed builds up rapidly and the controls stiffen a little under my hands. Around the edges of the canopy a dull, flat ghost whistle rides with us straight down. She points directly for the ground and the jet engine changes its shriek to a higher pitch. The force of the dive pushes me hard into the backrest, and on the panel the altimeter whirls into a blur. She picks up speed faster than I expect, no propeller to stir up a braking drag. I'm enthralled at the way she accelerates. I hang on in disbelief. With the whistle piercing through my ears, my stomach forcing against my chest, trying to suck in enough oxygen, I feel the fantastic speed she is gathering and I'm transfixed. I forget the Machmeter. What a way to commit suicide this would be. The earth remains a long way below. This is too good to stop just yet, there is lots of time.

A little more speed, a little faster. The jet dives powerfully, pushing the air out of her way as she plummets straight down. Accelerating as she plunges, churning up the air in her wake.

Then a sudden violent, hammering vibration jolts through the plane—a machine gun in rapid fire. I freeze. I'm stripped of ego, reduced to a startled child. She can't take the speed I've forced on her, she's hit the wall all right and she shakes on the edge of the destruction that surely lies ahead. The Sky God has caught us in his teeth and below me the earth quakes convulsively. She'll pull to pieces with this God-awful hammering . . . instinctively I want to slow down, to alter this wild dive to an easy flight altitude . . . power off . . . dive brakes out. The hammering beating is growing stronger. It is as if my body were afflicted with uncontrollable convulsions. How can it stay together, how can it? Hang on! Treat her gently, very gently. Get the damned nose up. I pull hard at first . . . God, that makes it even worse, the jolting is more violent. Keep your head; hold what you've got. There can be no increase in the angle of the dive. The wings will snap off for sure.

What can I do to slow her down? Think. What did they say Ed did wrong when he "dug a hole" last month? What did they say in the hangar about it? Remember the answer from somewhere in all the hangar talk. Remember a hundred things. What one of those hundred answers have I neglected to recall? One is surely the answer. The buffet is a continuous bolt of electricity buzzing through me. We're picking up speed all the way down.

For God's sake, try something! Pull a little and ease a little—that's it—she takes it. A little more, ease up, not too far! Leave enough room so you can back out quick if you're wrong. Anything to change the radical dive angle to something reasonable. That's it. Pull back, take the hard jolt that bounces the airplane, ease up. Got the nose up ten per cent that time; again, pull back . . . oh God, that hammering

. . . now ease up. Once more pull . . . ease up. The diving, buffeting plane that carries me in its pod tears wildly through several thousand feet more and the indicated air speed moves continuously up, the bottom of the ride is coming up closer.

The spring is being wound too tight; something is bound to give momentarily. Ways to save the plane are clouded now with thoughts of escape. how long can I wait before I get out, how many things can I try before I open the canopy and let her go? When is the proper moment of surrender to this thing? Just a little bit longer. Instinctively I feel I am handling the plane properly, but the ground is coming closer. I had better be right. If I decide to give her up I will open the hatch, kick the stick forward with my body—the negative G's enforced by this maneuver will hurtle me out into the air free of the tail section. Optimism! Chances of getting out are slim at this speed.

I wait. I lift the nose a little. Wait. The awful shaking is dying out! A little bit more . . . hold it! Suddenly it is quiet. Why? As abruptly as it began the buffeting stops. The ride is over; the wings stayed on. My head rolls forward on my chest; I can hear myself breathing deeply from the oxygen mask. Before my eyes close, I see the Machmeter needle slipping back .78, .77, .76, .75—there's the answer to the giant hand that shook the dive into a nightmare. The F-80 hums evenly now as if the 30 seconds never happened. I remember Roth's last warning: "The limiting Mach number on the ship is .8." The ship will buffet on the tender edge of the speed of sound. Inadvertently I have driven into an aerodynamic fact, a truth I was aware of but never bothered to investigate. If I had understood it more thoroughly, the compressibility phenomenon would not have occurred. I am a fool. This time an intuitive feeling of the plane's reactions got us through, and as she reached lower altitudes, although curiously she picked up speed, she ran away from the critical Mach number. Of course, at altitude you hit the high Mach numbers with less true air speed than in the denser, warmer air closer to the ground!

A test pilot comes to accept the unexpected, but this experience was something I didn't look forward to meeting again soon.

"Well, how did you like it?" The sergeant asked me as I walked away from the jet.

"It's different."

"Yeah, that's what they say."

Now that the plane was set down I could leisurely take out of the cubbyholes the problems that I had filed during flight. There was time now to think about them. The high-speed buffeting. One of the big reasons for the Skyrocket's design was to eliminate the "high Mach-number" phenomenon so that this "effect of compressibility" won't exist in future fighter designs. I had touched on the area the Skyrocket had been created to explore. This was a phenomenon that I had to become familiar with. To what severity and degree would it exhibit itself? I had to be prepared to recognize any abnormality. Quickly I had to become acquainted with this thing if I were to make discerning and complete testing reports. Flight in the jet had convinced me more than ever that the aircraft of the future needed careful and faithful study. This was the way to fly all right, but it involved new principles. The equations had to be thoroughly understood. The theories pertaining to jet performance I had been studying, the detached, slide-rule answers, took on vitality and meaning they lacked before. My respect for the engineers' problems was greatly increased.

CHAPTER X

Back at the Douglas hanger, I was hanging up my chute when Carder came out of his office. He waited for a reaction.

"Smooth as a kitten's ear," I told him.

"It went okay, did it? Good." Carder wanted to get me into the program as fast as would be safe. "Later in the week, Bill, let's try some ground tests on the rocket system," he looked over at the Rocket in her usual state of disarray, the maintenance crew probing into her openings. "It'll give you a feeling for the rocket engine."

They were letting me creep up on it. "That's fine with me, Al." I hung the mask, crash helmet, and clammy overalls in my locker. Right now I wanted to get someplace where it was cool.

"Incidentally, Bill, whenever the F-80 is available you've been authorized to take it up. You ought to get as much time as you can."

"I'll fly again tomorrow." I wanted to know the jet well. "If you want me, Al, I'll be over at the pool." The project coordinator was not reassured. So far he had to accept the judgment of the Douglas Testing Division that I was the man to fly his charge. He viewed me like a doting parent meeting his 16-year-old daughter's first date. My frequent afternoon visits to the pool caused him to shrug his shoulders patiently. He could only wait and see what happened three or four weeks from now.

In the heavily chlorinated water of the confining officers' pool I missed the freedom of the buoyant swells of the Pacific, but still it was a cool release from the prison heat of the parched and peeling base. Beside the pool the hot breeze carried the smell of the desert, sage, and the ozone that rose in waves from the sun-baked sand and rocks, like the smell of a washing dried in the back yard on a summer day. I thought about the flight I had returned from.

What forces act upon the ship to cause the buffeting at high speeds?

Into the cool cave of the officers' lounge that was set next to the pool, I continued the search for the right answers to the riddle of the Skyrocket, jamming and crowding into my mind all I could find in the books. I went over and over the intricate, unfamiliar equations of high-speed flight. Things I didn't understand I made a note of; the engineer and aerodynamicists could explain this for me.

And here was the answer to what I had touched in this morning's dive. The forces that cause buffeting and shock waves (compressibility effects) at critical Mach numbers: Perkins and Hage, Stability and Control, explained it.

During subsonic, level flight when an airfoil (a wing) is developing a normal amount of lift, a thin boundary layer of air flows over its surface. When the airfoil is subjected to speeds higher than it is designed to meet, shock waves will appear along its surface, disturbing this boundary layer. As a result the thin layer of air thickens and rips off in a turbulent flow that beats upon the wings, causing them to buffet.

The discovery of the 80's secret eased the frightening memory of her performance this morning. Her violent symptom had a simple diagnosis.

I turned to the Skyrocket's inch-thick operation manual.

I was relaxed from the long swim and the big couch was deep and comfortable. Through the sparsely occupied room ran the drone of conversation. There are times when the movement and hum of your fellow man is good.

Looking at the Skyrocket in segments like this, she lost her identity, she became merely a mathematical problem without reality, and I felt no apprehension.

But then a buzzer rang in my chest. On the wall in front of me hung a picture of the Skyrocket, trailing a river of flame from her rocket barrels—suddenly a big reality. She would be mine soon. My responsibility to harness and rein the powerful experiment into obeying me, to trick and train her into the routine of gathering accurate data. There could be no wild plunges into the unknown area like this morning, but small, orderly increments toward it. The unbroken stallion waited and I had yet to master the trotting mare, the F-80.

Every plane flying has an individual rate of change, as power and control surfaces are adjusted to meet a condition of flight that is sought. So it is with the smallest trainer or the 70-ton flying boat Mars. The length of time that is required for the pilot to adjust to each new ship depends on his experience in the particular brand of plane and his native ability. With the professional pilot, native ability is the lesser qualification: it is expected. Rate change has embarrassed many a seasoned bomber or transport pilot who has taken the family for a Sunday ride in a cub.

So it was with the F-80. But as days went by and flights went by, conditions were met and mastered, the slow response of the jet engine became less mysterious. The delayed response, though at first confusing, finally began to become second nature, a condition that is sorely needed by the test pilot so that he is able to divert his attention to the more pressing needs of testing.

From carefully read theory regarding compressibility, I began to study the theory in actual flight with the F-80. I took the ship above 35,000 feet and with great care rolled her into a shallow dive. As the Machmeter approached the critical Mach number of .8, at some value a little below, small accelerated pull-ups were initiated. This allowed the ship to reach, somewhat prematurely, its buffeting speed. By modulating the vertical acceleration applied to the aircraft and correlating the G forces closely to the indicated Mach number, a safe and fairly accurate study of light and moderate buffet could be made.

This studied approach to buffeting gave me a clear picture of what had happened the day I met the phenomenon in my first experience with the jet. Buffet can be controlled as long as the initial dive angle of the craft is not allowed to become too steep. A hard and fast law of nature had put me into the buffet area on that first flight, but a further condition of the same law had allowed me a safe retreat. As any Mach number versus indicated-air-speed chart with reference to altitude will show, Mach number or the speed of sound increases as altitude is lost and the big problem you had at altitude, in spite of a rising indicated air speed, disappears.

By nibbling at the buffet and using a studied approach the function was tamed. Actually the personal process I used to understand buffet is the essence of testing. It is the first rule set down by the fathers of the business—every new step must be explored a small increment at a time.

As the F-80 gradually slipped into the category of an airplane met and understood, some small degree of confidence toward the research ship emerged. Now that I was acquainted with a member of the jet species, the Skyrocket—the highly complex mutation—seemed less formidable.

When I had won some freedom in the jet, I had time to survey the Mojave Desert below, but not entirely for pleasure. I skimmed over the small, scattered dry lake beds, sizing up their terrain as possible sanctuaries in case of a forced landing in the Skyrocket. There was time for games, too. Get yourself in a bad spot, cut the engine, and glide in from the north, look for a place to land. A game played east, west, and south, covering the entire valley, learning the ground like a vast airport. Another game: Accelerate the jet engine beyond the limits it can function normally and force it to flame out. Then glide soundlessly through the cold sky in a solitary departure down toward the desert heat, where the engine can successfully be started once more.

Flights in the F-80 became increasingly enjoyable; the hours in the jet were a welcome break in the tedious occupation of constant study and a sudden release from the hot, dry desert floor. But after the F-80 flights, back on the bottom of the dusty Mojave, the pile of manuals and books was always waiting. I looked forward restlessly now to the day I would be allowed to fly the Skyrocket. The preparation for the big day dragged on.

Undoubtedly an annoyance to Al Carder, or more often Tommy Briggs, his assistant, was an irritating method of firmly implanting Skyrocket information in my mind. A schoolboy getting someone to listen to his multiplication tables.

"Okay, Tommy, ask me something about the rocket engine. Go on, anything. Ask me." Briggs would take a big breath, lean back in his chair, and in a resigned tone ask a question, usually in desperation and boredom the most complicated one he could think of at the moment. If I knew the answer Tommy would have to listen to the involved and sometimes lengthy discourses. If the question stopped me or came out slowly I went back to the books and got it straight. When I thought I had it, Briggs was ferreted out again. "Tommy, ask me the question again."

Eventually I managed to get the engineers into the one-sided quiz game. The first request for information pertaining to their section of the plane was usually met with a hastily extended manual on the subject. The manual would occupy me for a day or two and then I would appear before the authority once again, armed with a dozen or so more questions. The Skyrocket's corps of godfathers had frequent stretches of leisure time brought about by test flights unexpectedly delayed due to endless mechanical causes or the weather. My inquiring visits to their row of offices often interrupted nothing more than a coffee session or the organization of a football pool and it was with faint amusement that they stopped to answer my questions. When I had unraveled a particular problem I would return to disturb their meeting around the coffee machine with the quiz game. "Ask me a question about the hydraulic system?" Bored though they were with the idea, they would throw a question at me. After a period of conditioning they warmed up to the game, it became another pastime, like the recounting of ribald stories; and unsolicited they began inventing questions for me.

As I walked through the hangar they would call over to me, "Hey, Bridgeman, how many pounds of pressure in the emergency reservoir?"" If I walked by with a thoughtful look without answering, they were pleased that they had caught me. The next day when I ran into the challenging engineer, instead of a polite salutation I would shout the answer at him, ending it with some affectionate imperative obscenity—a scene that undoubtedly caused visiting Douglas engineers no end of confused concern.

Further preparation for the bout with the Skyrocket involved another device. Sitting by the pool, in the mess, or over a drink I constantly dreamed up emergency flight problems. In take-off the gear won't come up, what do I do? The gear on the Skyrocket is "placarded" not to exceed 300 knots. This warning is printed on a card and affixed to the instrument panel. According to Gene if this placard is not obeyed the inherent Dutch roll of the ship will become aggravated by the increased drag induced by the extending wheel. How do I keep the plane in the air? Answer: Get rid of the heavy propellants, cut off three rocket tubes, and pull the nose up. This will force the propellant rapidly out of the remaining tube and also reduce the speed.

Constantly I thought of things that could go wrong. I had to have fast answers prepared ahead of time. The ship would not catch me by surprise; I had to think ahead of her. And if the answer didn't work, I would have an alternate one ready to put into action. Old "Buzz" Miller Navy training—plan Able, Baker, Charlie, Dog, Easy, fox, and down the line. If plan Able failed, switch to plan Baker. Never be taken by surprise, have an alternate at hand.

The gearing-up process and the battle plan I was mentally mapping in preparation for the big day was temporarily interrupted with the rocket ground test run in the Skyrocket. Up until now Gene or McNemar, the crew chief, sat in on them. Now I would do it. After every 30 minutes of actual firing time in the rocket engine, which approximated about three flights, the system was removed from the plane and sent back East to Reaction Motors, Inc., for a complete overhaul. The power-plant engineers, Sorenson and Osborne, were taking no chances on fatigue failures that could easily cause the engine to disintegrate in the air. Spare engines were kept on hand to replace the used one and it was the spare that had to be carefully checked on the ground before it was okayed for flight.

A frequent danger was caused by the cylinder cooling system. When all four barrels are fired at once the 20-foot ground flame that shoots out of the Skyrocket reaches a temperature of 6000 degrees F., hot enough to melt the cylinder. If the cooling system is not functioning properly on all areas of the cylinder, the intense heat can melt a hole in the neglected spot in a fraction of a second. Occasionally, after a ground test, the inside of the barrels will show a rippling scar, indicating that the cooling system is marginal. This and the detection of a dozen other dangers was the object of the ground test, where controlled conditions allowed the greatest margin of safety to the costly ship.

Carder announced that a rocket ground test would be made on the static test stand at the east end of the runway. "We're shooting for 11 o'clock tomorrow morning Bill. Do you want to run through it for us this time?"

It was good that I was allowed to handle the rocket engine separately at first; in actual flight I would have the jet to cope with at the same time. It would be sort of a dress rehearsal on one function of the Skyrocket. What does rocket thrust feel like? Tomorrow morning I would find out.

The sandpaper wind was up the next day, blowing close to 30 miles an hour, scorching everything in its path. It scraped against my face and hands as I bent my way over to Kenny Frew, shop foreman.

"It looks like some time this afternoon now," the foreman explained. "Something went wrong again."

An old story in aviation. A part is missing or has given up unexpectedly and there is delay. The delay is accentuated in a test program, particularly in a highly controlled research program. Nine tenths of the time devoted to the project is spent in adjustment and preparation.

By three o'clock the wind had subsided a little and the necessary adjustment had been made. Everything was in order for the test.

The Skyrocket, steaming off her fuel in the familiar whistle, was facing into an adobe, U-shaped abutment, tied to the earth by heavy chains looped around her landing gear and fastened to cement posts on the ground test bed: the giant Prometheus bound to the rock. If the exhaust gases at the end of the 20-foot flame were allowed to hit the ground in back of the ship, the gigantic force would dig a hole ten to 12 feet deep in the course of a minute. As it was, the rocket engine pointed a flame over the desert and kicked up a storm across the terrain. Assistant power-plant engineer, Bob Osborne, tells the story of the time some attending engineers at a static rocket ground test run of the R.M.I engine in the East tossed a ten-gallon milk can into the exhaust gases of the rocket tubes. A minute later when the four barrels were shutoff, there was no trace of the metal can.

Fastened to the instrument panel was a portable red light, a warning device that would blaze on if it appeared to the outside observers that the engine was about to blow up. Two electric cords ran from the cockpit on either side of the plane 75 feet aft. At the end of the lines were stationed observers who watched the rainbow-colored flame with its diamond-shaped shock waves for any change in pattern that would indicate trouble. The second they see danger they drop the end of the cord they hold and run—the red light in the cockpit goes on as they release the button.

Carder left it up to me to decide what course to take when the light went on—I could get out quick or I could wait and shut down the rocket engine and depressurize. The latter decision could take a few seconds longer and would help to keep the fire down. But Carder didn't insist on it. He mistrusted the rocket engine; the same rocket system in the rival Air Force project had blown up one model in firing for take-off. And in a rocket ground test they had lost another plane; the pilot Joe Cannon was so badly burned that he was unable to fly again.

After the four rocket tubes are successfully fired and shut down, a residual fire remains in the barrels and immediate action is needed. A 15-foot-long, elbow-bent pipe with four long, thin prongs is shoved into the tubes, a twist and water is released over the blazing barrels.

Close in front of the Skyrocket, McNemar was to stand to oversee the whole operation, I was to watch him also. If he drew his hand over his throat I was to immediately cut the whole system off on the master switch.

Around the plane in the wind moved the mechanics in their cumbersome white protective overalls and glass-plated helmets, tending the fuel-pressure gauges. Carder approached from the circle of cars that shrank back, 200 feet away from the bound plane. From a prudent distance engineers and interested spectators from other projects came to watch the curious rocket engine perform. The key men concerned in the test circled about Carder. He addressed me. "Bill, I want a ten-second run on the first barrel, and accordingly on each barrel until they are all firing at once. Okay? When the last barrel has fired ten seconds, shut them all off." I nodded. The rocket-second counter, a dial on the control panel, works as a fuel gauge. It begins at 600, indicating there are 600 rocket-seconds' worth of propellant available in the tanks. If you fire two barrels at once, you eat up twice as many rocket-seconds—four barrels firing at the same time and the rocket-seconds are used u four times as fast. As each barrel is fired the rocket-second counter spins increasingly faster.

Into the circle of hovering men the project coordinator gave his instructions slowly, straining his voice above the rush of the wind. The listeners squinted their eyes against the sand and pulled their coat collars higher around their faces.

"Do you all know what you are going to do?" Carder looked into each man's face one by one. "All right, what are you going to do?" Around the circle once more. The men recited their assignments. Carder nodded his head in approval. "Okay, let's go!"

The men scattered into the wind to their posts and Al Carder hurried back to his radio car a safe distance from the test. There he would remain in contact with the performance by radio. In back of the radio car loomed the ambulance and the red fire truck.

It was my turn now. The mechanic rolled the ladder up to the rocket's side, the clamshell canopy, lay open on the fuselage, it was to remain open for the test. I stuffed myself into the confining and uncomfortable cockpit, there was just enough room for my legs and little room for movement.

Fred Iltner, the inspector, alerted the men at their positions. McNemar took his stand in front of the ship. Iltner gave the signal. The test began!

Mounted on the platform to the left and alongside of my thigh is the metal level of the rocket pressurizing system. I move it to the pressurize position. Next step, hit the prime switch and wait for 60 seconds while the liquid oxygen runs from the tank to the engine, reducing the temperature of the tubes as it moves through them. The heat of the tubes before they have been primed causes the first shot of liquid oxygen to evaporate. A white vapor appears from the engine the last ten seconds of the prime. Bob Osborne and Fred Iltner stand close to the cockpit, leaning in to advise me in the case of emergency and to watch the pressure-indicator dials. I listen to advice from the engineer and the inspector, keep an eye on McNemar ahead of me, watch the pressure dials, count the seconds, and remember what to do if the red light flashes on.

"Your prime looks good, Bill."

The four rocket switches are lined up alongside of me under the master rocket switch. I motion to the men below; I am ready to light number one. A glance at Iltner and I hit the first switch in the line. Click, the tiny level snaps forward. A muffled explosion, like dynamite in a tunnel, and then she roars with more noise than I've ever heard, all the roaring power of Vesuvius and Niagara Falls combined. She lunges fiercely in her chains throwing me back hard into the backrest. What if the chains don't hold? Is it all right? The noise. I had expected noise and power but nothing to compare with this. I forget about the rocket counter spinning before me as I glance quickly up at Iltner to make sure everything is going properly. No response! He doesn't appear alarmed. It's all right. The counter! The row of pressure dials! The pressure has to remain between 2000 pounds and 600 pounds during the run. The rocket counter in the middle of the panel in front of me is past 590, whirling into 589-588.

I'm off schedule. Hit number two! She bellows twice as loud and pulls harder at her chains. God, what keeps her from tearing out the posts? Check the pressure! Osborne leans in and screams something. Okay. The counter doesn't wait, twice as fast, 584-82-80-78-76-74--. Lost seconds again; number-three switch snaps. There isn't this much noise in the world, it explodes through my head like a violent blow about the ears, and it is exceedingly difficult to concentrate on McNemar, the men beside the cockpit, and red light, the dials, and the counter. The counter is spinning furiously. Let go number four! The noise of the power behind me in incredible and I have a feeling of complete shriveling, defeat in its wake; I am caught off guard. Shut them off, quick. Time's up. She jolts back abruptly into her chains and I am jerked forward violently against my leather harness. It is over; the noise is dead. But around the plane quickly the crew runs in, the long pipe prong is pushed up the rocket barrels. A second later, "Fire's out" . . . the word is called down the line, "Fire's out," and again, "Fire's out."

Osborne and the rocket company representative, Johnny Conlon, swarmed in to read the instruments.

"How did it look?"

"Looked good. I think we've got a good system." They peered up the tail.

"Barrels don't show any deformation."

Carder came up. "Well, that's it, huh? We should be able to get a flight day after tomorrow."

From the sidelines the visiting engineers and spectators were visibly impressed. They shook their heads, their mouths formed into exclamatory whistles, and they discussed animatedly among themselves the performance they had witnessed.

The project coordinator saw me standing alongside the plane, left the group of men clustered about the tail, and walked over.

"What did you think of it?"

"It makes a lot of noise, doesn't it?"

Carder was startled by my flippant answer. Yet I think he was pleased with the reaction.

The rocket engine had awed me far more than I allowed Carder to know. It had rattled me to a degree on this first run; I hadn't expected the violent noise. I had lost rocket-seconds by reacting to the noise and the fantastic amount of power, probably 20 seconds—an excess of reaction in testing. Soon the time would come when I would take her off the ground and there would be not only the rocket system to reckon with, but the jet engine as well. Next time it would go more smoothly.

Above: The Douglas A2D Skyshark. *Below:* Bill Bridgeman and the Douglas Skyrocket.

Above: Douglas test pilots: *left to right,* George Jansen, Bob Rahn,
Bill Bridgeman, and Jim Verdin. F4D Skyray in background. *Below:*
Aft view of Skyrocket shows four rocket tubes which furnish power
to thrust the research craft through the atmosphere at almost twice the
speed of sound.

Above: The Skyrocket in an air-to-air launching. *Below:* Bill Bridgeman in the cockpit of the Skyrocket. He's wearing a USAF high-altitude pressure suit. His helmet was specially designed by Douglas engineers.

Above: The Skyrocket being tailed by a "chase" plane over southern California. The F-86 directs the Skyrocket to a safe landing, "mothers" it during test flights. *Below:* Skyrocket in flight.

Above: The Skyrocket in a jet-assisted take-off (Jato). Jato enables fuel conservation during climb for high-speed runs. *Below:* Ground shot of Skyrocket.

Above: Trailer used to transport Skyrocket on ground. It travels at
40 mph. *Below:* Flight crew of Skyrocket gets together with Donald
W. Douglas (second from right, seated) who presented them with gold
watches for assistance in the plane's history-making flights.

Above: The Douglas X-3. *Below:* Clockwise from bottom: X-3, Sky-streak, XF4D1, Skyrocket. These are all Douglas aircraft.

A striking shot of the X-3.

CHAPTER XI

The Skyrocket flew Friday morning following the rocket ground test, marking the end of my first month on the base. The air was beginning to get chilly these mornings as late fall approached; the fleece-lined Navy flight jacket I wore felt good. I sat with Al Carder in the radio car, at the end of the eight-mile-long lake bed attending Gene May's current flight; still to me, even after watching five of them, an impressive show. Once more the Skyrocket had returned safely from her investigations.

Gene pulled the canopy back, took off his helmet and oxygen mask, and wiped his face with the sleeve of his G suit. He handed his big helmet down to the little group waiting below, scanned his instruments briefly, stood up high out of the nose, and proceeded to back down the portable ladder.

Orv Paulsen, the aerodynamicist, offered him a hand, "Nice landing, Gene."

May snapped, "The T5 went overboard again . . ." and quickly he returned to the car where Carder and I sat.

Before we began the trip across the lake to the hangar, Carder and May discussed the flight; Carder quietly and Gene explosively with a good deal of hand-waving.

"The rocket sounded good to me on the light-off." The pilot, empty and tired, began to reprimand the ground crew. "Although for a moment I thought that number two might have had a little squeal. You people are going to have to be a little bit quicker in letting me know how it sounds and appears to you just before lift-off. You know, you can tell more about it than I can. I haven't got all day to make up my mind whether or not to lift it off or stick her back on the lake." Carder listened patiently as May scolded on: "So make up your mind down here fast . . . sing out."

Carder made no comment but started up the car and began the trip back to the hangar. The conversation died.

And then after five minutes of silence, over his shoulder to Gene slumped in the back seat, Carder spoke. "I think next flight would be a good time to work Bridgeman in. What do you think?"

I sat up straight.

May stretched out and closed his eyes. "Yeah, sure . . . why not?" The decision was made in casual terms. The time was up.

"Next Friday . . . that okay with you, Bill?" Carder turned his head to me.

"Sure, Al, Friday's fine with me."

Friday. Did I know everything well? Had I anticipated every possible emergency and set of conditions? There were seven days to redouble my efforts, to review the lessons. I had to keep up with Gene, go over every bit of advice again, get hold of his squawk sheets, and see what was done about his complaints.

Through my mind questions and memoranda regarding the Skyrocket floated, one after the other—Carder pulled the company car up to the hangar and we were met by the corps of technicians who were waiting for the film and the miles of manometer and oscillograph charts. For the first time I was anxious for the ship to be towed in from the lake, I wanted to get into the cockpit at once, to look around again, get my hands on the controls once more. Impatiently I waited with the others.

There was the usual bustling preparation in the photographic laboratory. After days spent at a leisurely pace, the morning of a flight threw the film room and the flight office into intense activity. The film-room technicians wanted the film from the Skyrocket's camera that had recorded the instrument panel during flight. It took two to three hours to develop it and during the processing time the film-room door was constantly assaulted by the impatient aerodynamicists and engineers inquiring, "How much longer is it going to be before we can see the film?"

One of the technicians asked Carder how soon the ship would be at the hangar. "They were hitching her up with I left. She ought to be in pretty quick now," the project coordinator answered.

"Any trouble with the recorder?"

"Gene didn't mention any trouble."

Twenty minutes later the spent experimental craft was hauled gently into the hangar. The eager group crowded in quickly around her, pushing to get into the cockpit, and I found that I was among them, fighting for position; after all she was my ship.

As I was about to climb into the cockpit, the crew chief stopped me. "I understand you're going to take her up next time . . ." The news traveled fast. He had just now come in from the lake bed with the ship.

"That's what they tell me." McNemar regarded me with a curious, doubting look. He was reticent about having the present working combination broken up, everything had been running smoothly and now there was to be an alteration. The crew had a simple devotion to the Skyrocket, she was a personality to them. Their constant job was immediate contact with the ship, grooming and repairing her. Under their hands she lived. She was not the set of equations and the order of combined units that she was to the engineers. The mechanic's concern was as instinctively proud as that of a ship's crew that had weathered many hard months at sea.

There was nothing further I could say to the crew chief. He stood by watching me as I stepped into the plane.

Later in the week I sought out McNemar and the other mechanics in order to review with them the characteristics of the jet engine at altitude. They enthusiastically repeated the lesson for me, reassured somewhat. They had been consulted. They wished me well.

Then there was the dress rehearsal in the cockpit. Although I wouldn't need all of the equipment on first flight, I wore it in any case, in order to see if it interferred with the controls. I was a head taller than Gene May and I wasn't sure that the extra height, added to the necessary flight gear, wouldn't impair mobility in the cockpit.

In the tight G suit, fleece-lined boots, the big crash helmet, and oxygen mask I managed to use up the cockpit. To make it appear as close to actual take-off as possible I secured the shoulder harness around my chest and locked the safety belt.

And for the first time I asked one of the mechanics to close the clamshell canopy; the top of my orange helmet missed it by inches.

So this is the way it's going to be! Although the cockpit was tight as a coffin, I didn't feel any claustrophobia and yet I invariably got the sensation if I sat on the inside of a restaurant booth or between two people in a car. It must be a matter of visibility. From the wing-shaped, faired-in windows of the canopy I could see clearly across the desert to the foot of the mountains.

First flight in the Skyrocket would be a simple one: stabilized runs at 16,000 feet at slow speeds of 300 miles per hour, 320 and 360. No high-speed investigations this trip. I was only to see how the ship handled, approach the stall, and determine aileron effectiveness. The rocket engine would not be fired; instead, four small rocket-bottles, full of slow-burning, dry propellant would be used in a jet-assisted take-off (jato).

Sitting here, in full gear, staring at the instrument panel that I knew by heart, the answers all came readily enough. An imprint of the panel was stenciled in my mind, I could quickly hit any knob or switch with my eyes closed. Automatically, for the hundredth time, I practiced take-off procedure, rythmically rehearsing all the twists, snaps, and pulls over the mass of controls—the estimated time lapses and then the finale of the jato switch sequence.

I felt overtrained; I knew everything too well; maybe stress had been put on the wrong items. Perhaps the really important facets I had overlooked. It was like studying for an examination and then, on entering the test room, finding on the blackboard, questions you have neglected for others you felt the professor would surely ask.

Again the fire-emergency sequence. Okay. The gear sequence. This was becoming tedious, to the point of senselessness. I wanted to take it down the runway now. There had been too much preparation, too much talk, too much study. Let's move. I wanted to fly it now. These last days of waiting were the most painful. If it was too much airplane for me, I wanted to find out. If it wasn't, let's go. With luck, on first flight I was convinced I could handle her, but there were still four more days before I would know. Friday.

Wednesday afternoon—one day left before flight. Gene had given last-minute warnings about the ship he was turning over to me. The Dutch roll, a new experience the Skyrocket had in store, was the big thing Gene talked about.

"Don't forget the Dutch roll she's got . . . when she slows down to 250 knots she rolls and dishes from side to side," he shook his head once. "Kind of nasty, but as you flare out for a landing it dampens."

There was no doubt that the pilot had esteem for his ship and he advised me to have the same. "You've got a lot of flights ahead of you—have a lot of respect for the airplane." He remembered something else. "Come in with enough fuel so if you make a bad approach you can go around again. Get her right down on the deck before you slow it up too much—the aileron effectiveness become nil as the ship approaches the stall." And the jatos—the four little bottles of powder that hang on the underside of the ship that give the craft a big push in take-off—also cause a tremendous amount of drag in the air. Gene warned: "About the jatos you'll be using for this flight, if you can't get rid of them after you're up, you'll have a hell of a time keeping the plane in the air. The thing to do is make a broad turn and bring her right back in." May cocked his head in the quick motion of a bird and waited briefly for another thought to occur to him, none did, and he turned and walked quickly away. He was about to leave for Los Angeles and he wouldn't be back until the morning of my flight. Before he had taken too many steps toward the hangar a last warning came to him. His last words were: "Stick close to the lake, don't wander all over the countryside. It's a bad plane to have an emergency in. If there is anything you don't understand, just sing out. I'll be on the ground, I'll talk to you. I don't see why you shouldn't have a good flight, just be careful."

Be careful!

There was nothing more I could do now but wait for Friday morning. To review the lessons again would be a senseless and monotonous task. If I didn't know the lessons well now one last night or two would make no difference in the way I would handle the flight. Tomorrow night I would go to bed early but tonight I wanted to be occupied. Miss Tatlock's Millions was still showing at the base movie and I had seen it twice already; the officers' bar was too close. The only alternative was Pancho's. I joined a group of unattached Douglas personnel that was heading out to the airmen's oasis.

This was my fourth or fifth sojourn to Pancho's and I had no reason to expect any reception from the proprietor; she was all for the Air Force. There wasn't a Navy picture hanging in her bar and her favorite pilot on the base was Chuck Yeager. I possessed none of the qualities that would endear myself to the lady: an ex-Navy commander, flying a Navy project in direct competition to the Air Force's program and Yeager. Pancho had never spoken to me and I wasn't sure she even knew what I was doing at the base.

When we arrived, Pancho, in a tight white sweater and a pair of brown slacks, was standing by the piano with one arm around a portly major, smiling widely at her guests' spirited attempts at entertainment. A young lieutenant was playing a loud and embellished version of some Cole Porter tunes. Three other officers were trying to remember the words.

From her position at the piano Pancho watched us come in. And as we waited for a drink, she came up behind me. "You're Bill Bridgeman, aren't you?" I nodded. "I hear you're going to fly the Skyrocket Friday." Surprised, I told her she had heard right.

"You checked out in the F-80, didn't you?" I told her I had. "I'd like to have you sign the picture." She glanced up at the big inscribed photograph over the bar. "Hey, Pete, hand me down the picture will you?" The bartender lifted it from the wall. "Everybody who gets checked out in this ship signs the picture; a lot of famous guys have flown that beat-up old thing." Pancho's discourse on the F-80 was well punctuated with exquisitely graphic oaths. My companions were awed.

However I was pleased that I had been asked to add my name to the photograph of the second production jet ever flown in the country. Pancho had given me an endorsement of sorts and I found her approval somewhat gratifying.

We joined the circle at the piano, and for a couple of hours I completely forgot the Skyrocket and most of the Porter verses.

She didn't leave me for long though. Back at the base alone in the dark cubicle of The Shamrock, the same questions automatically drifted through my head. What do I do if an inverter fails? And the answer would come without calling it. What if the generator fails? I put the pillow over my head.

The mornings were cold now; the days didn't begin to warm up until noon and already I was beginning to miss the freedom of wearing only a cotton sport shirt. It was still early and Orv Paulsen, drinking a cup of coffee, was filling the only desk in the small aerodynamicists' office.

"Morning, Orv. Man, but it's cold this morning."

"It's damned cold—but, thank God, this weather'll help us wind up the rubber bands in that J-34. We can use all the push we can get."

On one of the empty desks lay Flight Plan Number 54. That's my flight tomorrow morning! I picked it up. These didn't look like the items we have agreed upon for first flight! The whole thing had been altered. What had happened anyway?

I turned to Orv. "What's this?"

He didn't lookup. "Oh yeah, Gene's going to take the flight tomorrow. The Navy's got a couple of items they're hot for right away."

No flight. I was ready to run the race and the race was called off. A whole week of waiting—for nothing. I wanted to shout at the complacent engineer for telling me the flight had been canceled. If he had said he was sorry about it, I could have challenged that, I could have let off steam; but it was an impersonal piece of news he had relayed. "Gene will take the flight tomorrow." A statement of fact. It was an unwelcome reprieve. All this gearing up, gearing up, to nothing. I had another week of this to look forward to, another week of wearisome anticipation.

Perhaps Carder would say more. Perhaps I could beat on Carder's desk. He was in his office. "I understand Gene's taking the flight tomorrow?"

Carder got up from his desk, "Yeah, that's right. The Navy needed some stuff. You'll take next flight." He was about to leave his office. "Do you know if Orv's in yet?"

There was nothing I could say; he had left me no opening. "I just left him; he's in." It was of no importance actually to Carder if I took the flight next week or this. There was no one whom I could logically expect to listen to my mounting rage, no one I could hold responsible for this alteration. Next week I would go through the torture all over again.

Outside, the sun was getting brighter and the early-morning movements were beginning; the cars were pulling up to the Douglas hangar. And the program was going right on as it had before without me.

Six weeks ago I had come to join the research project and now I wanted to get away from it. I threw some clothes in the back of my car, informed Carder I wouldn't be around for Friday's flight, and took the road back toward Los Angeles, down to Hermosa Beach and my beach shack.

It was supposed to have been a big week end—even a party for the triumphant return out of the desert where the monster had been neatly slain. I drove fast down the highway away from the base and the books and the Skyrocket, leaving the whole program—that small unit of men searching after answers—that already seemed my life, behind in a little spot in the wide valley.

Out of the desert, into the canyon, I felt better. I wasn't returning a hero, but practically speaking, I was returning. If Flight Plan Number 54 had gone according to the original schedule there may have been some doubt about that.

It was a big holiday in Hermosa, all right, but for none of the reasons anticipated at the beginning of the week.

CHAPTER XII

My next appointment with the Skyrocket was set for the following week. Again, the day before, Flight Plan Number 54 was called off. Gene May took it up for me. The Navy had needed some hurry-up data. And so it went for six weeks, each week the next flight was promised to me and each week I went through the agonizing preparation again; reviewing the lessons, reaching for the switches with my eyes closed and, at the last minute, the flight would be canceled.

Preparation for the Skyrocket became more and more tedious, my enthusiasm waned with the passing of the weeks. The process became embarrassing. In the mess, in the bar, interested pilots considerately stopped asking when the flight was to be after the first two cancellations. And on more and more frequent visits to Hermosa Beach, the friends who waited each week end to help me celebrate now waited for me to announce the news independent of the inquiries.

The sixtieth flight of the Skyrocket was set for a Thursday morning and once more it was tailored for the new pilot. Flight Plan Number 54, that had yet to be followed, hung again in Carder's office, the figure 54 crossed out and the number 60 replacing it.

May would undoubtedly be called in again just as I was buckling my parachute; there was really no need to spend much time in preparation. It began to appear that I would never be allowed to fly the ship; I would only be allowed to prepare.

During the six weeks that passed, waiting for first flight, I was occasionally occupied making rocket ground test runs that by now had become orderly, routine function. Several times a week, in order to remember what a plane felt like, I took the F-80 through its paces, "wringing" myself out in invented emergencies that I might meet in the Skyrocket when the time eventually came to fly the thing.

The Skyrocket comes over the fence at close to 200 miles an hour and she touches down at 160. I kept the 80 at Skyrocket landing speed and approached the runway in a wide turn, as if it were the lake bed, and then I would pull her up again. There was no way to simulate an actual Skyrocket landing in the F-80. The little jet couldn't handle Skyrocket landing speed; her sit-down speed is a slow 90 miles an hour.

During the time I waited outside of the program, training for the flight that moved away from me week after week, the Air Force's star, Captain Chuck Yeager, after an absence of several months, began flying chase for the Skyrocket. Yeager didn't hang around the officers' bar much, which would be about the only way I would run into him. He had a pretty wife and three kids living over in the base settlement, and when he wasn't giving a speech somewhere on supersonic flight he stayed close to home. Once in a while he was seen at Pancho's but never when I was there. And though the famous pilot had flown chase the last four flights. I had yet to meet him personally. When the Skyrocket came in for a landing he would bring his F-86 low over the lake, alongside Gene, pull up when Gene touched down, slide into a spectacular roll, and disappear back toward the Air Force hangar for a landing on the base runway. His slow, unruffled comments, softened even more by a West Virginia drawl, came over the radio along with Gene's staccato voice on those mornings the Rocket flew without me. Conversation and camaraderie were at a minimum between the two pilots and the comments were formal and brief. It was entirely possible I would have Yeager flying chase for me one morning; from the way things were progressing, it looked like that day would be some time in 1950.

It was Wednesday morning and the flight plan in Carder's office that now I had learned to check daily remained the same. It was the stabilized run at 16,000 feet; the rest of the schedule I knew without reading further. It was memorized. In the afternoon I checked again—Flight Plan Number 60 was still there! Still I felt no alarm, after six weeks of conditioning like an animal in a psychology laboratory, the appointed hour no longer caused apprehension or anxiety, the buzzer was losing its effectiveness and the once highly keyed reflexes were worn to a slow response. Once more it could be Gene's; save your fuel!

But still by Wednesday night no one had come up to me with the usual, "By the way, Bill, something's come up . . ."

Just to be on the safe side, tonight I would go to bed early. The flight was called for five-thirty tomorrow morning. Across from my bed in the narrow room of The Shamrock the big white refrigerator stood out vaguely in the dark. Seven hours away now and no one had come to report a cancellation. Perhaps the white Skyrocket sitting in the dark Douglas hangar waited for me after all.

I was shaken out of the total comfort of sleep by the clattering of the alarm clock. The room was black and I felt the cold of the early morning as I reached out and quieted the little clock. What was it? With the same awful surprise that I felt when I awoke in a tent in the Pacific and remembered that I had a strike, I recalled now that this was the morning I was to fly the Skyrocket. What an irrational action it was to leave the warmth and security of this bed to go out into the black, cold morning and meet a radical, ominous plane, to deliberately go out and face fear! Five-thirty. The strike was called. Miller was probably already on the field. Fear begins early in the morning when you are least prepared to cope with it. The war began at dawn on an empty stomach. It burst on you in ironic contrast from the security of sleep, miles away from the enemy. No one had come to tell me the strike had been canceled. The electric light bulb did nothing to warm the room and in the mirror I saw my face. "Okay, bright boy. You got yourself into this, let's see what you can do."

Down the hall behind the closed doors the other civilian test pilots and personnel were sleeping; out in the freezing desert dark on the gravel street there were no lights, the whole base was sleeping. I was alone as I proceeded down to the hangar and the enthusiasm lost by the continual postponement of this morning was remustered with "stay alive" instinct, an independent function.

The Douglas hangar was silhouetted by a bright shade of blue rising from the desert; above the roof line the sky continued black and crowded with stars. In the empty desert the stars hang close, thicker in number—like shy animals in a forest assured that they were unobserved.

There were more cars than usual in front of the hangar. Inside the building it was like the middle of the night, the neon tubes glowed off a blue, cold light. There in the corner was hot coffee in the vending machine, a scolding, black mixture in a paper cup. It helped to relieve the rubbery, weak, early-morning feeling. The flight would be made on this mixture alone, we would celebrate with breakfast later if the flight was a success.

Under the glare of the neon tubes the engineers and technicians were gathered in Carder's office. They sat, cold and pulled out of sleep, on the chilled metallic chairs and desks, clutching paper coffee cups.

"All this on account of you." Osborne greeted me with the joke as I entered the room.

Tommy Briggs wanly picked it up: 'Yeah, look at his eyes. What did you do, Bridge, wash them out with Mercurochrome?"

"Hell, they ought to be red, I didn't go to bed last night." And so the banter went. We had 15 minutes to kill before the procession moved out to the Skyrocket. The limp paper coffee contains piled up on the desks. We drank one black, bitter cup after another. The office was cold and the men were irritable, but they broke the silence with an attempt at good humor as if it were a duty.

Time to get into the gear. At the opposite end of the hangar from where my locker was, I was startled to see the large frame of Hoskinson standing next to Al Carder. Hoskinson is chief of the Testing Division for Douglas Aircraft; this was the first time I had seen him on the base. He was quite an addition to the audience this morning. The two men saw me getting into my flight gear, but went on with their conversation, utilizing the time in company business.

I climbed stiffly into my overalls, the big helmet was as cold as the inside of a refrigerator door. I checked the oxygen mask for leaks, went over the parachute; everything was in order. On my knee pad I looked through the small stack of flight cards. They were in proper order. Still it was not time.

Until Carder called I occupied myself with the paper in the empty aerodynamicists' office behind the lockers. An electric heater in the middle of the cramped windowless room tried dismally to give off heat and I crouched inside the fleece-lined Navy jacket in one of the uncomfortable metal chairs. From the open door of the adjoining room the voices of Sorenson, Briggs, and Carder floated, flat and monotoned.

"Ready to go?" Carder appeared in the doorway. And the movement began; men huddled around heaters here and there in the building left the little warmth and headed for the cars and the cold, thin, piercing desert dawn.

Carder looked at his watch, "Sunup is due in 30 minutes." We headed toward the radio car, the other green Douglas wagons were filling up with the usual entourage. Next to the radio car the Douglas brass were already to go, Hoskinson and Bert Foulds—and in the back seat, Gene May. There appeared to be a great deal of interest in this flight, a situation that added to my discomfort. It would have been far less awkward to perform alone. Why is it that one was rarely allowed to suffer unobserved, there was always a nurse or a copilot or an audience for whom you must assume a role? Men who are allowed the dignity of privacy are the creators, the scientists, the solitary workers whose product or function begins and ends within themselves.

Across the runway, we began the 15-minute ride. Along the bottom of the dark blue sky the margin of pink was widening. The radio car stopped at the small Air Force flight office and the officer received our flight clearance.

There was a pain in the bottom of my stomach from all the black coffee I'd poured down and I was not as controlled as I would have liked to be. My heart was beating faster than usual and I was conscious of breathing. A curious thing, I would withdraw from my body and in a detached manner observe these peculiar reactions that seemed to work independent of my mind. My mind seemed excessively alert this morning, but it had no control over these uncomfortable sensations.

There was little conversation. Carder was busy giving his orders into the stick he held, and the lake swam by eerily alongside us as we pointed toward the Skyrocket somewhere ahead.

There she was! A mile before us the Skyrocket, a large white bomb, was poised on the gray clay. Alone, with nothing to tie her in with the sparse surroundings; no hangar, no building, in violent man-made contrast to the mountains behind her and the line-flat lake, she squatted. This morning the plane had all the horror of a surgical table, an electric chair, and although I had seen her lying in the dawn many mornings, the sight of her now filled me with a kind of morbid fascination. I was seeing the Skyrocket for the first time and I couldn't move my eyes away from her as she loomed larger in front of us.

I was vaguely aware that someone was talking to me, but I could not turn away from the airplane that waited ahead. My stomach was complaining uncomfortably. I had to begin the enormous effort of relaxation and composure; I had to look away from the ship. The easiest way back was through the enormity of small, wry jokes. Again Briggs and Osborne entered into the banter.

Carder pulled to a stop 20 yards from the plane; the crew cowered from the stinging wind behind the shelter of parked cars and reluctantly they came out to meet us. Beside the ship McNemar squinted through the wind in our direction, got to his feet, and moved at a trot over to the car.

Carder rolled down the window and the cold air blew in. "You ready to go?" he asked McNemar.

The crew chief leaned in the car; his eyes fell on me briefly and he nodded, "Good morning," and to Carder; "Yeah, she's all set as soon as Iltner gets out of the cockpit." In the cockpit the inspector's head bobbed up and down as he checked the equipment with the beam of his flashlight.

It was time. Awkwardly I gathered up my equipment; Briggs offered me a hand with the parachute. Outside on the floor of the lake the cold rose through my shoes and the wind was like ice water blown against my neck. Carder stood beside me.

"Do you want to talk to Gene before you go?"

"No." Now I just wanted to get out of the wind and into the plane. The crew had emerged from behind their shelter and they offered their brief good mornings. Across the lake and east toward the mountains the sky was lit with yellow and orange and the day had arrived. The sun would slide up fast now over the rough edge of the eastern range.

"We're all set," McNemar was delivering the Skyrocket. One of the mechanics gestured, "She's all yours."

As I had done many times before in preparation for this day, I climbed the ladder into the cockpit, and for the first time that morning I was more myself. The wind was off my legs and the performance of the preflight routine had a settling effect. I plugged into the oxygen supply and turned the valve on, strapped the knee board around my leg, adjusted the harness under my chest, and ran down the preflight check list. Carder waited in the wind below me, the mechanics stood by to plug in. Rechecked the oxygen lines. Okay. The helmet was tight against my temples. All the circuit breakers were in . . . how easily my hand dropped on the proper switches; it was as if I knew this plane better than any I had ever flown. The switches and buttons were more familiar to me than the DC-3 I flew for two years. I laughed at the joke I'd played upon my ego . . . I ought to know them; I've only practiced for two months, it really isn't such a feat. The sudden laughter from the cockpit surely alarmed the men working below, they must have thought the strain was too much for me . . . and I laughed again. Carder probably gulped down what was left of his bottle of aspirin.

Below me he shouted up. "Ready for the chase plane?" I nodded and Carder retreated to his car. He fumbled with his microphone.

The voice of the dispatcher in the control tower eight miles away at the other end of the lake crackled through my earphones. He called the chase plane at Carder's order.

"Air Force 120, you are cleared to taxi to the duty runway." Colonel "Pete" Everest, chief of the Air Force test pilots was flying chase today. The dispatcher now cleared him for take-off. Two seconds. A dot over the lake, the F-86, headed for us, thundered 40 feet over my head, and then bent steeply into a climb for altitude. Everest's playful salutation vibrated through my helmet against my skull. He called down, "Okay, Gene, whenever you're ready."

Carder came on in an irritated tone, "This is Bridgeman. Remember, we briefed you yesterday."

"Oh yeah, the new start," the chase pilot's voice drops. "Let us know when you're ready."

I was as ready as I'd ever be. At the sight of the circling motion of my hand the mechanics plugged in. She whined a protest and the engine started. There was no way out now and in a minute I'd know what it was that I had armed against for three months. The dials and gauges responded normally, I was not cold any more despite the fact that my head and shoulders were exposed to the wind; the palms of my hands were even a little damp. Okay, bring the canopy down, I motioned and at once Iltner and two mechanics were on the ladders. It took three men to lock the shell over my head. Once it was locked the only means of escape in the air was to pull the lever at my feet and break the nose off the ship. Before the clamshell was secured Iltner, the first one to do so, wished me well but in a none-too-confident manner. "Have a nice flight," he shouted over the engine and then he added, "damn it, bring her back. It's our seven bucks per diem, you know."

Bring her back! Below, the crew scattered away to the sheltering trucks and cars. The Skyrocket and I were on our own.

Let's go. Bring the engine up to 12,500 rpm full power, she vibrates very gently under me. Turbine out temperature--850° F., the green needle on the fuel pressure wavers on 15 psi, oil pressure 50 psi. Number 1 bearing temperature, 90° F.: Number 2, --120° F.; Number 3, --150° F., check hydraulic pressure, generator warning, and fire warning lights. Okay.

Behind the small transparent door by my left foot is the cockpit jettison handle, the escape device. When it is opened a red light bleeds on, indicating I can expect a successful ejection if it becomes necessary to pull the handle. I reach down, open the door; the light glows on. The cartridges are in the firing chamber and they are effective. The apparatus is not comforting but I am too busy now to reflect upon it. Jato master switch is off. All the temperatures look good. Now!

She rolls smoothly forward. She's got me now. I call to the F-86 above, "Starting to roll." My voice is a pitch higher although I try to keep it normal. Every nerve under my skin is alerted, every sense reaches out to pick up a sound, a change in balance, a vibration or one of the warning lights that will automatically flash on the panel before me if a fire starts or there is a failure somewhere.

You're in it now; hope for some luck; you've got to have some luck on this flight. The unforeseen has a big advantage on this trip and I wait for it to happen. A mile of runway is eaten up and she hasn't hit 100. Up to 80, now 90, there it is, 100. Hit the first two jatos. A second, and a kick in the fanny, and another kick as the remaining jatos fire off. She's up to 180, roaring down the lake bed. This is the time; pull her nose up . . . she won't go. Pull back more, more yet, it is almost a prohibitive angle, at least 18 degrees, but she lifts off, bites into the air, and shoots low over the desert. Get rid of the jato bottles now; the designated spot is a second away from here. Without glancing down, I let my left hand fall on the small metal jato jettison switch. The jato indicator light goes off; the bottles have cleared the airplane. Turn the jato master switch to off.

Everest's voice comes into my helmet, "You look clean from here; four bottles away."

That much is out of the way and it hasn't happened yet. Still, I am ready. Keep the field in sight. The visibility is bad from the sliver windowpanes at my shoulders, I can't see the wingtips, swept back out of sight the way they are. I am guided by the long white nose that determinedly points the way, splitting the air in front of it. Move the long nose into a slight turn and level up the wings, feel for the climb speed, it takes at 260. This is no F-80! Without her rockets, climbing on jet alone, I can feel that she is far underpowered; she handles like a truck, heavy and large. I've got hold of something new all right. Still the thing I am expecting, that I have waited for and armed against for eight weeks, doesn't happen. It is almost vaguely annoying; any fool can fly a ship that behaves! Twenty thousand and still nothing. Like any other plane she got here, no warnings. And I relax against my parachute, but only a little. There is some testing to do. The stabilized runs—they will require great attention, they must be straight and level at exact speed. Steady, very steady. Don't get too far away from the field, leave it in the middle of your run path, rather than at the end, where it is more accessible in an emergency.

The nose obediently turns in front of me back toward the field and the precision run begins. Keep it steady, feel the air as it flows. Air is like a river, it's never still and like a river, however calm, it has swells and sudden eddies. In the air you can feel the swells as you move through them. To hold a straight and level path it is necessary to make constant adjustments. When the altimeter trends one way you trend the other. Now as I steady out across the lake she is lighter because of the fuel used up in the run, she wants to go with her lighter load and she leaves the lake quickly behind. Watch the oil temperature and pressure; this is a bad spot to be in, heading away from the big safe lake bed. There is enough fuel for a run back. The ship performs adequately again on the second run; she is fulfilling her function at my direction—but still I wait for the moment to come when she will balk. One more run—I measure the task against the remaining fuel—two out of three is good enough, there are only 115 gallons left in the tank.

"I'm going to make some stalls!"

Quickly Carder comes through with the warning. "You mean approach the stall, don't you?"

"Yeah, yeah—approach the stall." I call over to the chase pilot, "Going to slow her up and see how she feels."

Again Carder watches over me: "How much fuel have you got?"

"One hundred."

When she buffets I'll call it a day. Flaps down, gear down. She will react the same in a landing, but up here I've got altitude and room in which to recover. In an actual landing you guess wrong and there's no where to go but into a hole in the ground. The air-speed indicator slows to 200, 190 . . . when does this thing start to shake? No sign of buffet; an F-80 would be shaking like a rivet hammer this close to the stall. Now 180 . . . ahead the nose vibrates just a shade, and then like a hammock on a summer day she starts to rock gently from side to side. What in hell is this? What freak of design can produce this crazy reaction? There is nothing I can do about it, the ship is flying me, gently rocking back and forth, back and forth . . . no ship I have ever flown has reacted like this; the rocking increases. My throat is dry as I move it to call the chase pilot . . . before I can speak, Everest observes, "Guess you give up something when you sweep the wings."

"I'll clean it up now and we'll go on in." I apply power in a hurry and the rocking dampens.

"Why stop? That was just getting interesting."

Although I think we are going to be friends, the feeling of control in this ship is a complete departure from anything I've ever flown. She handles more like a transport than the fighter-size plane she is. But she is neither fighter nor transport; she's a result of mutation, and from her will evolve a new line of airplanes that will take all her strong characteristics and the discoveries she's suffered and leave the rest like a shell. This plane will take understanding.

It's all over now but the landing and it hasn't happened yet.

"Hey, Gene, you ready to go in?" Pete Everest calls.

"Yeah, Sol, let's go."

From the ground, Carder who is glued to the radio car speaker relaxes: "Boy, boys. . . ."

Everest laughs and Carder asks me, "How much fuel, Bill?"

"Sixty."

"Better bring it back."

The control tower interrupts without waiting to be called. They also are attentive to this flight. "Navy 973, you are cleared to land on the lake bed using the Douglas east-west runway, landing to the west. Wind is west at 15 knots."

The sun is now in back of me; to my left are the mountains. Just the landing now and below I know the audience holds its breath.

I'm on the final approach. This has got to be good, Bridgeman. Keep ahead of the speed she "rolls" at. The prospect of a hammock ride over the ground makes me wince. But as the flaps drop it starts, the uncontrollable swing back and forth low over the hard-baked lake at 250 miles per hour. She is fast and a little high and my muscles feel as if they will burst through my skin. A little pressure. Not too much. She is tender. Steady. Ease off power. My hands, restrained, seem to perform independently over the controls. Let down now. Easy. And still she swings closer to the ground that is rising fast below me. Where does she get this speed? She is still going . . . 200 mph. I tug at the nose a little and there we are . . . she flares! The roll drops off at once but I'm still a little bit high.

"You've got ten feet yet, Bill." Everest's observation comes before I can make the correction and I am irritated by his promptings.

Just as advertised, the ailerons become weak as I let down. God, the speed this thing still has. There! The ground is met as if the Skyrocket were a feather, but the speed she's tearing down the runway with—twice as fast as the F-80 comes in! Brake it, brake the power she's still got left.

Everest approves the landing: "I bet you wish they were all like that." It is probably one of the best landings I've ever made, thank God.

Her power finally dissipated on the wild roll across the gray adobe lake, she stops. Far behind me the dust from the Douglas cars racing out to meet us fills the air.

The cockpit seemed very warm and I was suddenly aware that my helmet was like a vise against my head now that the flight was over. The oxygen mask pinched at my face and I wanted to get out of this cubbyhole. I unlocked the canopy, unhooked the mask, and gulped down the clean desert air. It was like a long drink of water.

And now that it was all over I slumped into my parachute and found

I was trembling. The thing I was prepared to fight never happened. My body unwound. It was all over! I was glad for this moment alone; there was no one to watch me, dropped into the silence of the desert this way. No sound but the sound of the Skyrocket panting steam under me; we breathed together; the breeze, now warmed by the sun, dried the sweat off of my face. And here was peace for as far as I could see: that phenomenal combination of parts in balance with one another that can touch the thing that lies waiting in every man—an inexpressible kind of bliss.

Seven-thirty in the morning and my work was already completed, my day was done. I would have liked to sit here uninterrupted, but alongside the ship the Douglas cars had caught up with me.

Iltner was the first one out of the cars, he brought up the stand. Briggs came up behind him and I began to hear bits of conversation. "Congratulations." "Nice flight." McNemar was calling orders to the crew. Ten feet away from the plane, Al Carder stood waiting as Briggs climbed up the ladder to hand down my helmet and gear. As I prepared to leave the ship, Iltner called up, "Well, you brought back our seven dollars a day." With great effort at composure, I tried to appear unscathed by the flight. Perhaps the audience would not notice. But my legs caused the ladder to jiggle a little as I backed down to the ground below. A dead giveaway.

Carder greeted me: "Nice flight, Bill." His tone was one of relief rather than praise.

In the rear of the radio car, Hoskinson and Foulds were waiting to ride back with Carder, Briggs, and myself. Disgruntled, they made room for my pile of gear at their feet.

"Well, what do you think of it?" Hoskinson, a large-framed man with dark heavy hair, asked.

"It scares me a little." And then quickly I added, "but not too much."

Hoskinson leaned forward, "Listen, when it stops scaring you, that's the time to quit flying it." Hoskinson was the man who would decide the amount of money I would get for the remainder of the Skyrocket contract. "I think you'll work it out, Bridgeman."

It was over. The day had come and it was over. There on the runway the Skyrocket stood harmless and still, and I was back on the ground again, driving to breakfast. There was little conversation as we crossed the lake. The sun was in our eyes. I didn't feel like talking and my companions were empty and unresponsive. Foulds appeared to be asleep.

One last look at the ship left behind. There was a match here after all! I was not outweighed. She had her weak spots, and through these weaknesses I could bend her into doing things my way. It was a fair match.

CHAPTER XIII

The Skyrocket was officially turned over to me with Carder's succinct "okay."

"We'll plan a flight for next week, Bill. That's about as soon as we can go." If the project coordinator was pleased that I had brought his airplane back in one piece, it was not apparent. It would take many more flights before Carder would display any confidence in his new pilot. He was anxious to get the program going again, squeezing out the data for the aerodynamicists who waited for precise high-speed information in order to design faster and faster military aircraft.

"I guess you'll be taking the week end in town? While you're there, better go up and see Hoskinson about the contract."

So far there had been no talk of money. Monday morning I would go in and find out definitely what the job would pay. Despite the project coordinator's lack of enthusiasm I felt good. The big day was over and there was no doubt left in my mind that I could handle the Skyrocket. At last the Hermosa crew would have something to help me celebrate. First flight had been easy; the tough ones were coming up but that morning I didn't look any further ahead than next week. A long seven days away.

For the first time in several months I found that I was able to relax, that I could sop up every minute of the week end at Hermosa. The party lasted three nights and two days. Beginning at my cramped apartment that had the beach folk overflowing out onto the sand, the group progressed to Frank and André Davis' waterfront lair and then on to Bill and Betsy Boyd's. Lighting the party were girls, shiny-eyed and suntanned with that evenness of golden brown that reaches into the sun streaks in their hair, healthily pretty from days spent surfing and swimming. Saturday and Sunday were without fog, the sun was out bright and big for late fall, and the water was cold and sparkling. I put the program and the desert out of my mind.

Monday morning I went in to see Hoskinson about the contract. Hoskinson's office was considerably more plush than any of the other Douglas offices that I had visited. It was by comparison fairly spacious, with windows along one wall, a leather couch, and a row of expensively framed Douglas airplanes hung above it.

"Well, Bill, here's the contract." He offered me the papers and then he added briskly, "12,000 dollars is all that's left in the kitty. Do you want to take it?" A year's testing is worth less than two nights of a crooner's Las Vegas booking. The contract was worth more and the chief of the Flight Test Division was aware of the fact. He also knew that I would take it because now I wanted to fly the airplane.

"Of course, you'll receive your regular monthly salary on top of that, Bill, you understand."

I signed the contract.

Now that I was at last the official test pilot for the Skyrocket investigations, the program didn't slow up a bit. Carder saw to it that the flights were tailored so that the less tricky ones were approached first, but still there was no flight time allowed for me to personally become familiar with the ship. If she was in the air, she was working, bringing back the precious data, following to the second the program of testing that had been mapped out in the master test plan, the bound pamphlet, *High-speed Investigations for the D-558-II Skyrocket,* that lay in Carder's office. Flight time was a precious commodity.

Thirty minutes in the air was all we could get at a time. The brief half-hour of flight a week was the result of a fabulous amount of man-hours on the ground. This precious use of flight time in the experimental ship is unique in aircraft testing. A prototype production plane has ample space for fuel; it is not necessary to plan a test so carefully that every minute brings back data; there is no frantic race against time or fantastic cost involved. But with the highly complex Skyrocket this wasn't so. Because of the seven miles of instrumentation wiring, jet engine, and added rocket system with its two huge ton-and-a-half tanks crowded into the sleek body and razor-thin wings, there was not much space left for jet fuel. She held enough fuel for 30 minutes of flight and that was it. She wasn't designed to "go" anywhere or carry a pay load; she was a brief explorer of speed, running into it for a few minutes at a time, using her jet engine to carry her to altitude and then blasting into a high-speed run with all four rocket tubes firing at once. Then she was through, her rocket fuel spent, and she had to get back home quickly on what little jet fuel she had left.

Back on the ground, it took a week to put her in shape again— there was the recording instrumentation to be readjusted, the rocket engine required the attention of a whole crew even if it wasn't used for the flight, and of course the jet engine was torn apart and put back together again.

Because her fertile period of data gathering was so brief, the engineers took no chances on wasting a flight due to unforeseen conditions that might make it impossible to complete a scheduled test. They worked out three plans for each flight in order to allow an alternate for items that might not be obtainable.

My first five flights, without rocket power, were devoted to low-speed stability tests—studying stall characteristics, control effectiveness, accelerated stall recovery, and some buffet checks. There was no time to be apprehensive; I learned as I went. The remark Bert Foulds had made last summer, "None of us know much about it, get in and get your feet wet," held more and more truth for me. I was getting my feet wet all right, and all the time spent in gleaning knowledge from my books was paying off. But it was actual flight time that was the real education—five minutes in the air with the experimental ship was worth ten hours of study on the ground, and gradually I understood the magnitude of the horizon that lay out there, unknown, waiting to be probed in the rocket ship.

One of my first concerns was getting test items completed more efficiently and faster in order to get the most data out of each costly flight.

Time unfruitfully spent during the meager 30 minutes of flight showed up embarrassingly on the film that recorded every move I made from take-off to landing. The record brought the engineers right into the cockpit with me. It was a matter of integrity to get their stuff for them without any blank time lapses showing on the film.

It took five flights before I developed a routine that would utilize the flight time, so that every second in the air brought back valuable information. I found that the transitory period between one flight condition to the next in order to gather succeeding items was taking too long, resulting in a waste of the energy I controlled. After each flight a careful study of the test film made it possible to perform faster in the next flight. One way was figuring how much thrust was needed to attain a given air speed. I could pick up time in flight by setting the throttle to the required position for the next item on my knee board.

In order to fill in points on the blank film that existed between items it was necessary to understand thoroughly the big master plan and what regions the investigations were to encompass. Sometimes it was impossible to perform any of the three alternate tests at a scheduled altitude because of an unexpected turbulent layer of air or a cloud bank that showed up. I developed alternate plans for the engineers' alternate plans. Familiarity with the over-all program made it possible for me to immediately transfer the scheduled test to another that I had filed in my mind, requiring another altitude. The flight brought back something and was not wasted.

It was a challenge draining every possible drop of data out of the ship and on to her recording instruments. It became a consuming game that required a great amount of conditioning. It involved weeks of poring over the master flight plan, learning what future tests were required to fill up the waiting envelopes and growing rows of data notebooks. I carefully studied the individual flight plans as they came up and the steps that surrounded them, fitting them into the over-all picture, making it easier to fill in extra points along the way. The reward was a bigger load of news.

Before every flight I sat in the Skyrocket going over all the moves and settings that I would perform in the actual test, each time gaining a little more speed. *One, two, three. Too much time. Try it again. . . . That's better.*

It all helped. The big job of bringing back information with the supersonic airplane moved uninterruptedly along, more and more smoothly, but the problem of handling the plane itself still existed.

She was one of the only two supersonic airplanes in the world at the time. Her predecessor, the X-1, beat her through the sound barrier by a slim six months. Her design was radical, she was a research tool carved strictly for high performance, her sole function was to experiment in high speeds in the big laboratory above the Mojave. As a result her stability and handling characteristics came second—if she behaved erratically it was of no particular concern as long as she brought back the news and continues to fly. She would never be the prototype for a new military fighter; she was not a gun platform; so what if she had a Dutch roll? You didn't stop the program to rebuild the ship, working the "bugs" out, the way you would in a military-ordered fighter, you merely learned to fly with the phenomenon. If the Skyrocket's unruly behavior hampered you from getting a particular test run, you modified your flying technique so you could "get around" the undesirable characteristic and complete the test.

This was a whole new concept of testing. In routine military testing, the sort of thing that the Flight Test Center here deals with, the stability characteristics of an airplane rigidly have to meet set standards. The Skyrocket did not. She sacrificed controllability and easy management to the quest of more and more speed. The study of stability in the Skyrocket was wide open! And the prospect of how she would behave as the program began to reach out for higher and higher Mach numbers was something I looked forward to with a kind of dreadful fascination.

So far her top speed with rockets had been a shade past the speed of sound. Mach 1.05. Her rival, the X-1, had beat her again with a top speed of 1.4. The X-1 conserved all of her rocket fuel for her high-altitude speed run by the means of air launching. instead of burning up part of her propellants in a ground take-off, she was carried up to altitude in the belly of a B-29 and then dropped out for her high-speed sprint, actually a safer way of handling the rockets. The further you are away from the ground the better off you are.

Now that she was truly my ship she managed to occupy all of my time. Between the weekly flights on the jet engine alone, I memorized the endless amount of data points I could pick up between scheduled items. One half-hour a day was spent faithfully in the cockpit rehearsing my performance for the next flight, formulating whole sets of alternate plans in the event the three scheduled ones didn't come off. Doing a more accurate job crowded my mind; what corner remained was concerned with self-preservation and the safe return of the costly ship.

There were the flight emergencies to think about and their separate set of alternate plans. Still more alternates. Again I called on Miller's solid combat training: "Always have an answer prepared and you'll get your ass back in one piece." An emergency is treated the same in war or in testing—expect it!

During dinner, over a drink, the sharp questions of flight emergencies nudged my brain, and in the middle of a conversation I retreated with the problem and silently repeated the answers like multiplication tables. For every emergency I had devised three or four alternates. There seemed to be no room in my mind for anything else but alternates; there were so many things I should be able to carry in my mind—valuable charts and graphs. The alternates were easier to remember, they were a natural progression of thought, like a chain, one was associated to the next, but the graphs were isolated lines and figures, and hard to stamp on the mind. I could only hope that I would remember the answer when I needed it.

A fire emergency! Do I jettison the fuel and take a chance it doesn't spray on to the fire or do I keep the explosive stuff in the tanks?

What points can I pick up between the second and third items dropping from 32,000 to 30,000? What alternates have I prepared for 20,000 feet? What is the throttle control setting for the thrust needed on items number four? There is so much to remember, so much to calculate.

Only after a flight was over could I begin to unwind, to feel that I could safely forget the dartlike ship that was now my life.

And so the first five weeks, the first five flights, went by. The anticipated emergency hadn't happened on these slow-speed stability tests and the chase pilot's job of bodyguard was uneventful; he had no trouble at all keeping up with the Skyrocket on her jet engine alone at speeds between 180 and 600 miles per hour. Time made me more confident with the ship; her strange flight characteristics became less strange; her responses became part of my own. And although she had the power to momentarily freeze me with an unexpected murmur, we established a close relationship.

So far the most uneasy moments in the Skyrocket were spent when a test led her as far from the lake as Tahatchapi. If I had had to make an emergency landing in a hurry, I couldn't have made it back to the big, safe lake bed. An ordinary runway isn't long enough to accommodate the ship; she comes over the fence hot and she eats up three miles in a landing—one of her more inconvenient features. A forced landing on the desert floor was inconceivable.

My new-won confidence toward the plane soon led me into tentatively offering suggestions on the improvement of the engineer's flight plan, small suggestions at first. The advice was received with some eyebrow-raising, but by the fourth flight I was pleased to see that some of the alterations were put into practice.

Carder was vaguely surprised at the effrontery of his new boy. "I see you changed a couple of items around already. Well, I guess the pilot knows more about the airplane than anybody else—but you'd better be right." If my reshuffle of items proved beneficial, Carder would no doubt be pleased. If I was wrong, the next time I wanted to make a change it wouldn't be so easy.

The rocket take-offs came six weeks after first flight, when Carder was sure I knew the plane. The project coordinator characteristically took the big moves in small steps; there was no unnecessary hurrying in his program There would be no accidents as long as he controlled the project.

It was on the ride back across the lake from the fifth jato-assisted flight that Carder suggested we use the rockets on the next trip.

"I think it's about time that we get on with the program, Bill. We'll fire up the rockets on the next one."

It had been a long while since the old wave of anxiety had swept through me. I thought of the intricate, highly explosive rocket system. Here was something new again. Just as I was beginning to feel somewhat at home in the ship that had brought me through five successful flights, the whole picture was rapidly changed with Carder's announcement.

"We'll pick up some buffet information in the transonic area at Mach .95 in a high-speed run with the rockets, Bill." In a way the step forward toward the high-speed stuff was an endorsement of sorts. Carder was a very careful man. "After a couple of transonic flights, defining the buffet boundary on this side, we'll take a look on the other side in the supersonic region. It'll probably take a week or ten days to get her in shape for a rocket take-off; that'll give you time to prepare."

A rocket take-off involved around 30 highly specialized technicians, each assigned the responsibility of one small function. The men concerned knew their job well. It was largely a matter of timing and synchronization. For her high-speed run she would use her rockets at altitude. The added two tons of fuel she carried to feed them weighted her down heavily in take-off. In order to get her in the air it was necessary to light two of the rockets to help the puny jet engine with the tremendous added burden. Once the ship was in the air the rockets would be shut off, conserving fuel for the important test at altitude; it was up to the jet engine to carry the load the rest of the way up. If the rockets should stop firing at take-off, the jet engine, left unassisted, would not be strong enough to keep the ship in the air, she would drop back on the lake bed with her belly full of explosives, straight into a half-city-block-wide hole in the ground.

Each afternoon before the flight I climbed into the cockpit with a stop-watch. I ran through a practice drill of the movements involved in the complicated rocket take-off, checking the stop-watch to see if I had crammed all the steps into the ten seconds that I was allowed. After 30 minutes in the cockpit I could hit all the switches and read all the dials in the allotted ten seconds. If I failed to do so the morning of the flight, the whole elaborate show would be halted and the flight would be called off. Ten days of preparation lost in ten seconds.

Beside my leg I was aware of the escape lever. It had been some time since I had considered what would happen if it became necessary to pull it. So far the Skyrocket had behaved. My anxiety toward the next flight was not lessened any by the sight of the lethal-looking metal lever gleaming behind the transparent door. Actually I would just as soon take my chances with the Rocket if she got into serious trouble. Hurtling through 20,000 feet of sky in an uncontrollable pod, perhaps blacking out before I got to bail-out altitude, was not a comforting thought. No one had ever tried the escape device. No one could say whether it was practical.

The day before flight Carder informed me, "Yeager is flying chase for you tomorrow, Bill." The Air Force's pride was going to ride herd on my flight! It had been Yeager's pattern to take a look in at the program from time to time to see what the Navy boys were up to. Since Gene had left Yeager hadn't been too interested—the rocket flight had brought him out.

The prospect of Yeager flying chase was certainly reassuring; there was no doubt about his guardian abilities. The current Yeager story circulating around the base is how he shepherded the unfortunate contract pilot who became separated from his oxygen supply. His sloppy flying at 20,000 was a warning to Chuck that the pilot was in trouble.

The squat little experimental plane was going through some slow-speed stability tests at altitude when it happened. As is his custom Yeager was flying alongside within shouting distance of his charge.

The two planes were cutting along together at a modest speed when the research plane weaved erratically instead of maintaining the strict straight and level course required for the test. Yeager crawled into the cockpit for a better look; the pilot's head was rolling loosely on his shoulders. Alarmed, Yeager called into him. He got a slurring, nonsensical answer. Again the chase pilot called, "Hey, boy, how do you feel?" There was no answer. Another try and again no answer. For some reason or other, Yeager figured, the guy was out of oxygen, another minute or two and he would pass out altogether. Trying desperately to get through to the pilot in the faltering plane, Yeager urgently suggested, "Check your oxygen-supply gauge, flip over to 100 per cent."

The incoherent flyer replied irritably, "Never mind that, will you . . . I've got to finish this run." The run was erratic and meaningless weaving, and Yeager, really worried now, urgently repeated his request for the dazed pilot to check his oxygen. His charge, made belligerent by insufficient oxygen, curtly told Yeager to "shut up" until he finished his run. The danger was imminent and Yeager tried desperately to coax the stricken pilot down to a lower altitude where he could get oxygen. The pilot of the research plane would not respond and the two planes headed further away from the safety of the lake bed.

Yeager, in a last effort, attempted to get through to the rapidly blanking-out pilot with a cry for help himself. "Hold off before you go into your next point. I've got a problem here. I can't keep this thing running even on the emergency system. I just flipped over and she flamed out. I'm going to put her on the lake bed. Follow me down." Yeager moved out in front of the weaving plane and made a turn down. No response. Yeager now roared into his microphone, "Look, 'my devoted young scientist,' follow me down!" It worked. The cry for help cut through the fog closing in around the test pilot and obediently he dropped down behind his chase plane.

At a safe 12,000 feet, Yeager began to circle and his charge followed him without question. Yeager kept up a running conversation until he noticed the pilot's slurring voice returning to normal.

"How do you feel?"

"I feel better—what happened?" The contract pilot was amazed to learn of the danger he had just escaped. When both ships came in for a landing with near-empty tanks, the pilot discovered what caused the trouble at altitude. The oxygen tube had pulled loose and lay dangling, unattached in the cockpit. Without Yeager he never would have returned from the flight.

I awoke with the siren in my ears. A raid! Five years ago seemed like this minute. A little time to remember what it was, and the whistle that shrieked overhead was not a siren in the Pacific—it was the Skyrocket being fueled for her rocket flight in two more dark hours. The shrill whistle struck more response in me than the infrequent sirens in the Pacific. There, it was a warning to several thousand men, never a personal one—the danger was thinly spread about and surely you would escape with those odds. The whistle that whined across the desert was a singular call.

A block away in the cold and drafty Douglas hangar, Al Carder was already up, meticulously overseeing the fueling procedure. The men moved cautiously about the plane, shrouded in their awkward white, hooded suits. Carder would be nervous today. Today there was a good chance he might lose his plane: a tire could blow on take-off, the rocket system could fail, his pilot could make an error, and countless other unforeseen enemies lay waiting. He sniffed at the wind occasionally; if it suddenly shifted the wrong way he would call the flight off at the last minute. But because the fueling had started, as the whistle announced in my room, the chances of a flight were good.

I had developed, in five flights, assurance toward the Skyrocket, but the hard-won condition was lost this morning as I contemplated the rocket engine. Whatever this energy was that filled me . . . apprehension . . . I had to get it harnessed somehow, use it in some way for the flight ahead. All the bodily activity the mind touched off by apprehension seemed a senseless dissipation. Anyway it had alerted me out of sleep, and the flight was still three hours away.

Since I was a boy I have always been able to escape into sleep. That night at Pearl Harbor I had slept soundly on a wooden board. It must be age. This morning I couldn't retreat into the anesthesia of sleep . . . or perhaps the whistle was really as loud and nerve-scraping as I imagined it to be. That night at Pearl I was 24; this morning I am 33—ten years of flying, ten years of emergencies. The same pattern. It reached out to something and despite the discomfit of fear I could do nothing else but follow.

Before the alarm had a chance to tear up the silence, I shut it off, there was no need for its prompting. I was already awake, waiting to go.

This morning the tension surrounding the flight was more apparent to me. The operation appeared in sharper focus than it ever had before, although on many cold dawns I had followed the mournful procession across the wide lake bed to attend Gene May's rocket flights. Today I was aware of the nervous control in the faces of the men who worked around the steaming plane, tending the frost-covered lines into the tanks of highly explosive propellants. Twelve men intently performing their part of the flight, anxiously watching a piece of equipment or an operation so that it was not their portion of the day's performance that failed or snarled, abruptly canceling the flight. They looked for trouble and hoped not to find it.

The pace had changed this morning. There was no allowance for adjustment or last-minute consideration—the movement was all quick and meaningful, no leisurely steps, no easygoing conversation or a relaxing waste of five minutes here or there. It was more difficult than ever to maintain a relaxed approach under these high-gear conditions. Every man on the ground knew his job and performed it with great efficiency—I hoped I knew mine as well.

The radio car pulled up to the scene: the Skyrocket with the lines in her sides, the huge trailer, the red fire wagon and the ambulance, the men in the grotesque plastic suits moving in and out, the gases that whistled off into the pale dawn sky—a scene that had the sickening atmosphere that surrounds an accident on a cross-country highway. I left the car at once and headed for the plane, buckling my chute as I walked. Briggs gave me a hand with the helmet and oxygen equipment as I mounted the ladder into the steaming Skyrocket.

I reshuffled the cards on my clipboard to the new "rocket take-off" card. On the floor of the cockpit I dropped the map I had made of the flight. The map was a detailed diagram of my flight path from take-off, through the rocket run, and into the landing; it was carefully marked along the way with notations to check climbing speeds, fuel and temperature readings, "data switch on," "data switch off," at the correct altitudes and positions—a crutch for my memory. I couldn't take a chance that I would remember every detail.

From now on every single move counted. The big bundle of energy wanted to go somewhere now that things had progressed this far. All the time she sat here she boiled off her energy. In any other take-off you can delay, if necessary, until an item is altered to suit you. There is time to assure yourself that everything is in order. But not here, not with the four tubes waiting to go—you've got to move rapidly.

I made a quick cockpit check. The wind was cold. I motioned for the canopy to be clamped down. Beside the plane Carder, in sign language, asked if I was ready for the chase plane. I nodded. While the chase plane was getting up, I signaled the crew to plug in the power cart and I started up the jet engine; she whined gently like a buzz saw going through a thick log. Low over the lake the chase plane pointed toward us—Yeager! The F-86 went into a lazy roll and then moved into a slow, graceful Immelmann above the tense knot of men and machines below.

"Okay, light off that torch and let's go." The quiet, West Virginia drawl came over my earphones. An incongruous sound amid the urgent orders on the ground. The fancy quip irritated me. Things would happen fast now.

I called out to the ground crew, "Okay to pressurize?" The enormous scurrying activity that was lost behind me darted into my slit line of vision from the side of the nose where I could see. Why don't they answer? Again I called, "Okay to pressurize?' Silence and then, "Okay to pressurize" . . . the command was repeated down the line: "Okay to pressurize . . . okay to pressurize . . . okay to pressurize." The scurrying became intensified and the figures darted in more number back and forth into the slit at my shoulder.

Now. "Okay . . . *pressurizing*." I slammed the value into position and the pent-up tanks released the gases with an explosive rush into the propellant tanks. Carder called in for the readings. The needles on the three pressure systems had swung up to 30, 60, 450.

I'm ready to prime. "Okay to prime?"

"Okay to prime . . ."

This was the big moment. It was now that I'd see if I'd learned the lesson well. I had ten seconds.

"*Priming!*" There was no time to think of anything now but the quick movements I had to make. I hit the stop-watch clipped to the kneeboard at the same time that I hit the prime switch, part of the routine I'd practiced every afternoon for ten days. I had exactly ten seconds now in which to prime the rocket system, bring the idling jet engine up to full power, check all the temperatures and pressures to make certain the jet engine was performing properly, begin the 60-second roll down the runway, and light off the two rocket tubes. Just ten seconds.

Now. Fast release the brakes—thumbs out—two heads disappeared under the belly and brought out the chocks. *Work fast! Bring the jet engine up to full temperature, full rpm, and correct fuel pressure, oil temperature, oil pressure.* It is a frantic race.

"You going to fly it or blow it up, son?" Yeager wryly called down. He was circling overhead, burning up fuel.

Five seconds left. *Faster, if I'm going to get it all in.* There are three engine bearings to be checked. I hit the switches and read them "*okay.*" *Watch the gauges carefully for fluctuation or temperature change in the jet engine—if they respond erratically—kill the flight. Rocket power alone will get me up but it's the jet engine that will bring me home.* All are normal. Three seconds. I called for a prime okay. *Have I forgotten anything? God, have I forgotten anything?*

"Prime looks good." Ten seconds on the stop-watch and the time was up. I let the brakes off.

The Skyrocket doesn't shoot down the runway with a violent thrust; in ludicrous contrast to the intense activity and frantic preparation, she lumbers forward slower than ever with her great added weight of rocket propellant, limping down the runway. The crew runs alongside and then ahead of me into the waiting cars. The superspeed Skyrocket is outrun by her ground crew.

Fifty-five seconds left before I hit the tiny rocket switch . . . and as the seconds tick off, the jet engine faithfully begins to pick up power and thrust. Jostling along the runpath waiting for the number 70 to come up on the stop-watch, once more I recheck the dials and gauges. Okay. All the pressures of the rocket engine read in the green. Now she is rolling up to 100 mph and the second hand is coming off on 60 seconds . . . 65 seconds and now . . . 70 seconds!

Hit the first small metal switch, like the light switch in your living room . . . an innocuous *click!* And 1500 pounds of kick rams into the back of me, jerking me hard into the backrest. She lunges wildly forward, chewing up the lake bed behind with a gargantuan roar. For an instant the violence of the power that has added half again as much thrust to the jet engine, slamming the ship almost at once into twice the speed she had—momentarily shrivels me. On the panel before me the dials and needles wave in a row, back and forth, and the number-one green rocket light glows on ominously. The delicate system reacts to the shocks like my own body. There is no time for reaction. I am caught off guard by the sudden unleashing of power but I catch my breath fast. . . . Is the intricate rocket system taking the enormous shock suddenly imposed upon it? The pressure needles are sinking back together. She is taking it. A call from the outside startles me. "Number one is firing, Bill."

Here goes number two. I reach over and unleash 1500 more pounds of thrust, another violent kick in the fanny. The dials jump all over the board and the second green light comes on. A tiger by the tail! Now I've got an airplane that wants to go somewhere, her reflexes are tender, just touch the stick now and she'll nose up into flight. I can feel it through my hands, the harnessed power I control is so taut it can be manipulated with my fingertips, just an inch back now would do it.

A last look at the jet-engine readings before I pull the stick. It would be embarrassing to get off on rockets into the middle of the desert and find I had no jet engine to complete the flight. One hundred and ninety miles per hour, the lake bed is a brown-gray blur rushing past and I am pointing toward the mountains at the end of the valley, the needle spear in front of me tearing a path ahead.

Ease back on the yoke, about six and a half pounds of pressure and, *pufft*, she's into the velvet. Get the gear up quick. She's up to 300 miles in a couple of seconds, already I've burned a good part of a minute's worth of rocket-seconds as she climbs up at 400 miles per hour, steady and firm. That is enough. That is all I can afford; the jet engine will have to take over.

Quickly I shut off the two rocket tubes and immediately I've robbed the Skyrocket of half her thrust. The sudden drop of power throws me forward into the harness and the tender, firm control in my hands turns to mush. The Skyrocket wallows under her heavy load, struggling to continue the climb like the overloaded B-24's we begged off the runways in the Pacific on bombing missions. The desirable thing would be to stay over the sanctuary of the field, spiraling upward above it in tight turns to altitude. But this protection is impossible with her load; I am allowed only one course and that is to head far out from the lake, ascending gradually in a wide turn. I consult my schedule. Data switch on here for a segment of the climb. The camera cannot be allowed to run at all times, there is not enough space in the ship to carry that much film. The data switch is turned on only when a particular section of the flight is to be recorded, then it must be turned off immediately again. I have a haunting fear that I will forget to turn the data switch on at the right times and part of the flight will be wasted. The schedule I have drawn is marked at the various altitudes and speeds where the data switch is to be turned on. The schedule also marks the altitude where the rocket pressures are to be read and the jet fuel is to be checked. As the lake slips further away beneath me, I think of a dozen possibilities for trouble. If I take too long in the climb to altitude I'll burn up the jet fuel and I'll have nothing to get home on after the run. The rocket pressures might not hold up; if I take too much longer in the climb they will drop and the rockets won't light off when I get there. Or what if she won't pressurize at light-off? Either consequence and I'll have to jettison the tons of rocket propellant in order to try for a long glide back. What if she doesn't jettison? No answer at all for that.

"Where are you, Bill?" Carder. What does he want? I'm busy. "Twenty-seven thousand," I tell him.

A minute later: "Where are you now?"

Oh, shut up, will you? I don't answer this time.

I need altitude badly. I'm pushing with my head, holding my breath for altitude, and the curve is taking me further and further from home.

"Now, now." Yeager playfully reprimands. And outside the slit windowpane I see the chase plane glued to my wing. I had forgotten about Mr. Supersonic. The sun is directly in my eyes. I can't get a good look at him but he is close enough to shake hands with. I squint in his direction trying to make him out.

My eyes take a second to become adjusted to the shadowy cockpit again: 27,000 feet . . . check jet fuel. Looks okay. Pressures up. Speed down to 210. Data switch on. It's difficult to read the instruments with the sun burning in my eyes.

I am startled as a shadow falls, unexpectedly, across my face, blocking the glare out of the cockpit. Slightly ahead and above me Yeager is dipping his wing in front of the sun, shading my eyes.

"Is that better, son?"

"Yeah." And for a minute I'm without a retort—the captain's reputation is not exaggerated. "Would you mind scratching my back with your other wing?" He flys! The bastard. He has made his point and he couldn't have picked a worse time, but his cool, brilliant piece of horseplay eases the tension and I laugh. This is quite a boy. He continues to hold his position, blocking the sun out of my eyes until I have turned out of its glare, coming up on 30,000 feet, dragging the load at a painful 200 miles per hour. The pressures are holding out as she wallows sickly up the curving path and she is behaving. Yeager slides under me, then to my wing, then over me. He rotates his position closely, looking for trouble.

"What's your system three, Bill?" Carder calls up.

"Pressure's 1500."

"Discontinue the climb while you've got enough system pressure."

"Okay, I'm at 31,000 feet, pressurizing!"

"Right."

"Pressures up and holding steady." Here we go. "Starting the prime now." Below, George Mabry, Carder's quiet new assistant, will start his stop-watch at the moment I start mine. Sixty seconds left before I light all four tubes at once for the high-speed run. Yeager advises me, "Prime looks good."

Mabry calls, "Thirty seconds." And, as I have instructed him, he reminds me, "Data switch on."

I pull back the jet engine 500 rpm to allow a cushion against its overspeeding and flaming out at the high speed the rocket engine will take it to in a few seconds.

"Twenty seconds. Data switch on."

"Okay, data switch on."

I nose her over into a shallow dive to drain the last puff of power out of the jet engine before lighting the rockets. She is picking up speed all the way down. Yeager is right with me: 30,000 feet. This is where we get off.

"Ten seconds." Pressures holding steady. George begins the the count . . . "Nine, eight, seven, six, five, four, three, two, and one!"

Light number one! Slam. The explosion bounces the ship and we are shot through the thin, chill air at a fantastic rate of acceleration. She takes the power gracefully at altitude where the air offers less resistance. The air-speed indicator spins forward.

"One is going," Yeager calls.

Give her some more. Hit the second tube. Another explosion.

"Two looks good." Yeager is falling 'way behind the 40-foot flames that are burning a bright wake in the sky. He can barely see the number-three tube fire, "Three's firing. Come on back and I'll have a look at number four . . ."

Four roaring rivers of flame are ramming me across the sky. This is the payoff! Seven thousand five hundred pounds of thrust. The yoke I hold tightly in my hands is in a delicate balance. *Keep the run straight and level*. Again I can feel the gigantic mass of power coming through my fingers. The needle on the Machmeter moves steadily up--.65, .7, .75, and the only sound is a low rumble as I run away from the ear-splitting noise. This is worth it, worth all of the preparation, the boredom, and the anxiety. This is her promise. And what I feel is ironically akin to the feeling I experienced sitting motionless, alone in the empty desert the morning after first flight. It is a welling of exhilaration that floods my stomach, chest, and head.

Shock waves will form now, causing drag. The rapid acceleration is diminishing. Mach .8, .85, . . . the tender edge . . . .9, and I'm jolted back to business at once by the sudden vibration that disturbs the smooth ride—a nibble and it's gone. Apprehensively, I suspect the jet engine of overspeeding and I search the instruments for an indication. They read okay. The rocket instruments are all in order. I can't worry about it now; there is no time. Mach .95, only a whisper under the speed of sound, and there is work to be done, the purpose of this flight—the measuring of forces at this speed, to define the buffet point at Mach .95 pulling 3 G's. Sixty rocket-seconds gone and a ton of fuel is burned up. The maneuver requires an accelerated turn into the buffet. *Data switch on.* Hold 3 G's in tight; she balks into a jarring buffet, a hammering, vibrating complaint that I press hard on to her—a controlled torture that can be stopped at will. Data switch off. I straighten out and the buffet falls off.

The low, sustained rumble behind begins to sputter and then *pop, pop, pop, pop.* The rockets quit, hurtling me forward into my harness as the thrust disappears. A puppet dangling by its strings. The ride is over.

There are things to be done. There is no time to contemplate the experience and I return to my knee pad. I cannot readily remember the next sequence of events—the excitement of the run. The next move along the flight path, following the accelerated turn, is marked *Depressurize.* I let them know on the ground; "I'm depressurizing." Jettison the volatile dregs of fuel remaining in the tanks.

I am not directly over the west end of the lake in a good spot for a landing and below Carder reads the white vapor sheet I've sprayed off in the jettison.

"Jettison, okay," he calls.

"How's the wind holding?"

"It's shifted around to the west."

Below, the big, broad lake bed lies. Home. I pick out the long east-west runway and circle so as to approach the east end. In a minute or two I can walk away from her, my job will be completed for another week. The ocean will feel good.

The chase plane catches up with me and Yeager comes on; "D'you hold with rocket flying, boy?"

"It's mighty sudden, ain't it, Captain?" Yeager is right at my elbow and for the first time I can really see his face under his helmet. It's a wide Texas kind of a face, and I can tell by the eyes squinting above the oxygen mask that he is grinning broadly.

So far today I've won the game. I have been able to handle her with her rocket power and I head for the field feeling like a returning hero.

"Navy 973." The tower has heard my transmission to the company. "We have an emergency! Project Baker is returning with a possible fire. He'll be landing on the east-west runway in approximately two minutes. Will you remain in an area south of the lake bed during the emergency?"

My moment of triumph dissolves. Something more urgent is going on in the sky. Today I am not the only test pilot doing a job. The Air Force has its boys up running exacting tests on new jet fighters, checking out new engines, and running fatigue marathons on new military designs. NACA has its stable of test pilots investigating the flight behavior of other experimental research aircraft, exploring different and radical design features. The Skyrocket is not the only plane in the sky.

I've got 30 gallons of fuel left—three or four minutes of flight. I begin a long, slow glide to the south of the runway and hold a speed that will allow me to stay in the air as long as possible. At the altitude I have and with some judicious throttle manipulating I may be able to get four minutes out of her.

From the east below me I see the stricken plane racing toward the lake dragging a trail of black smoke. I switch from the company radio to the control-tower frequency. At once the wire is alive with the static flow of conversation between the chase pilot and the project plane.

"Ah . . . the smoke's getting thicker, Pete, some is coming from your right-hand wheel well . . . you still got altitude. Maybe you ought to leave her."

"Gear coming down." It's Pete Everest's voice. The project pilot ignores his chase pilot's suggestion to abandon the craft. He is going to try for a landing.

The chase pilot checks his gear and warns him, "No nose wheel."

"Gear coming *up*."

"You got it up, boy. She's clean. you going to take her in?"

"Yeah. On the belly."

The chase pilot calls the tower. "Tell the fire equipment they're going to have this plane on its belly in 60 seconds."

Below me the two planes streak by. The smoking one levels off over the lake bed and settles on, digging a long trail of dust and black smoke as she rips the ground, straight and then into a turn. The three fire trucks that have been waiting for me converge on the sick, smoking plane. A beautiful job by a seasoned pro. I hope I do as well someday.

Back into my own world. There's a landing yet and I've got one short spiral left in the fuel tank.

Yeager is committed also. His fuel is gone. "Chuck, coming out of this turn, I'll have to land."

"I've had it too. Let's check your gear and we'll set down. Take the left side, will you?"

In loose formation we touch down together, the graceful white research plane and her blunt-nosed guardian.

CHAPTER XIV

One of the most important phases of investigation in the Skyrocket was to establish her buffet boundaries—the boundary lines that were waiting to be drawn on the big charts in the aerodynamicists' office. There were two. One on this side of the speed of sound and one deep on the other side of the speed of sound, leaving a dark valley to be explored in between.

At 1 G, in level flight when an airplane is lifting its exact weight, my predecessor, Gene May, had established that she would buffet lightly at a Mach number of .9, the first point on the chart. The knowledge that the Skyrocket shook at .9 was the one piece of information that had escaped me when I was preparing for my first rocket run last fall. In that flight the brief tremble was unexpected and had given me a nasty moment. It hit so fast and disappeared so fast it was difficult to diagnose. My mind was at once filled with a hundred ominous reasons for the reaction. After the flight I discovered that it was her normal murmur at .9. At the speed of sound the Skyrocket doesn't buffet. Where the production airplane might fly to pieces at such speeds, the Skyrocket has no problem—this is what she was designed to do and she does it with little complaining. With the exception of a left-wing heaviness and an increase in drag, she slips through the sonic wall easily.

My job was to find the points in the sky where she would buffet as increased G was put upon her. The more G forced on her in the subsonic region, the sooner she would buffet; and as each point was found in the sky, it became an ink mark on the chart until the line began to curve up from Mach .9 at 1 G to Mach .6 at 4 G's—the region was mapped then for buffet on the subsonic side.

The theory is, and was tentatively substantiated in Gene's few flights into the supersonic regions, that the plane would buffet going through the transonic region at a given G and should continue to buffet as it accelerates until the aircraft has crossed through the transonic region into the supersonic area, fencing off a neat no-man's-land of buffet. It is the Skyrocket's mission to define absolutely where the border lines of this no-man's-land fall—outlining the "envelope" they call it.

Two or three points had been inked in by Gene's flights on either side of the big envelope. It was left for me to fill in the many points in between, to prove the theories that the aerodynamicists have based on wind-tunnel tests. So far in the last two months the wind-tunnel data had matched pretty closely what we had found in actual flight on the subsonic side.

Now I was due to take a look on the other side. The supersonic side. January, 1950, and the engineers had come up with a flight plan that would take me through Mach 1 at 1 G in level flight. This would mark the beginning of the curved buffet boundary and its margin that I would draw on the other side of the speed of sound—the narrow end of the buffet envelope. As more G's were applied, the wider the envelope would grow.

If such a flight had been suggested to me a year ago when I was checking out the AD's at a top speed of 400 miles per hour down at the El Segundo plant, it would have caused me considerable alarm. But after a half-year of study; detailed conversations with Gene May, who was one of the handful of men in the world to go through Mach 1; and personal knowledge of the ship herself I was, without doubt, merely curious. The Skyrocket had gone through Mach 1 on many occasions without incident and there was no reason to believe she wouldn't do it again as effortlessly. I knew what to expect in the Skyrocket; Gene May had already cleared the path and there were few thorns along the way.

The sound barrier, that had taken the life of English Test Pilot Geoffrey De Havilland four years ago when the DH-108 he was flying disintegrated at or near the speed of sound, has been pretty well designed away by the pioneer X-1 and the Skyrocket. They have been molded and shaped to cut easily through the wall of compressed air. Like the sharp bow of a boat sliding through water, cutting a bow wave that angles off on either side as she goes, the supersonic plane at Mach 1 pushes a huge shock wave that bends back in a similar pattern as the spear nose of the ship rips through the compressed air. The big shock wave causes a tremendous amount of drag on the ship and she needs a giant power to fight the load. All that remains of the sound barrier since Chuck knocked it down is this great increase in drag. Designed with the same principles as the X-1, the Skyrocket with the added advantage of swept-back wings has no problems to speak of at Mach 1. It is in the transonic areas where she protests so far. According to my pile of aerodynamic textbooks the explanation based on wind-tunnel tests with subsonic airfoils is simple enough:

Local velocities on an airfoil (a wing) traveling through the air at subsonic speeds (below three fourths of the speed of sound—500 miles per hour) are all less than the speed of sound and are relatively consistent. The boundary layer of air that cushions the wing is undisturbed and causes no loss in lift.

But in the transonic area (Mach .75 to 1) velocities over the same airfoil are both below and above the speed of sound. In order to pass over the object moving through it, the air reaches the speed of sound so that it can meet the slower air on the other other side once more.

The supersonic speed of the air traveling shock waves tear up the boundary layer of air that has been cushioning the airfoil, resulting in loss of lift—buffeting.

Once into the supersonic regions, the shock wave that developed on the airfoil at transonic speed has moved aft of the ship, like a wake, and the nose of the aircraft has caught up with its bow shock wave that had been building up ahead of it at transonic speed.

Armed with all this theory and the knowledge of the Skyrocket's innate ability, I approached the Mach 1 flight with nothing more than curiosity. The only fear I had was not getting through Mach 1, of lousing up the two weeks of work by the 30 men on the ground. It was just a matter of getting up there again, dragging the two tons of fuel to altitude, the long, tedious grind to 30,000 feet—another chance to make a mistake, to forget to turn on the data switch—another half-hour of intense concentration and responsibility. Once I got there the Skyrocket would take over and I would merely ride her out to the other side, then, at the end of the run, bend her into a turn for G's.

Yeager was up for the trip; the man who did it first would stand by for me. The captain, who handles an airplane as well as any man I have ever seen, had been flying chase for me off and on for the past two months since Everest had taken over the X-1.

We're up to 30,000 priming to go, the jet engine is behaving and the rocket pressures are holding. George Mabry, glued to the radio on the lake bed, starts his count and on ten: light one, light two, light three, light four. The ride begins again. I am amazed as I always am at the phenomenon of the speed, the thrust, and the solitary experience that I share with only a few pilots. The needle moves: .85, .9, she buffets and is out of it into .95 and now I am too occupied with the controls to see when the Machmeter needle creeps upon 1. Her left wing wants to go down hard just as advertised and I hold right aileron against it with all my strength to keep her straight and level for the run. The air-speed indicator and the altimeter jump as I hit the bow shock wave and that's it. I'm supersonic. There is no time to reflect upon the feat; there is the turn now. Before I can get into it, number-one tube stutters, gasps, and *pop*—it quits! In rapid succession two, three, and four follow—*pop, pop, pop*—and at Mach 1.02 she hits a brick wall. I lunge hard against the leather harness that saves me from going through the control panel as the Skyrocket shudders fiercely against the sudden drop in speed. I have not expected this tremendous deceleration and it takes me a couple of seconds to recover, to get my breath back, and to take control of the plane once more. She decelerates rapidly down to .85, buffeting back through .9, and the chance for the turn at supersonic speed is lost now. It is this sudden cessation of speed that restores my respect for the Mach number the Skyrocket has reached.

In the long turn back to the base on the jet engine Yeager catches up with me; the pilot who proved it could be done three years ago when the word *supersonic* made most pilots wince, calls, "Did you make it, son?"

"Yep."

And in the tone I have learned to expect he drawls low, "Terrifying, wasn't it?"

Going through Mach 1 became a regularity during the following months; the right-hand buffet boundary slowly grew on the charts very much in the manner the engineers had predicted it would curve. in order to get in the turn for buffet at the end of the high-speed run, I began to move into it before the rockets stopped firing, when the rocket-cylinder-second clock read 40. The Skyrocket was performing her duties well, bringing back the data, filling up the books, and so far I had met no emergency. The program moved along.

One day, after two years of being the sole occupant of the big Douglas hangar, the Skyrocket moved over for another plane, the A2D, a revolutionary new prototype of a carrier-based fighter scheduled for delivery to the Navy. The Skyrocket's new stable mate, an offshoot of the old AD's I knew so well, was the first plane to use a counter-rotating turbo-propeller. And the pilot sent up to see if she would fly was my old teacher of the coffee-pot sessions under the stairs of El Segundo, the oracle of flight—George Jansen.

George moved into The Shamrock with a carload of books and the same studious and careful approach to airplanes that he always had. His enthusiasm for the tricky little fighter was only exceeded by his store of academic aerodynamic knowledge. The A2D was just the plane for Jansen, a complicated piece of engineering, possibly the forerunner of a whole fleet of turbo-driven transports. George was a demon for detail and the plane was an assignment that would try his particular talents.

I hadn't seen George since I had taken over the Skyrocket program. It had been almost a year since he had patiently and lengthily explained engineering facts to me. I remember at that time his complete distrust of the Skyrocket. When he saw me again, he was standing in the middle of the big hangar beside his awkward-looking little A2D.

"Hey, Bridgeman, it's good to see you. How's everything going in the white bomb?"

I was glad to see the big, serious kid on the base. A fraternity brother. There was little *wild-blue-yonder* about George. He was married and had a baby son. Flying to him was a serious profession.

"We're moving right along with it, George, and she hasn't blown up yet."

"What Mach number are you up to?"

"Mach 1.1," I tossed it off. George hadn't gone supersonic. It was an exclusive club for the jockies of the X-1 and the Skyrocket. It seemed incongruous talking in terms of high Mach numbers with the young engineering pilot who so recently helped me through the fundamentals. I enjoyed it. There had been times when George was inclined to be effusive, although he never pushed it too far—you could kid him out of it. I remembered how he would readily admit that he couldn't answer some of the questions I eventually put to him during the period of my study of aerodynamics.

Now, in a cozy voice, he pulled up close. "Is it true what they say about her, Bill?"

"Ah, come off it, will you?"

He laughed and was serious again. "You slipped through it okay, huh. No trouble?"

"Like nothing," and then I took off: "Although she does demonstrate some asymmetric Mach effect on the way through . . ."

"Get him, will you . . ." George stepped back a foot. "Hey, really, down below I hear that you're doing a hell of a good job. No kidding." And to verify his point he waves his arm toward the Skyrocket at the end of the hangar. "Well, there's the airplane—and there's you. That's proof of something."

I looked at the ship. It was proof all right, proof that I had had luck and that the Skyrocket wasn't the harpy she was supposed to be. With respect and caution she could be kept in line. I hadn't thought about the ejection level in a long time.

George had been on the base two months now. Winter had eased into spring and the air smelled of sage and of the scattered patches of pale wild flowers. The emergency I had anticipated all these months still had not happened. It was Friday and the flight plan called for buffet turns at Mach 1.03. Chuck was flying chase for me.

Thirty-three thousand feet. Her ears are back, shooting through the sheer air at a Mach number of .85, approaching the buffet with the rockets lighting a flaming rainbow path aft. Yeager is lost somewhere 15 miles behind. The sound that comes through into the pod I sit in is a sustained, low rumble, the s-s-shosh of a giant blowtorch. The jet engine firing too, taken beyond the speed it can normally attain, emits a painful pitch-whistle cry. And again, although it is no longer discovery, it is a lonely, secret, three-dimensional world of these sounds. It is also a world of dials and pressures and purpose. Twenty-three seconds before I go into the turn.

Wrrr-eee-eee . . . Wrrr-eee-eee . . . the warning siren splits through the quiet of the cockpit as if the giant laugh of Pan suddenly filled the still sky, and out of the control panel a solitary red eye glares. There is a fire somewhere in the ship. The siren wail touches a set of nerve endings in my body and I am paralyzed.

"*Hey, skipper, there's a flock of fighters at 11 o'clock high.*"

I am numb. Out of a vacant sky six perfectly bore-sighted machine guns are pointing at me, their sole function to knock me out of the sky. I stare fixedly at the red light as if there was all the time in the world, as if I were totally removed from the reality of the danger if flashes. Calmly I look down the barrel of the gun. You never see the bullet that hits you. As long as I see the red light I'm alive. I leisurely consider the possibility that the red light will be the last image imprinted on my mind. The next second the ship may explode.

A long, luxurious dream-second and independently my mind begins to struggle out from under the weight of inertia. The inaction is over. Once more activity begins in my legs and arms and answers break out of a dam into my mind. There is no decision. The emergency and a combination of 20 different complications of the same situation have already been met two months ago in the safety of my room. There is no need to analyze the emergency; just follow the plan, start the turn back toward the base.

Pull the jet engine off slightly, check T5 temperature, manipulate the throttle. Oil temperature okay. I cut off the siren. The red light continues to glow. There is nothing more to be done. Just wait for the explosive propellants to be pumped out of the tanks. Until they are, I must sit with the loaded gun in my face. It would be so easy to disregard my decision and cut off the rockets, to panic. I begin the long turn back, keeping away from G by rolling over into it. Off to my left and far below, Muroc lies remote, an enormously long distance away. All of the people whose job it is to help me, the ambulance, the fire trucks, are five miles below. My preconceived judgment had better be right. I cannot allow myself to listen to last-minute decisions or arguments now. I must trust the plan I have already diagramed on the ground.

I have decided, before this minute, that to jettison the fuel would be an error. When there is fire in a ship, there is no way of knowing the extent of the damage; to jettison the volatile propellants from their tanks may bring the fluids into immediate contact with the fire. Also, such action would take longer to get rid of the stuff. It will take less time to let the fuel burn off at the rate of a ton a minute through the rocket tubes.

Before the flight I have given George Mabry printed emergency plans and their alternate procedures. When I have completed the steps here, I will call down and George will read the steps to make sure I have not omitted one.

Somewhere a fire is eating and licking its way toward the tanks, but the Skyrocket gives no other indication of the danger than that of the round red light shining urgently among the rows of dials. Twenty-three seconds and the run will be finished, the tank will be emptied.

The altitude is in my favor; I have a better chance of leaving the ship if it becomes necessary. I will try to determine how bad the situation is before dropping down. When the rockets stop firing, Chuck will be able to pick me up. He can take a look at her.

Plan Baker—continue the speed run, head for the field—and wait and see if you blow up. Plan Baker—old Miller stuff, every detail carefully thought out ahead of time. Never be surprised—you presented your plan and its alternates to the Old Man before a strike—if he could poke holes in the plan, you didn't make the trip: "Come back when you get it figured."

It seems an inordinately long time before the rockets pop off. They've stopped firing and she throws me forward in the harness. I throttle back on the jet engine; the light continues to stare, the manipulation has no effect on the fire, wherever it lies. There is still a little residual fuel left sloshing in the tanks, but according to the plan I won't jettison it either. It is time now to let them know on the ground. Before I press the mike button to call the ground crew I count to ten out loud to assure myself I still have a voice.

"Metro One, I have a fire warning. I am heading back to the lake."

At once the control tower, monitoring the frequency, issues orders. "All aircraft in the local flying area—there is an emergency in progress. Remain clear of the Muroc Dry Lake." The formal, deliberate voice of the dispatcher is reassuring now that I have committed myself to the plan. Order is being established where things are badly out of order. And then to Al Carder out on the lake bed listening to the emergency, the dispatcher calls, "Metro One, you have fire trucks and ambulance standing by, have you not?"

Carder's voice—thin—joins in: "Yes, we have them standing by on the lake bed."

Chuck's voice now. "If you stay in that left turn a couple of more seconds I'll be able to close in on you."

"Right, Chuck, let me know how it looks as soon as you can."

At any minute the ship may blow up and the thing that keeps me from abandoning it while I still have a chance is ego. If I pulled the ejection lever and the plane remained in flight for another ten minutes before it exploded—ten minutes would be plenty of time for me to have set her back on the ground—I would be a fool. Four million dollars' worth of airplane lost because I did not wait to determine the damage.

Fifteen seconds and I see Chuck, a speck on the horizon. He calls, "I'm almost on you now; are you going to jettison?"

"No."

"No?"

I repeat, "No . . ."

The radio is silent. I wait for Chuck to inspect the plane. ". . . From what I can see it looks like you've lost part of your tailpipe fairing."

I am not encouraged. I begin to spiral down and in the turn I cross over a stream of black smoke. "Is that black smoke me, Chuck?"

"It ain't me, son."

Perhaps I can get her back on the ground before the fire reaches the tanks. There is a slim chance, the only one I have. It is an easier choice than pulling the ejection lever.

Chuck calls into me, "Manipulate your throttle, Bill, and let's see what it does." He is calm. Al Carder on the ground listening, is no doubt straining to keep from asking what is happening. He leaves us alone. "That's it, Bill. Ease her back again . . . when you pull back it tends to diminish the smoke. Maybe you had better cut the jet engine."

The suggestion causes Carder to break his silence. "Are you sure he can make the field from where he is, Chuck?"

Yeager answers. "He can fall over the side and make it from here . . ."

I shut off the jet engine and it is quiet in the cockpit, the Skyrocket will glide in on the thin, swept-back wings. The fire is in the jet engine. I reach down and trip the CO bottles in the jet engine—the fire extinguisher.

"What's that, the jettison?" Chuck asks.

"No, the CO." The red light on the panel goes out. The fire is temporarily controlled—according to the ingenious buttons.

I call down the news to Carder who wants to know, "Are you going to restart the jet?"

"No."

"How about that?" Yeager moans in disbelief at Carder's request.

The control tower offers the wind directions. Now Mabry calls, "What's your approximate position?"

"We're ten miles south of the lake bed. We'll be down in a couple of minutes." Chuck does the talking.

"Bill, while you're bringing her home, would you mind picking up that side-slip we've scheduled on number-two card?" Mabry calmly asks.

Well, I'll be Goddammed! I ignore the request.

"We might start our turn in from here, Bill, the wind is probably stronger up here than on the ground."

"Captain, you are lousing up my approach."

"Okay, hot-shot. Suit yourself."

I move the spear nose of the soundless Skyrocket around into an S turn, pop the dive brakes, and level off over the lake bed that lies waiting beneath me now. hold on, just a second more . . .

"You got it made," Yeager reassures me. "You've got eight feet, four feet, two feet . . . That's a boy." He makes a noise like wheels hitting the dirt. "Scurpt, scurpt—you're on. Nice job!"

She touches the runway and we're home. Across the lake the fire trucks and ambulances head toward me, churning the dust behind. I point toward them.

There is just enough time to speak to Yeager before I leave the plane. "Thank you, Chuck."

"My pleasure. Any time at all." And he is gone, back to the Air Force runway and the base.

Thirty miles an hour and I open the canopy; the fire trucks skid to a stop and wheel around as I skim by them. A Keystone Comedy of cops and robbers. She stops and I leap over the side on to the ground, breaking the lines that connect me into the ship. Carder's car appears out of the dust along with the rest of the ground crew. The Skyrocket is the center of attention and excited bits of the engineers' conversation float over to me, "Now that we've got the rocket firing, the Goddam jet's got to foul up." They look anxiously up her tailpipe, into her hatches, looking for the mistake, the miscalculation, the unforeseen combination of events that has almost destroyed their charge.

My legs feel alive with nerves; I laugh louder than normally at the dull jokes the maintenance crew self-consciously offer me. In a couple of minutes Al Carder, pale, comes over to the truck I lean against. He hesitates as if he were searching for something to say and then with a shake of his head, "I'm glad to see you like to fly around without any engines. It makes a wreck out of me."

Muroc Air Force Base is no longer called after an early California settler. In honor of the Air Force test pilot Captain Glen Edwards who died in a crash of Northrop's huge experimental Flying Wing a few years ago, the dusty, rundown base has been renamed Edwards Air Force Base, after a new kind of pioneer.

Yeager turned over the last phase testing on the X-1 to "Pete" Everest and went on to try Consolidated's delta-wing prototype, the XF-92. He continued to fly chase for me, alternating with Everest. So far, George and I were the only two Douglas pilots on the base.

My flights in the Skyrocket averaged no more than once a week for a period of 30 minutes; there was more time for leisure now that I was beginning to know the ship so well. I could get away from this temporary, unpainted, tar paper-and-wood base with its few permanent buildings. The base had not kept up with the function it performs. The Air Force and Navy aircraft of tomorrow streak through its skies and the world's fastest planes are being developed in its hangars; supersonic flight for military aircraft is pushing into reality in a dilapidated remnant of the last war. According to the Air Force pilots who are obliged to remain on the base day in and day out, no money was allotted for the construction of permanent buildings and the flight-testing program was badly handicapped.

After a flight I could get away from the dry desolation of Edwards—a freedom not shared by the military test pilots—and when I had to be on the base, I could complain to George. We were together a good deal, at the officers' bar or down at the hangar.

George's favorite topic was intricately describing how his A2D was performing—a proud father with a pocketful of pictures and behavior characteristics—and mine was bitching about the desert.

But as the months went by and the flights went by, I managed to spend less and less time on the base. The trips down south were not altogether an escape, I spent some of the time practicing for flights that were coming up in the research ship.

Things had changed at El Segundo. Brownie had three new young pilots working for him, and although the pace was not as frantic as when Brownie and I used to clear the field, the boys were up and down most of the day. Compared to my 30 minutes a week, they spent a lot of time in the air. When Brownie introduced me to the new production pilots it seemed a very long time ago that I was one of them, and I remembered how I felt when I first encountered George Jansen and Russ Thaw.

The flights out of El Segundo helped to keep me in flying shape: the brief, highly controlled flights in the Skyrocket had a tendency to make me rusty. In one of Brownie's little AD's I could spend an hour or so wringing myself out, exercising unused flying muscles in acrobatics, loops, split S's—maneuvers there was neither time nor fuel for in the Skyrocket.

The other sort of wringing out I did was physical; it is easier to maintain a relaxed approach toward the Skyrocket with a well-used body. I was swimming longer and harder and the walks through the hills were more frequent.

Summer was coming and the weather was warm at the beach shack; the chill was leaving the water. As the world in Hermosa became more lush and inviting, Edwards Air Force Base became more distasteful. The heat that hadn't seemed so bad the first few months on the base was now oppressive and debilitating. A year at Muroc, a year of gearing up, had become a secondary reflex; and although I was almost completely confident in the ship, the reflexes she had developed in me remained. Always there was the acute awareness of the flight ahead.

The Skyrocket and I were up to our fifteenth flight together and the big thing we seemed to have discovered for the slip-stick artists is that although the rate of drag increases drastically at supersonic speed, it reaches its peak there and tends to drop slightly, remaining even, so far as I had gone into the new area. The engineers were encouraged and felt that the Skyrocket was capable of attaining higher Mach numbers. Until the line, past Mach 1, began forming on the drag charts, at an even rate, the aerodynamicists had supposed that the drag rise would increase to a prohibitive angle, precluding any possibilities in the Skyrocket of hitting speeds greater than Mach 1.05. I had heard some veiled talk around the hangar about launching the Skyrocket from a B-29 the way the X-1 was dropped into flight at 35,000 feet. However, the flights for supersonic information continued as before.

Flight Plan Number 75 hung on its nail in the aerodynamicists' office. Item Number 2 read: *8000 feet. Pull to the stall at 300, 280, 260, and 200 mph.* The engineers were asking for high Reynolds Number investigations entailing turns at high lift coefficients—their request would bring the plane close to the stall at an altitude of 8000 feet—5800 feet over the terrain.

I turned to Orv Paulsen at his desk behind me, "It's too low, Orv."

The aerodynamicist got up from his chair, walked in front of his desk, and leaned against the edge. "Just get in and nibble at the buffet, Bill, that's all." He tried to convince me.

"Orv, I think you had better get it up to 12,000." At 12,000 I'd have a chance to recover if she kicked up her heels. Orv was disturbed.

"We can't do that, Bill; it'll ruin our Reynolds Number. It'll change the whole scale of the investigation . . ."

"So it changes the scales!"

Orv said no more but headed into Carder's office. The conversation came through the door and as I turned to leave I was surprised to hear Carder's emphatic voice, "If Bridgeman says it's too low, it's too low."

The next morning I approached the altered flight plan with great assurance. Yesterday was the first time Carder had unequivocally displayed confidence since I had taken over as pilot for his project.

It was all low-speed stability work, no rockets this time, just the jet engine and the jatos.

The stinging cold desert dawn is beginning to warm with the early summer months and the days start earlier. At 4:30 A.M. the flight day begins. Chuck meets me in the air on take-off, glues himself to my wing, "Morning, Commander. What've you got today?"

Item Number 1 on my knee pad calls for 20,000 feet: low-speed runs, three to four minutes each. The first run is at 200 miles per hour. She is nose up, dressed at a high angle of attack, and she's hard to manipulate. The controls are mushy. Three minutes. Back again on the same path, slower this time, 180 miles per hour for another three minutes. I continue the series of runs, decreasing the speed until she buffets. Until this flight the complete stall has been left unprobed. Today Carder wants a thorough investigation. In previous flights I have been allowed to bring the Skyrocket up to the edge of the stall, backing off at the last second. Today I will go all the way into it.

I remember Gene May's repeated advice, "Treat her with respect; if you don't, she won't forgive you." It has been established that the Skyrocket will not withstand a "spin"; according to the aerodynamicists she will not recover from such treatment. Another instance where she must be handled respectfully. Today we are going to push her a shade more than we ever have before.

One hundred forty miles per hour, on the edge. Nose up, flaps down, gear down . . . data switch on. I ease a fraction of an inch back on the stick to 139, 138 . . . she protests, rolling laterally, and she shudders along the road I hold her on. She doesn't like it . . . a little more . . . a little more . . . easy . . . she becomes wilder . . . I walk the rudder to the stall. That's it   She stalls.

We drop flat through the sky, at 2000 feet a minute. She rolls and pitches violently all the way.

"Got a mind of her own, hasn't she?" Yeager's voice floats calmly into my helmet. "You exciting any of that stuff . . . you trying to damp that out?"

"I'm attempting to, Captain." She'll take it. A half an inch more and I'll really have it. They can't ask for any better than that, this should impress Carder. I press back on the control column—and immediately I know the movement is too sudden. The stick hits against its socket.

Holy God . . . here we go! A wild lunge and she pitches up, rolls to the right, then points her nose toward the ground. She is in a spin. I swallow a gulp of air—a fist in my stomach—and hang on as she cuts loose from me. She's on her way down, corkscrewing crazily through the sky with a whip-lash motion, building up speed terrifically and the earth revolves rythmically below me. This time I've pushed her too far; she didn't take it. A spin! According to Carder, the book, the men who built her, a spin will destroy her. According to their careful estimation she won't recover. With both hands I grab the gear and the flap handles and clean her up. It's all automatic movement now, all feel, no theory. Apply full opposite rudder, neutralize the stick. There is no pressure on the rudder, no response, it is as if the ship had no rudder. The solitary thought I have is: will the corrective action take effect fast enough, is the rate of "rudder-pressure" return greater than the speed at which the ground is coming up? Come on, answer me, will you! A little pressure against my foot now, a little more, she's coming around. I can feel the pressure building on the rudder. The rolling and twisting stops and the Skyrocket straightens out into a steep dive. Once more I've got an airplane under me. She recovered. They were wrong, only this time the error in prognostics was in my favor. She has lost 7000 feet in ten seconds as I start the long pull out and my breath returns heavily.

"Oops!" It's Yeager's voice and on my left wing there he is—a big orange helmet with a big kid's grin. He had been right with me all the way to the bottom. When the Skyrocket is straight and level, as if the last two or three minutes hadn't happened, Yeager asks, nonchalantly, for the benefit of the engineers on the ground listening attentively to the radio, "How are the stalls progressing?"

"They're finished. I'm going in. Fuel to 40 gallons."

In a reflective tone the chase pilot sagely replies, "I would say they were finished . . ."

There was no more talk. Chuck escorted me home and disappeared off toward the base. Summoning great composure, I climbed out of the Skyrocket. It would be difficult for them to tell that there had been any trouble, that is if no one saw the ladder shake against the side of the plane when I first put my leg on the step as it always did after a rough flight. Carder didn't seem to notice it, but he was right there to meet me.

"What happened?" he demanded immediately.

"Nothing." There was no point in telling Carder about the spin— it might put him in bed. I got away with it all right. She was back; she came out of it okay. She forgave me.

"Are you sure?" Carder looked at me curiously, "Yeager sounded kind of funny. What was that 'Oops' all about?"

"You know Chuck and his repartee . . ."

On the way back to the postflight conference George Mabry also asked tentative, indirect questions. My answers left him puzzled. If the "slip" didn't show up on the film they would never know what I had put their ship through. There was little talk on the ten-minute ride to the hangar.

After the postflight session I stationed myself in the developing room to be around when they read the news.

Orv Paulsen had his head under the black hood reading the day's trip. Al Carder was looking over the oscillograph sheets when Paulsen at last called him, "Hey, Al, you want to take a look?" He glanced briefly at me and returned to the film with Carder. From under the blanket I heard mumbled exclamations and then, "Hey, Bridgeman, this might interest you. You want to look?" It was still possible that they hadn't found the spin; there was still a chance I could divert their attention perhaps.

Under the hood the film ran before us—there on the panel the artificial horizon was spinning like a top. I attempted to divert their attention to the stick position but Orv pointed out the telltale dial. In disbelief he slowly let it fall. "Look at that artificial horizon . . ."

"I'm looking at it," Carder said painfully.

I was still trying. "Some of these stalls get rather violent, don't they?"

Carder pulled back the hood and straightened up. "Yes, they do." He looked directly at me. "How far did you spin?"

"I wouldn't call it exactly a spin, Al."

"Whatever you were exactly doing, when did the airplane

become controllable again?"

I gave up. "Fourteen thousand feet."

For a second or two Carder didn't speak. He looked calmly at me, and then finally, "You're a pretty cute pair." He left the room without any further word.

Carder didn't let the matter drop altogether. There was a perfunctory investigation the next day, and among other lines of inquiry Chuck Yeager was called in to recount his version of the near-catastrophe.

We were gathered in Carder's office when Yeager showed up to answer the engineers' questions. It was the first time that I had ever seen him on the ground. Although he had been flying by my side for the last six months, all that existed of Yeager to me was an orange helmet and a Southern accent. When we shook hands it was like meeting someone I had been corresponding with on very important matters for a long period of time. Yeager was a stocky, medium-tall man, around thirty, with close-cropped, black curly hair. His hands were big and his face was broad and there was an amused look in his eyes.

With easy assurance he pulled up a chair, crossed the big hands over his chest, and smiled benignly at the serious assembly of engineers and aerodynamicists. It was apparent to me at once that Yeager was a pilot's pilot. He was on my side, but for no other reason than the fact that I was a pilot in an awkward spot facing a line of engineers. He didn't help them a bit and the matter was at last dismissed with the verdict that I was to go up and see "the man." Hoskinson, at the Santa Monica plant next time I was in town.

CHAPTER XV

In June the Korean war broke out. The effect on the base was immediate. Security tightened up at once, radio frequencies were changed, familiar faces one by one disappeared from the bar, brass floated in and out in greater number and stature; mysteriously projects arrived on the base under wraps and were swallowed up by the hangars. It was now impossible to know what was going on in the next building; each company's project had a barbed-wire fence around it; and the only restricted project at the Flight Test Center that i was aware of was the Skyrocket and her investigations.

The request for more and more high-speed data reached a new urgency. The demand for faster and faster airplanes was no longer a security measure, it was a necessity. North American's F-86 took to battle and was proving herself well against the Communists' MIG's. But there was still more speed to be had, and so far there was no supersonic plane flying operationally. The designers needed more information; there were still too many bugs to make supersonic flight practical.

Six years of standing still structurally, and overnight the base was pounding with activity. A new 10,000,000-dollar-rocket-engine test facility was under way 17 miles east of the main base. At the far end of the lake a 1,000,000-dollar experimental parachute test laboratory was going up.

The demand for higher performing aircraft presented new problems of escape at high speed. The Communist MIG's weren't the only danger facing the young jet pilots; many lost their lives trying to abandon their stricken crafts. The Air Research and Development Command was searching for the answers to this big problem of speed. They moved in a human-deceleration project from the Aero Medical Laboratory at Wright-Patterson Field, Dayton, Ohio; testing seats, belts, and harnesses with volunteers. The "Agony Gulch" project, as it was known, simulated G forces received in aircraft crashes by use of a rocket-propelled car mounted on a track. The same track was to be used to test seat-ejection equipment at supersonic speeds with the aid of a specially designed car.

Amid all the rumbling of activity on the base, the ambitious talk around the Douglas hangar grew more persistent. More frequently I overheard conversations about the higher Mach numbers that could be reached if the Skyrocket were able to carry more fuel. It was the "drag-rise" curve that had the engineers and aerodynamicists enthused. Instead of getting into more trouble past Mach 1, as they had expected, the feared drag rise appeared to hit a peak and tended to level off—the Skyrocket had remained controllable into the supersonic region. That is, so far she was controllable and so far the drag rises had leveled off. Nobody on the face of the earth could be sure what would happen past Mach 1.4. But the Douglas aerodynamicists were inspired to find out. According to their newly acquired set of facts and figures and charts the whole picture had changed. The Skyrocket's current flights into the supersonic area proved they had been wrong in their original "prohibitive drag-rise" calculations for speeds past Mach 1. Now they felt confident that the Skyrocket ought to be able to hit Mach 2.

It seemed to me that it was quite possible that they could be wrong again—but they were all set to send somebody in deeper to find out, to prove or disprove their new theory.

Around the first of December it was officially decided. The Skyrocket was to be air-launched in order to try for the higher Mach numbers, following the routine pioneered by Bell in the X-1. The idea, the big departure from the original program, would require a contract extension and the Navy would have to be convinced of its practicality. Carder, Gene May, and Chuck Pettingall, chief flight test aerodynamicist from Douglas' Testing Division, took off for Washington armed with the following argument: The Navy didn't need to construct a new, fantastically expensive research ship to reach Mach 2; with modification the Skyrocket could do it. All that was required to attain the higher Mach number was a hollowed-out B-29 and two modified Skyrockets—one an all-rocket version.

Gene May, the senior pilot on the project, now assigned to the Santa Monica flight-test office, was the logical choice for the contract extension. As for me, I was having quite enough adventure as it was with the rocket take-offs and the supersonic flights. I did not yearn to be in Gene's shoes. The plan, from what I could pick up around the flight office, loosely followed the Air Force's X-1 methods. Gene would be carried to 40,000 feet, then dropped out into the blue with nothing but a rocket engine that fires for three minutes—from there on in, after the rockets quit, he'd come home dead-stick, quiet as a bird.

George Mabry held things down for Carder the week the trio spent in Washington. The base was thick with Army and Navy brass checking into the many programs that were under way. Over at the Fir Force hangar every military test pilot on the field was taking his turn at wringing out the new all-weather jet fighter, the Lockheed F-94, in round-the-clock shifts. Accelerated service testing they called it, six months of war-type flying jammed into one month to find out what failures to expect in the field. Some of the pilots I had talked to in the bar had flown as many as six hours a day. The attitude of the men has changed; now there was new purpose. The easygoing air of last year was gone and the waiting climate disappeared; suddenly the men had a job. There was a war.

Part of the Navy brass on the base had come to take a look at George's A2D in the Douglas hangar. Jensen considered their visit a little premature; there was still a good half a year of tests to be completed before the tricky little carrier-type attack plane would be ready for service.

Commander Hugh Wood was one of the three pilots assigned to make check flights in Jansen's A2D. George had thoroughly briefed him on the ship during the few days that he had been on the base. At night George would sit up composing written tests to give the young Navy flyer the following day. As is the case with test pilots, George was worried that he hadn't explained everything well enough to the man who was to fly his ship for the first time.

The afternoon George had to turn over his ship to the commander for a trial run, I was in the hangar talking to McNemar. It was two weeks before Christmas and the wind was coming in sharp from the snow-laden mountainsides onto the desert floor below. Two radio cars lay out on the parking strip with the doors open. As I walked out of the hangar I could hear the pilot calling down to George who sat in the front seat of the car nearest me, holding a mike. George was tense and all business. He nodded silently to me, attentively waiting for responses from the man who was flying his plane. The A2D project coordinator sat beside him listening, watching the metallic sky. Then loud, out of both radio cars, came the voice from the plane that was sucked up out of sight by the sky.

"I'm at the south edge of the lake, starting a shallow dive at 20,000 toward the north edge . . ." The men in the car bent into the speaker. The radio was quiet once more.

Again from the open car doors the remote voice sounded over the strip, "I'm having trouble with the turbine engine. It seems to have only partial power."

A quiet call of emergency. George sat up straight, his mouth moved a little as he stared at the radio box. Out of it came the voice once more, "I'm going to make a turn into the lake for an emergency landing . . ." The box was still. The voice didn't call again.

I moved aside as George sprang out of the car. He searched deep into the sky for the plane. We picked it up against the sun. Far to the south, the speck in the sky came at us, plunging toward the lake at an unnaturally rapid rate of descent. The life, the energy that was about to be stopped, was held for another minute in the eyes of the men that followed it in a steeper and steeper line down the wild dive path. In a brief second we watched the A2D roar nearer to the lake and then stop. From the place it ended a billowing pillar of black smoke bloomed gently against the sky.

"Emergency on the lake . . . emergency on the lake . . . emergency on the lake . . ." was repeated like a buzzer, evenly over the radio. The announcement was joined by the clang and scream of the fire wagons and ambulance. Lonely sounds of disaster. We followed the noise and the dust to the black smoke on the far edge of the vacant lake and I thought about what the young commander experienced as he rode those long 60 seconds out, watching helplessly as the bottom came up. It was impossible to get nearer than 100 feet of the wreckage, the heat of the fire held us back. George didn't speak. He stared into the flames boiling out under the black cover of smoke and watched the white-suited men in helmets and big gloves move in and out of the red foam, pulling hoses that spit feebly into the flames.

Without turning his head from the fire, George groaned angrily, "Oh God, why couldn't I have been in it?" He repeated the question over and over, as if he were beating himself with it. From out of the pyre the white figures emerged carrying the black, charred thing that had been the voice I had heard ten minutes ago.

"Why couldn't I have been in it, why couldn't I have been in it? Maybe there was something I didn't tell him, maybe that was it . . ." There was no answer; there was nothing I could say to help George. All of his careful, pains-taking instruction on the plane he knew so well couldn't have saved the man who took it up less than an hour ago. Maybe if the Navy pilot had known the A2D as well as George knew it he would have jumped, but in first flight it is impossible to know the moment of surrender.

Nevertheless, George was eaten by the idea that perhaps he

could have prevented the disaster if he had explained the airplane's warning signs more thoroughly. There was not a test pilot in the business who was more conscientious or articulate than George, but it happened in his ship anyway. In first flight you need something more than instruction, and knowledge of the airplane—you need luck.

One of the engineers complained, "Well, there goes six months shot to hell!"

The group of men began to speculate on the cause of the failure. After the long period of saying nothing, each had something to say. Something to justify what they had witnessed.

"The turbine trouble he was having probably caused the props to disturb the air stream enough to make the elevators ineffective." If what the engineer said was true, there was nothing the pilot could have done to recover from the dive. There was a moment for surrender— but chances are the pilot did not recognize that moment.

By the following week, when Al Carder returned to Muroc, the crash of the A2D had become merely another incident on a field where tragedies are common. That is to everyone but George Jansen. It was difficult for him to put the crash out of his mind, to justify it; and left abruptly without a project, he had nothing else to think about. All new designs were assigned or weren't out of the shop yet. It would be almost a year before the company could put together another A2D, but the project and its engineers and pilot would remain at Muroc acting in an advisory capacity until the new ship could be delivered. George's period of waiting began, and he was restless and more sarcastic than usual with the time on his hands.

Once more the Skyrocket was alone in the hangar and her program was more ambitious than ever.

From Al Carder's cheerful countenance on the morning of his return from Washington it was apparent to all in the Douglas Hangar that the Navy had approved the request to take the Skyrocket deeper into the supersonic region. A B-29 was on its way to be converted into a mother ship, two modified Skyrockets were already on order at the El Segundo plant—an all-rocket version and a jet combination. The all-rocket Skyrocket would carry double the previous load of propellant; and the Skyrocket's guardians felt pretty sure that this fact, coupled with the advantage of extreme altitude, would have their ship passing the X-1 soon to be the fastest airplane in the world. The jet-rocket combination would be the same airplane that I was flying now, but by means of the free ride to altitude in the superfortress' bomb bay, she would have a full tankful of rocket fuel when she got there and so would have a much greater period of testing. Well, that would be a big break for the program. There was nothing about a launch in my contract and it looked as if my end of the project would soon be over. A year of the Skyrocket—it had been quite enough adventure.

I was sitting on a desk in the pilots' stuffy stall, going over the week's flight schedule, when Al Carder walked through on his way into the hangar.

"Welcome back, Al. I hear you did all right back in Washington."

"Hello, Bill," and then, as if I had recalled something to his mind, he stopped. "Yeah, it turned out very well; they were very cooperative . . . . Bill, I don't know whether you've heard or not but Gene May isn't going to take the launch program."

That was all. He waited a minute for a reaction and then continued his way into the hangar. I mumbled something like, "Is that so?" but I knew what Carder meant. The group had their eyes on me. Off-handedly I as being informed of a decision I hadn't been consulted about. With Carder's brief words suddenly, with no warning, another man's dilemma and challenge became mine. After months of secret talk, talk I was diligently excluded from the red-hot coal was tossed to me. For months the big flights had been discussed; I had heard snatches of conversations and then silence as I approached a huddle. And now with no build-up, no chance to think about it, the whole package was handed to me. It would be the Santa Monica office that issued the formal invitation but Carder's news was the first hint.

I wasn't prepared to think about it; I had my hands full at the moment and I was more irritated than alarmed by the abrupt news. Another decision. I wouldn't pull it out and take a good look at it until I drove home from the lake that week end. The long, uninterrupted drive through the orderly desert would be the time to decide.

Along the road the Joshua trees, angular-trunked with branch-arms held up like the warnings of scarecrows in a field, stretched in irregular lines back into the sand. The irritation I had first felt when Carder singled me out to fly the new program was gone. In its place slowly came a feeling of pride that I should be entrusted with the assignment.

Still this was something unknown. They were trying for speeds and heights nobody had ever attempted. Here there would be no one to tell you what to expect. I would be alone. And I thought of excuses to turn it down.

During the war I had picked up a book in Honolulu by a French pilot, Antoine de Saint-Exupéry, and I remembered the words: "There is no liberty except the liberty of someone making his way towards something." No matter what arguments I set up against the advisability of this new program, I knew I would accept it. This was the kind of freedom the French flyer talked about that subconsciously I had sought all along, and here before me was a big chunk of it. All I had to do was take it. Here was the choice: going toward something, freedom—or security and stagnation. One or the other, the two were incompatible; there was no compromise. If I turned down this "freedom" I knew that later the knowledge that I had would never leave me alone.

It was a couple of months away. There would be time enough then to worry about the big flight. It would be approached in stages. Easy. The first one would be a rocket-jet combination that would just poke around the edges. Yeager had been doing the same kind of stuff and getting away with it—the Skyrocket should behave as well as the X-1. She didn't have quite the lift with her swept-back wings, but that was to be seen. There was a big cushion of time between me and the launch. Also, there was the comfortable reward of money. At best, if I delayed facing the moment until the morning of flight, the discomfort could only be an hour or so. What a little piece of time to suffer fear; it moves fast and is behind you.

I would put off facing whatever it was until the day came. It was a long time off. Two months, maybe.

Now it was necessary to ask for the job; although it had already been agreed among the engineers and my superiors that I would be the pilot, it was arranged so that I must approach them. They would not ask me to take the project. I had to ask them.

Monday morning after the usual long, lazy week end, a barbeque and the beach crew and a brown, laughing girl, I appeared at the flight office in the Santa Monica plant to receive the official bid from Johnny Martin. Russ Thaw and Larry Peyton were filling me in on the local picture. Russ was about to go into some advice about pullouts when Martin walked through the pilots' office on his way out into the plant. I excused myself from the discussion and approached the chief test pilot.

"Johnny, I understand Gene isn't interested in the launch program." Martin stopped beside the filing cabinets.

"Yeah, that's what I hear." And then as if he were offering me the last cold potato in the dish he lifted his eyebrows and asked, "You want to do it?"

"Yes. I want to do it." Now I had closed the door. The bargain was sealed.

CHAPTER XVI

The Skyrocket program hit a lull while we waited for the converted B-29 and the modified versions of the rocket ship to arrive. The original task had been accomplished; the transonic areas of flight had been probed well. Now we waited for the necessary alterations that would allow the Skyrocket to push deeper into the unexplored dark land that lay ahead. The area that she would fly into would require extreme altitudes where the air is thinner and less resisting, somewhere near 70,000 feet. Such extreme altitudes require special equipment. In order for a pilot to endure the low pressures at such altitudes, altitudes that the X-1 had already attained, the Air Forces Aero Medical Laboratories of the Wright Air Development Center at

Wright-Patterson Field had devised an elaborate protective pressure suit. Chuck Yeager had worn the first one and as other Air Force test pilots took over test phases of the X-1, they were also custom-fitted with the suit. So far the only airplane that required the use of a pressure suit was the X-1. Again she would have to move over for the Skyrocket.

Carder sent word to Wright informing the Air Force that the company would be needing a couple of pressure suits. George Jansen was also to be included in the fittings at Dayton; his new A2D under construction to replace the original was expected to do some altitude work.

George and I waited around the hangar for word from Dayton that the Air Force could accommodate us at the Air Development Center for the indoctrination period—from what we had heard, a two-to-three-week period learning to live in the pressure suit.

George, waiting around the hangar to be on hand if the A2D project crew wanted to consult him about the new model that was being put together, was like an actor between pictures; and with no plane of his own, he became more and more curious about the workings of my project. He became as engrossed in the data as one of the Skyrocket's engineers and it was not uncommon for him to join in the informal conferences.

It wasn't long after I had taken on the launch program that George came up with an idea. "What do you think about me flying the B-29, Bill? I'd like to handle that end of the program if it's all right with you."

"George, that 29 has got to arrive at the right altitude, at the right time, at the right speed and heading to allow the Rocket to make a run and return to the base with enough margin to allow for a malfunction or maybe an unlucky turn here and there and . . ."

"'It's even more complicated than that, old boy. You want to talk?" George was enthusiastic again; once more he had an airplane to figure.

George was assigned as pilot of the B-29 but before we could get very deep into the planning of the launches, our appointment with the pressure-suit boys came through from Wright Field. We flew back to Ohio and the Midwestern heat in a DC-6.

Wright Air Development Center is nothing like Edwards. It looks like it has been there a long time; green lawns, paved streets, and large substantial red brick buildings like a well-kept campus. A clean, ten-mile city of laboratories—Armament Laboratory, Power Plant Laboratory, Propeller Laboratory, Materials Lab, Photographic Lab, Air4craft Radiation Lab, and many others, 13 in all. The Aero Medical Laboratory was where George and I were to be checked out in the suits.

Upstairs in the two-story building we met the man in charge, Colonel Walter A. Carlson. I remembered him from his frequent visits to Edwards checking over the acceleration sled operation. Like most of the personnel connected with the laboratory the colonel was a doctor.

"When do you need these suits?" he asked.

Al Carder's parting words were to get the operation over with as soon as possible and get the suits on their way. "We'll need them in two weeks, Colonel."

The colonel replied with the usual military answer to a request for equipment, "Two weeks? It's too soon." He explained the time involved. "We just can't fit you and turn you loose. You've got to be indoctrinated into this equipment. It will take at least two weeks before you can handle the suit. You'll have to learn to breathe in reverse before we can put you into the tank." He pressed a button on his desk and a Captain Mahoney appeared, another doctor, the man in charge of the "suit" department. The colonel didn't try to convince us further; he would let the captain show us what we were up against.

Mahoney took us down the elevator into the basement. The elevator door opened on to a line of Martian troops, a row of dummies rigged up in weird and grotesque uniforms that man had devised to adapt himself to the sky and to space. Down the hall were the three pressurized tanks, round steel balls with reinforced double portholes in a line along the sides. Oblong doors at either end were closed and sealed like submarine hatches. Inside the spheres, rows of light bulbs down the middle lit the sparse array of masks, telephones, a few chairs, and an instrument console. A mike hung from the ceiling.

The little room had the spare aura of an execution chamber.

Mahoney steered us around the confining basement with its crowd of air-manipulating wheels and pipes, desks and charts. The captain appeared none too proud of his cramped quarters but was noticeably proud of what his laboratory had accomplished.

"To give you a clearer idea of what function the suit provides, we'll run some films for you." He led us into a small projection room and the feature film began. For two hours George and I watched films of men in the tightly laced suits and diver-like helmets going through tests in the tanks.

The pressure is dropped to simulate conditions at 70,000 feet. For a second the man in the film passes out and then jerks convulsively as the suit takes over and automatically fills up around his body. Slowly his eyes return to normal and he is asked to count to ten and to go through the motions of flying a plane. There was a "Mickey Mouse," a color cartoon of the human body showing in clear and simple terms the physiological processes which the body goes through as higher and higher altitudes are reached, and what devices are needed in order to withstand the imposed conditions.

Up to 15,000 feet the pilot adjusts to his surroundings without any aid. Above this altitude he needs an oxygen mask in order to operate his craft efficiently. He could manage without a mask but he would soon become overly fatigued. At 30,000 feet, if the pilot is in good shape, it is possible he can operate close to two minutes without a mask before he passes out. Any higher than 30,000 without oxygen and the pilot blacks out in a few seconds.

At 40,000 to 45,000 feet the pressure is so low that if the pilot is going to spend any time at that altitude he has to start "pressure breathing" in order to get enough oxygen into his lungs. Pressure breathing is breathing in reverse. Instead of sucking in the oxygen, as he does at the lower altitudes, pressure in the oxygen tank forces the air into the pilot's lungs; to get rid of it he has to force it back out.

Altitudes above 50,000 feet, from eight to 12 miles up, where the air is a near-vacuum, the region of extreme low pressure begins requiring the use of the pressure suit. Without one—if the cockpit pressurization failed—a man's blood would boil, the saliva in his mouth would bubble, and the pressure of the vapor rising from the water under his skin would cause the tissue to blow up like a balloon. Chances are his intestines would burst.

By the time the film ended I was convinced to the practicality of the Air Force's suit. They would get no argument from me. We began the fittings early the next morning.

Seven-thirty we were in the basement trying on the gear under the expert eye of Captain Mahoney. The helmet came first, a large metal sphere with a thick, curved face-plate. The oxygen hose hung like a long snout directly in line with my mouth. Around the neck an inflated bladder sealed the helmet so that when the pressure suit was inflated it wouldn't blow the helmet off your head.

Mahoney warned me. "Be prepared . . . it tightens down on you—the air will be forced into your nose and mouth. Let it come in through your mouth, count five, and blow it out. Don't worry about bringing more air in. The helmet will do it for you." Mahoney had me practice reverse breathing in the helmet alone.

The pressure in the helmet was enormous. It was as if the globe were filled with water forcing its way into my lungs. I blocked the oxygen off in my throat with my tongue to hold it back while I counted to five, then with a great deal of effort. I forced the air out of my lungs into the helmet. The sensation was like that of strangling. It would take a lot of practice before I would be able to wear this thing easily.

Five minutes of struggling inside the helmet and Mahoney brought out the rest of the practice suit which has a separate system of its own. It took him and two other guys 45 minutes to get me into the sausage-tight casing. Deflated, the pressure suit felt snug, like well-fitting long underwear. Before I was allowed to try the rig out in the tank under actual reduced pressures, the suit was manually inflated a little at a time.

"Now, Bill, instead of sucking in the air, rest against the suit. Let the suit do the work; don't fight it. once you trust the suit you'll be all right."

One thousand one, 1002, 1003, 1004, 1005 . . . I gasped out the air and let the pressure, like an air hose, blow up my lungs. The inflated suit tightened down, squeezing me in a vise. Al Mahoney gradually adjusted the knobs on the instrument panel that operated the suit. It was more difficult now to breathe, trying to adjust to the weight against my chest that pushed the air out. For 15 minutes I sat in a chair going through the contortions of getting oxygen into my bloodstream. My arms hung out in curves from my body as I sat and the doctor periodically asked me to count aloud to see how I was doing.

After four days of practice breathing outside of the tank, I was ready for the chamber.

The suit would remain in its deflated state as long as the pressure in the tank held under 42,000 feet. At first the pressure was reduced in the chamber gradually. As the chamber pressure dropped, the doctors manually pressurized the helmet and suit so that I became accustomed, in easy stages, to the strenuous grip of the suit. In an actual failure the pressure in the suit would hit me all at once. When I had been thoroughly initiated in the tank and had learned to adjust the knobs to match the system pressures with the chamber pressure, the doctors left me alone to manipulate the practice suit by myself. They peered through the portholes and asked for answers over the loud-speaker that hung in front of my chair.

Then the day of graduation came. The final test of suit and pilot. The pressure in the chamber would be instantly dropped from 38,000 feet to 70,000 feet to simulate a cabin failure at that height. The suit was then supposed to take over automatically, preventing me from splattering all over the tank.

Three doctors stood by while I was stuffed into the suit. They used the time to ask me questions, to make sure I knew what I was to do. My heart was checked, my pulse was counted. Beside the main door into the big tank a table was spread with cold metal and glass medical equipment. Every precaution was taken. During a test the year before they had lost a man.

Graduation day drew a crowd. People I hadn't seen during my two weeks of indoctrination arrived to watch the decompression show. Even with the suit hanging comfortably to my body it was an effort to stand up straight. I walked, slightly bent, into the chamber, supporting the heavy helmet evenly on my neck. Because the helmet was on its own system it was set ahead of time for extreme altitudes and would remain so, as it would in actual flight. It would be necessary to partially pressure-breathe all the way up. The contortion of pressure breathing was easier than it had been two weeks before. But still it was a matter of gasping and heaving convulsively, although I did it fairly automatically now. I no longer had to count.

Everything was in order. The tank was divided into two sections separated by a thick wall with a round opening in the middle sealed tight by a plastic membrane. On the side I sat in the pressure would be lowered to 38,000 feet.

The pressure on the other side of the partition in the larger chamber would be reduced to 90,000 feet. At a signal from Mahoney a trigger would be pulled which would break the membrane and let the enormous vacuum in the next chamber suck the pressure out of the tank I was sitting in. This would simulate conditions of an actual failure at 70,000 feet in the air.

Mahoney calls into me, "Are you ready, Bill?" I nod.

"No. Answer me out loud."

"Yes, I'm ready." I have taken a copy of the *Reader's Digest* in the tank with me. The operation will probably last over an hour. The big pumps outside the tank slowly suck the air from the chamber. Over the loud-speaker inside the tank I can hear Mahoney's urgent voice. "Everybody ready?" Everybody is ready. "Okay, Bill, you're going up to 38,000." The captain calls again, "Main chamber going up." The pump engine hums and vibrates through the chamber. But the exaggerated noise that fills my helmet is the loud, unnatural sound of my own breathing—like a man fighting ether on an operating table I go through the steady process of getting the pure oxygen into my lungs. The light glares down on the pages of the compact, optimistic magazine I read. It's a story about a little old lady left alone in the world, who fights back at the tremendous odds set against her. She starts a plum-canning factory that becomes a howling success. Now isn't that nice. The chamber is quiet except for the noise of my breathing and the hum of the pumps.

"Hey, Bridgeman, count for us . . ." Mahoney and the faces at the portholes want to make sure I am still with them.

"One, two, three, four, five, six, okay?"

The little old lady has netted 200,000 dollars the second year. Over at the windows the faces have changed for new ones. Fort-five minutes have gone by. "Bridgeman, count for us, please." I count between breaths. It is difficult to talk and breathe in reverse and I lose my place in the magazine.

Mahoney calls at last, "Ready everybody?" This is it. "Ready for decompression."

The faces at the portholes are like fish in an aquarium moving around the tank. I have finished the story. What is about to happen now is supposed to happen at 70,000 feet in the Skyrocket if there is a leak in the cockpit. For an instant I find I am fighting the air coming into my helmet. But it is all right again—I count to re-establish the cycle: I00I, I002, I003, I004, I005—push it out now, let another blast in, enough. My tongue shuts the air out of my throat. It is going properly again.

A click! The trigger is pulled and beside me the weight falls, forcing the metal-pointed lever to rip the membrane and the dam breaks! The air that rushes out turns to fog and the casing around my body tightens up like a boa constrictor dropping on its prey. It works! My entire body and my head feel as if they are weighted down with tons of water and the reverse breathing is more difficult to manage. I resort to counting again. According to the instructions I have received before I entered the tank, now I am to go through the motions of flying the Skyrocket. Okay. I move my fingers and then my arms and legs. Now I reach in front of me and pretend to handle the controls. The faces look in at me intently. It is enormously undignified, sitting here in this grotesque costume, gasping and panting like an animal and flying controls that don't exist. Five minutes.

"Okay," Mahoney tells me, "we're going back down." Fifteen more minutes in this vise and it will be over. The 15 minutes squeeze by and then Mahoney calls that school is out.

"Okay, Bill, you can spill the suit; 38,000 feet." By my side I push a valve and the suit lets go of me. Fifteen more minutes and at 10,000 feet, I can take the tin can off of my head and breathe properly again.

It was ten o'clock in the morning when the operation was completed and I was thoroughly exhausted as I retreated through the sticky, hot Ohio morning back to my hotel. The first step toward taking the Skyrocket into the unknown regions was accomplished. There was now the reverse breathing and the pressure suit to think about.

On the flight back to the Air Research and Development Command's frontier base in the desert, George and I relaxed with the other passengers in the DC-6. We were cruising along at an easy 23,000 feet when the man across the aisle from us shakes his head and exclaims, "God, we're high, 23,000 feet." He asks George earnestly as one passenger to another, "Do you think they'll ever really get much higher than this?"

George shrugged his shoulders and I smiled as we leaned heavily back into our plush seats.

CHAPTER XVII

George Jansen attacked his part of the launch with the zeal and thoroughness of a general deploying an army. He had little faith in the old Skyrocket as she was, and any credit that he might allow me was based mostly on the premise that it took more guts than intelligence to fly such a foolhardy assignment. However, he was going to see to it that nothing went wrong at his end of the ride.

It wasn't that George lacked an exploratory spirit; he was just smart. He couldn't see the point in risking your neck in an airplane that, to him, was a bad risk. Test pilots who did were damned fools in his book. Probably when I knew as much about testing as George did, I would have a similar attitude. In testing, as in most anything, the more you know about the subject the more room you have for doubt. Unconscious courage is an easy achievement for the uninitiated. They don't know any better.

Being sure was George's major testing characteristic. He was by far the most active engineering pilot in Douglas' flight test office, but he judiciously picked—when he could—the airplanes he would test. There was no patty-cake with Big George. If he didn't like the looks of a program, he said so. When an airplane did come off the boards that interested him, he would go after it and from there on out that airplane would become a part of him. Every facet thoroughly explored, each flight carefully planned and approached with caution, an inch at a time.

Now the big pilot spent hour after hour with me in the confining pilots' office of the Douglas hangar in the desert, going over the launch and drinking the scalding synthetic-tasting coffee mixture from the vending machine. He didn't push ideas about how I should handle my end of the operation. He took the role of advisor, only giving his opinion when I asked for it. It was up to me to determine how I wanted to handle the Skyrocket and at what spot I wanted to be dropped. From there George plotted the B-29's course, figuring out how to get me into the position that I had designated.

My drop was to be at a point that would leave the lake bed in the middle of the high-speed run path: if the rockets or jet quit during the run I would be in a good spot to glide back home. It was George's job to jockey the B-29 up to the exact speed that would allow the Skyrocket to drop clean. It had to be precise. A slight miscalculation one way or the other and the Skyrocket could take the B-29's tail section with her as she left her berth.

Synchronizing the two airplanes at the drop was George's biggest concern. According to the diagram of the converted superfortress, the hole cut for the Skyrocket was a pretty close fit over her tail section, almost like a slot. It would be up to George to hold the B-29 absolutely steady at the moment of drop; a jolt this way or that would be enough to break off the Skyrocket's high, graceful, swept-back horizontal stabilizer.

The men who would fly with us in the B-29 were an all-volunteer Douglas crew, Jack Robinson, Roger Allen, Don Pruitt, Wally Adams, and McNemar. Most of them had never flown at altitude before and none of them were experienced airmen. They were mechanics.

While George had no faith in my plane, I had little in his. B-29's were flying torches as far as I was concerned. The things were always catching fire. One little spark near the two rocket propellants heavy in the Skyrocket and both planes would be dust. This was something else we had to take into consideration as we fitted the plan together.

The plan was to spiral up wider and wider over the field. If the 29 sprouted a fire, which it was notoriously capable of doing, between take-off and 8000 feet, everybody was to get the hell out and let the whole works blow up. It would be futile to try and save the Skyrocket with so little altitude to maneuver in. From 8000 feet on up if the superfortress began to smoke George was to press the pickle and get rid of the Skyrocket. If the "bomb" itself began smoking, past the altitude I was to board her, it was decided that George would give me a five-second warning, then get rid of the bundle of explosives. I could take my chances and stay with it or get out. It would be up to me.

Although I was sure that George's volunteer crew considered the Skyrocket a menace that they would be relieved to part company with, I thought of my airplane as a kind of lifeboat that offered escape from the inflammable superfortress. That is, if she dropped free all right. We would be testing the launchable jet-rocket version first and, once it was free of the mother ship, it would be identical to the airplane that I had flown this past year. I wouldn't need the pressure suit for this one. It was to be a long-sustained stability run at a modest 40,000 feet. If she dropped away successfully I would have two power plants: jet and rocket. After 50 flights in the Skyrocket I knew that if the rockets failed, the jet engine would get me home. So far she had been on my side. Once she was in flight I could handle her. It was the moment of the drop, the great demands the engineers were making of her, that caused me anxiety. She might not drop clean. George and I had our doubts. There was the possibility that one of the hydraulically controlled latch mechanisms that held the Skyrocket in the superfortress' bomb bay might fail—a situation that would leave the Skyrocket hanging by one support, jammed in the B-29. This dire possibility and the question of drag in the Skyrocket at the moment of the drop, that might cause the little plane to move forward or aft into the belly of the mother ship, instead of falling out, sent George and me into the aerodynamicists' offices for reassurance.

With great patience the aerodynamicists carefully showed us on paper that the Skyrocket had been calculated to drop and drop she would. We were not altogether convinced. Everything the engineers drew for us, that they insisted could be done in practice, we checked ourselves. Engineers are right 90 per cent of the time—it was that narrow ten per cent of the time that they were wrong we searched for.

An aerodynamic problem in itself was the superfortress that was getting its guts cut out at the El Segundo plant. Would it fly with the large hole in its belly? Again the engineers tried to convince us that the bomber would hold together. But George and I delved into engine charts and equations in order to verify, for ourselves, the engineers' calculations. Things were moving closer to the day we would find out for sure if the figures were right.

Carder and his crew of engineers and technicians were at the peak of enthusiasm anticipating the launches. They figured their ship could beat the Air Force's X-1 by a big margin. They talked about Mach 1.8 or even Mach 2, twice the speed of sound, once the jet-rocket-version launches were out of the way and we were into the all-rocket model. Like expectant fathers, the men in the Douglas offices were pretty confident of the results—it figured on paper—there was nothing more they could do but wait for the day. They interfered with George and me very seldom now. How to do it, the physical end of the feat, was left almost entirely up to us. Periodically a bright face would appear through the door of our office asking how we were doing. George would look up from his desk: "It's coming . . . "

Four months after it had been ordered, word came up from the El Segundo plant that the gutted superfortress was ready to go. George and I flew down to bring it back. El Segundo was a cool departure from Muroc. The wind was coming in from the ocean and it felt cold against the sticky khakis I wore . . . I could smell the salt water five miles away to the west.

Across the field the huge bomber sitting beside the Douglas hangar was ready to go. Two scanners were to ride with us. From their posts in the tail section they would attentively watch the four engines for fire. It had been a long time since I had felt the weight of a four-engine bomber, a formidable military aircraft like the B-24's in the Pacific—bigger and emptier, no guns, no bombs, nothing but a large, drafty hole in her middle—an old warrior maybe, who had flown through the flak-pocked skies of the Pacific at the close of the war. She had a new purpose now.

The midsection that once held tons of black bombs had been reinforced lengthwise with narrow aluminum beams that were supposed to hold her together while she performed her strange mission. George and I inspected the conversion. We pessimistically speculated how she would handle in flight.

Reluctantly, we got aboard, feeling like heroes about to embark on a suicide mission. George motioned down to the mechanic standing by to start number-two engine. "Well, Bridge, I guess this is it."

The four big windmills tore up the air in front of us. The shell of a bomber rumbled down the runway and lifted off into the shallow sky over the field. We weren't going to take her right out. Cautiously we circled the field once to see if she actually meant to fly or if the butchered-out hole they had dug from her belly was too radical a wound and the forfeit in drag proved to be too great.

She behaved! The engineers were right this time. With some relief we settled back into our seats and pointed toward the sharp-edged mountains and, on the other side, Muroc. Alone in the big glass nose, with the summertime valley, mountains, and desert flowing under us, we talked of the time we flew four-engine bombers out into the dawn over the ocean, George in Europe and me in the Pacific. We talked of the war. George had flown 24's for the Army, he had been shot up in the Ploesti raid. We compared wounds and fought the war over again, high above the peace moving beneath us.

There was some preliminary testing to be done. "Let's dive her a little and wee what we bought when they damn near sawed this thing in half," George suggested. We returned to the business that now held us as comrades. George carefully dropped the oval glass nose slightly down toward the bottom of the desert 12,000 feet below.

Aft, beyond the round door that separated us from the huge opening, the sky scooped in and roared over the naked sides of the bomber, whistling across the myriad wires and tubing there. Through the porthole into the bomb bay I checked her new ribs— just the extreme edges of the aluminum alloy vibrated slightly in the breeze—no twisting or skin rippling, no tell-tale signs of unsupported stresses. The engineers were right again. George lifted the angle, "That's enough for now. We'll see how she held together first before we put any more strain on those girders." Twenty minutes later at the base that sprouted unobtrusively out of the empty desert around it like a pioneer outpost, we brought her in.

We were satisfied with the way the B-29 had handled. All that held us up now was the arrival of the modified Skyrockets. While we waited we went over the plan, adding a precautionary measure here and there. It was going to be a tricky flight; it was the preliminary contest leading up to the morning of the big bout, the all-rocket version that would take the Skyrocket as far as she was capable of going. I had been able to successfully put off thinking about the morning of the big flight the last couple of months. There was no good thinking about the reality of the moment that was waiting to happen. It would be time enough to face it when it arrived. As if they were for someone else, I looked at the plans with detachment. In one year's time I had managed to get myself into successively complicated and radical phases of my new profession. First the Skyrocket herself—a weird, sterile departure from anything flying at the time, unstable, an explorer; then the complication of rockets, and now she was to be carried, a swallow in an eagle's claws, up to altitude where a restricting suit was required in order to exist.

As it was before on the more complicated flights, there was a build-up, a kind of inadvertent conditioning. This time it was the jet-rocket combination. Although there was a definite place for the jet-rocket combination as an investigator in transonic areas, the three successful launch flights on the dual power-plant model required by the Navy and NACA allowed me to ease up on the tougher flights waiting for me in the all-rocket Skyrocket. It wouldn't be so bad; I wouldn't have to face the whole problem at once. We would be able to determine the practicality of the launch first and whether or not the rockets lit off successfully. There would be no push for extreme altitudes or speeds—they would come in the rocket ship. In Al Carder's project there was no abrupt jumping-off place; you crept up to it. And then when there was no further choice, you reached. The jet-rocket was good preparatory training.

The combination launch model was trucked up from El Segundo, soon after the 29 arrived, to take her place beside the original sister ship. Except for the eight-inch hooks fore and aft on her back—the hardware that attached her to the mother ship—she was identical to the Skyrocket I had been flying. When the ship, held in place by its hooks and four pincers from the bomber, was snug in the B-29, George would press the pickle, the same mechanism that he had used to drop bombs over Europe. Supposedly the hooks would be released and disappear, automatically sealed off by tiny doors, into the Skyrocket's back.

In order to test the drop mechanism, the superfortress was put on giant jacks so that the Skyrocket could be moved under it into place. She was then "pickled" off to the ground a couple of feet below. When the bomber was actually ready for take-off, without the jacks, the Skyrocket would hang about 18 inches from the runway.

George and I figured on the worst—if the Skyrocket didn't let go all the way or moved up into the B-29, Jansen would order the crew to jump. He would pull the B-29 up sharply away from the "white bomb," as the crew already called it. If that didn't do it, we would both get out the best way we could.

First flight was called for two weeks after the new ship arrived. It was time to go through the performance we had planned on the ground. While the mechanics had her under the 29, checking her fueling accessibility, I practiced the sequence of moves I would make during the flight. George in the B-29 above me joined in the rehearsal.

Tomorrow morning the cushion of time would be gone. The

launch was scheduled for eight o'clock; I had caught up with it. We didn't need the dawn tomorrow; the ground wind was relatively unimportant to the flight of the big superfortress. It was the wind at altitude where the Skyrocket was to get off that would be a determining factor. It would be a long flight. The Skyrocket would be able to make an hour's worth of points once she dropped clear of the mother ship. She'd have a full tank of jet fuel after the rockets quit. Tomorrow there would be no long grind to altitude, she had a free ride and four times the fuel to spend in exploring. It would be a big day for the Skyrocket—if she dropped clean. There was nothing to reassure me about the drop. Tomorrow we would see.

To think about the moment of drop was a senseless thing. I was committed. This was the path I chose, it moved and I moved with it, the time had gone. Every possible plan had been laid to insure the flight's success. Tomorrow at lunch the flight would be swept behind and the next one would move toward me and I toward it.

Outside of my room the air-conditioning hummed, and around the hot metal bed lamp over my head, hard-shelled desert bugs buzzed and hit against the shade with little snapping noises. They crawled over the magazine propped against my legs. It was ten o'clock and the only relief from the buzzing and snapping and crawling was to turn out the lamp.

In the dark heat of the room the persistent doubt came over me again. No matter how well prepared I had made myself, perhaps I had forgotten something. Lying somewhere in the plan there might be an undiscovered flaw; the one that would trip me. *Oh, bullwhacker* I was annoyed at my anxiety. The flaw I worried about had surely been discovered in the two months of planning. *To hell with it!* I could sleep.

I was pulled out of the anesthetic of sleep by the whistle. The same awful wail, right on time, that woke me as it had for every rocket flight for a year now. Three-thirty. The sheet was hot and dry around my body as I turned over. One day I'd sleep right through the Skyrocket's call.

Two hours more of forgetfulness and the alarm brought me back. It was time to go down to the field that was shrouded in the half-light that covered it before dawn. The ground was damp and the air was thick and moist as I walked onto the Air Force runway toward the fueling tanks and the intricate operation of priming the Skyrocket for her launch. It must have rained during the night.

On the edge of the desert past the twin Air Force hangars the B-29 loomed dark ahead of me. Beneath her was the polished white Skyrocket hanging like a giant winged bomb from her bomb bay. Around the violated bomber that dominated the Skyrocket so, the crew, like members of a secret cult in their gleaming white plastic suits and hooded helmets, fed the Skyrocket her fuel from the huge main tank that held the liquid oxygen. The hose that crawled along the concrete into the side of the ship was heavy with frost from the --297° liquid oxygen. High up into the mother ship the Skyrocket's tail was compactly fitted; from her round, sleek, belly-sides her fragile wings protruded below the B-29. The black lines of the hydrogen peroxide and the alcohol dangled beneath her. So far no trouble, according to McNemar. She would be ready in a couple of hours. There was plenty of time for breakfast before I checked the wind.

A light breakfast in the nearly empty mess and I headed down to the Douglas hangar. The blue stripes of fluorescent lights burned over the row of engineering offices. The project members were all in attendance, going over last-minute details as I passed by on my way to the locker outside the pilots' room.

"You been down to the field yet? How's the fueling going?" George looked up from his desk inside the little office.

"It's going fine. How's the weather holding up?"

"Cover'll be less than four tenths." George returned to his charts. We were bound closely together by today's flight but there was little left to discuss. It was now a matter of following the plan we had established and we retreated into concentrating on our own responsibilities.

I dressed for the flight. No pressure suit. A G suit like an OD-colored glove, a year old now, familiar, unmistakably mine—the parachute I had worn on 50 flights in the research plane, the scratched and dented red crash helmet sitting on the desk beside the knee pad that held all the steps I would follow. The used gear, well seasoned now, an integral part of the program that once seemed so remote, was reassuring.

"See you down on the strip, George."

One of the Douglas crew, Elmer Batters, project secretary, volunteered to drive me down to my plane.

Along the way toward the end of the runway, along the flight apron, the silver-skinned Air Force experimental and prototype airplanes sat in the streaks of mist, glinting off the early light. A weird flock. Great, fat cargo ships squatting beside frail-looking little fighters, the rows of aircraft look out of order. A side-show of experiments.

And ahead of me was the biggest experiment of them all. Batters pulled up close. Two mechanics greeted me with self-conscious joviality. They solicitously offered me a hand with the gear. Under the shadow of the bomber's big wings I crawled up the ladder hanging down from the cockpit, into the dark cavern of her nose. The crew passed up my gear and I moved aft to take a look at the Skyrocket in her berth. Behind the window in the round door the Skyrocket hung snugly from the B-29, locked in place by the hooks and gripped along her sides by the big heavily padded, pincer sway-braces attached to the bomber. The canopy was laid back and she was whistling off her fuel.

In the event the explosive Skyrocket acted up and it was necessary for George to get rid of the little ship to protect the rest of the crew, I had practiced getting out in a hurry. I would blow the canopy up and jump on to the sides of the bomber, straddling the Skyrocket until she fell away, then I would climb the short ladder into the nose and join the rest of the party.

Two months ago Pete Everest, flying a launch of the X-1, barely got out when a fire warning in the rocket ship forced the B-29 pilot to pickle it off fast. Just in time, he grabbed the ladder and was hanging out of the bomber when the X-1 dropped away. The rocket ship didn't explode, as was expected, until she hit the desert. It wasn't hard to find where she hit, she had blasted out a 50-foot hole a half-block square.

George Jansen's voice came up through the bomb bay, "Is Bridgeman up there set to go?" The captain was ready to board his ship; he gave rapid instructions to the crew as the top of his helmet appeared through the hatchway into the cockpit. His face was set. Things had better be right. He nodded to me and rapidly made an inspection as he climbed aboard. His novice crew had known his disapproval and sarcasm and tried diligently to avoid it. George found nothing out of order. Before yesterday's preflight meeting, he had had a preflight meeting of his own with the volunteer Douglas crew—every man aboard had been thoroughly briefed on what action to take in a dozen situations or emergencies. The crew listened well to their skipper. It wasn't the sort of crew George had had in the Ploesti raid; these men were not experienced airmen. They had never flown on a bottle of oxygen and George felt a great responsibility for their safety. It was possible to lose a man through the misuse of his oxygen equipment.

"You're all ready to go, huh?" George continued to look over the cockpit; the rest of the crew crawled up the ladder behind him, two scanners, Vern Poupitch, the copilot, and the two men assigned to help me into the Skyrocket.

No time could be lost now. The Skyrocket was steaming off fuel that I would need in the climb after the drop. Arrangements had been made with the tower that the 29 take off immediately when George called that he was ready. Outside in the brightening light a crowd gathered to watch the take-off: Douglas personnel, Air Force people up early for tests themselves, and engineers from other projects. Today the Skyrocket would be the second research plane in the world to be launched.

George dropped behind the big spread of instruments and with his head half turned, he told me, "The wind's out of the south. We can use either end. That's a break, huh; it'll save us some time."

"Ready to turn two!" Jansen announced and to Vern, "Clear on your side?"

"Clear over here. Ready to turn."

The big props wound up. Hoses and lines were pulled from the Skyrocket and the spectators moved back. Down below us the men followed the motions of George's hand, one and four engines joined in the roar, and the chocks were pulled.

"Tell the tower we're ready to taxi out," George instructed his copilot. Before the superfortress began to move toward the runway

George checked his engines. Okay. We rolled out into the open.

"We're ready to go, Vern." I heard George tell his copilot over the intercom. The big ship was cleared for take-off.

The crew is silent. In our bomb bay the vessel full of explosives hangs low over the concrete runway. We sit along the narrow benches that curve with the sides of the bomber. Across from me the two line tenders sit side by side—one watches the pilots, the other stares past my shoulder. The big bomber joggles along the runway, heavy with her freight; she lifts off and hovers momentarily over the end of the field. George is giving fast orders as he manipulates the controls and we are on our way up the long spiral to altitude and the drop point.

It's a laborious pull. Carefully George regulates his speed and climbing angle, milking the power out of her. Fifteen minutes up: 10,000 feet, plug into the 29's oxygen. Another ten minutes and the altimeter beside the navigator's desk reads 18,000 feet. In the vibrating, roaring fuselage the intercom that connects the crew together is quiet. George will speak only when it is necessary. I have no desire to make chitchat; my mind is full with the details of the drop. The bomber is drafty and I move my arms and legs against the cold.

Eighteen thousand feet! Twenty minutes to go before we reach 30,000 feet, where the bomber will head out on a straight course. This is the altitude at which I am to make my way back to the Skyrocket hanging below. I motion to the men across from me, breathing heavily in their masks. They leave their bench to help me with the long oxygen line that will reach into the Skyrocket. George turns his head: "Have a good one, Bridge." Beside him "the Navy" raises his hand in a parting gesture and I head toward the bomb bay followed by my tenders. The door is pulled back from the drafty, bitter-cold hollow, and as in the vestibule of a train the roar of the wind screams around the protruding plane that lies three feet directly below me. Even in her captive attitude she looks good to me. Here is the plane I know. She won't be captive for long. She'll be away on her own.

Feet first, I ease myself through the opening into the hole below, sliding on my chute down into the canoe-like cockpit of the Skyrocket. The men hold the oxygen line out of my way as I turn around and stuff my legs down into the nose. A big suck of oxygen. I hold my breath and disconnect the 29's oxygen line and plug in from the Skyrocket. My tenders pull the hatch down over my head and lock it in place. Cozy as a tomb. The familiarity of the Skyrocket helps to make me less jumpy and the activity of starting the jet engine is a welcome exercise. Twenty minutes to go.

Through the slits of the Rocket I see the oxygen-snouted faces of my tenders above in the doorway of the 29. It is extremely cold and the light is a dim twilight in the dark belly of the B-29. If it works on this first one, it is safer than a ground take-off with rockets—there is all that sky below me to fall into.

The jet engine is just below full power. Under the roar of the superfortress the Skyrocket sounds like a sewing machine going in a closet. There is a little bit of everything on this flight—four reciprocating engines, one jet engine, and, in 15 minutes, add four rocket tubes.

I am aware of the sound of my breath rasping in and out of the snout dangling in front of me. At my left, in the corner is the oxygen indicator, breathing with me, a black circle with two white slits that click together as I suck oxygen from the bottle on my right side. A fish mouth opening and closing. While I wait I amuse myself by breathing faster in order to watch the little mouth move faster with me. It clicks rapidly, then slowly as I regulate my breathing.

Between the Rocket and the superfortress there is a margin of sky a foot wide and from the slit windows I can see down 28,000 feet to the ground below. The mountain looks recognizable, we are over Lake Arrowhead. No, that isn't it. The game makes me curious. Where the hell are we then? I call to George, "George, where are we going now?"

"I'm flying this one; you fly that one." George doesn't like chitchat over his intercom.

Carder breaks the monotony. He is out on the lake near the spot where I will eventually head for a landing. "How's the T-5 temperature holding out?"

"Holding steady, Al."

George comes on, asking for wind forces and direction at 32,000. The tower sends up the figures. "Okay, Bill, we're heading out." We have stopped climbing now and we are on the straight course away from the lake. The number of minutes that it will take to put us over the drop point is measured by George against the true air speed and the prevailing wind forces and directions.

Today is Friday. When this flight is over there is the week end at the cool beach, surfing, the evenings in the patio around a barbecue, and the irrepressibly lit face of the girl who surfs better than I do. It's all easy and slow and vital on the week ends; everything good is intensified, sharp, and exhilarating. The jokes are enormously funny and the smoky-flavored steaks are a wonderful experience. A week in the desert is too long. God, I hope we don't abort. Any minute now. I'm sick of the lake and the heat and the faces of men. Come on, let's get this over with.

"Okay, Bridge," George calls into the dark box I sit in, "here's your five-minute warning."

Five minutes before he lets me drop. There is flying to be done. Automatically my mind slips into another gear and there is only this moment, this series of steps in the world. On my knee are the cards, the road map. The one on top reads: Four minutes: Begin prime, I know the steps cold but I follow the cards anyway. The stop-watch is ticking. I watch the rpm and turbine out temp on the jet engine. Four minutes. Prime. Together in a row the instruments wave up across the dials and stop.

According to our flight plan George has now made a 180-degree turn back to the lake, he will go into a shallow dive to build up his speed to maximum so that the Skyrocket won't stall when she drops. At the point of drop the B-29 is almost at her critical Mach number, a speed that is just a shade above the Skyrocket's stalling speed. Yesterday's performance and tomorrow's touch lightly at this frail juncture.

Three minutes. Two minutes. With an attempt at nonchalance I toss a "kiss-off" gesturer to the two men staring down at me from the door of the bomber. It is a self-conscious gesture that is designed to show them I am composed, part of a role I play. It also has a personally reassuring effect—I manage to kid myself a little.

The pickle that let go a bellyful of black bombs over Ploesti will feel the pressure of George's thumb and release me from this dark closet. It is hard to read some of the instruments that are placed lower on the panel. I'll have to tell Al to have a light put in there.

"You're on your own, Buddy," George announces and begins to count down, in a flat, stead voice: "Ten . . . nine . . . eight . . . seven . . . " My hand is on the data switch waiting for him to reach "five." "Six . . . five." There. One hand on the wheel, one wrapped around the throttle. "Four . . . three . . . two . . . one . . . *drop!*"

And the trap door opens—down a glaring white shaft through 400 feet, an elevator dropping through the sky. From out of the dark, protective belly of the 29 the world bursts over me in bright light. She's free. I'm away from the mother ship clear and free. It works. No time for mental celebration. Rapidly I click on the four rocket tubes. They blast on and I've got a big hunk of energy to control. She heads out, still losing altitude but trimmed nose-up. Squinting through the glare of the blinding sun, I check the rocket pressures. In the green. She hits bottom and the altimeter shows a loss of 2500 feet and I point her upward again in the pullout. According to the plan, I let her pick up speed in the drop, holding the nose down slightly, and at the right moment I pull it up and begin the climb. Before me the long pole of a nose quivers, my invented stall indicator; I use the degree of its quivering to tell me how far I am getting into the stall. Too much. The nose vibrates like a taut string. I drop the nose a fraction. Too far. Up again; it is now a matter of calculation and feel. If I take too long in the pullout I will use up rocket-seconds that I want for the high-speed run ahead of me at 40,000 feet. If I pull out too fast she will stall. We are in the climb now, going almost straight up at the angle that will give me a Mach number of .85, a hair below her critical Mach number of .9. She climbs like she was sucked up through the 10,000 feet. On the panel the altimeter creeps up on 35,000, 38,000, and 40,000 feet. I push her nose over for the speed run. She accelerates rapidly in the thin sky-meadow of the higher altitude.

The buffet! Okay, that's .91. But she doesn't stop; she still buffets although we are through into .92, the other side, where she smooths out always. The buffeting continues . . . .93, .94. Perhaps the increase in altitude . . . it's a vaguely different kind of shaking. It becomes more urgent. I search the instrument panel and there's the answer—the turbine out temperature is overboard by 500. At once I jerk the throttle to idle, but it is not fast enough; the engine gives up. She flames out, loses thrust, and pitches over, throwing me into the harness and against the panel as if she were impatient with my stupidity. At once, in rapid succession, the rocket tubes fail.

Now there is no sound but the sound of my breath coming faster into the snout hanging from my face and the wind splitting over the canopy. For an instant I have let the familiar buffet at .91 disguise the trouble. I have sat here for ten seconds while a warning sounded and I have not heard it fast enough. My lack of alertness infuriates me. She has tricked me this time. There are enough things that can go wrong without the pilot adding to the errors. It is so obvious. The altitude is too much for the jet engine. When she pitched forward she unported the rocket fuel, starving off the tubes—all in a matter of ten seconds.

She carries me at Mach .8 silently through the lonely sky in a long glide path down, and the only life and sound in the world now is mine and the noise of my breath and the wind outside at the edge of the canopy. It is a dream. A soft, floating kind of dream, at the bottom of which is terror, but I make no move to rouse myself. The terror seems unreal.

I move the controls on the dead ship and feel the independent speed and power she still has coming through my hands. The dream state evaporates and it is an emergency.

Chuck is a mile from me. We have anticipated this one. I can glide in easily from here. Through the window on my left the field lies not too far away. As I look down, I am unprepared to accept what I see happening and I stare curiously at the white layer of fog that is rapidly filling the space between the windowpanes. It moves fast, hardening into a frost curtain blocking out the sky, the ground, the horizon, the field.

I cannot see out of the airplane as she rips her way down through the sky. The impulse to get on the ground grabs at me, the same reaction I felt in my training days when there was suddenly a little trouble. The instinctive reaction has always occurred in such moments as this. Even after years of flying, the original, almost overwhelming, impulse is still with me but it is controlled now. A man never becomes entirely conditioned to fear. He merely learns to live with it. It becomes less of a distraction from experience, but it is never any more comfortable. It has always the same face.

I need time now in order to think my way out of this. I've got to get into a position that will give me time. *Okay. Slow up. Wait a minute. I'm not on fire. The longer I can stay up here, the better chance I have of getting the windshield defrosted. There are two things I know: the sun and the lake bed are behind me.*

Through the frost-filled windows it is possible to determine light and ark. I make a 180-degree turn at 250 knots, the best glide speed, into the position where the sun glows full into the cockpit. I should be heading in the direction of the lake. Chuck can direct me down. Before I call him I count out loud. My voice is high on one and by ten it is almost normal.

"I'm all smucked up, Chuck. I can't see out of this thing. Pick me up as soon as you can and give me my position."

"Right, Bill."

Chuck is probably in close now, sliding underneath and over the powerless Skyrocket, checking to see what is wrong. He tells me straight without the usual flourish, "You're passing north. The field's right . . ."

The sentence is cut off. The radio quits. The last lifeline is snapped away from the blind and helpless ship. Almost more than fear, I have an overwhelming sense of loneliness. I am helplessly and neatly bound up by an irrevocable steel chain of rapid events. One part of the machine fails and in second-timed sequence the other parts cease to function.

I am heading into the sun, perhaps over the lake into the mountains on the other side. There is no way of knowing now. *Think ahead beyond panic. There's a way out. Get rid of the propellants. Think a way out of this opaque, tight tube I am wrapped in that carries me noiselessly through the enormous sky.*

I begin the jettison. Fast, I check the circuit breakers. They are all in. The generator is not putting out. When the jet unwound it took the juice and radio with it. That's it. The answer comes in pieces. There is a relay that is supposed to automatically throw the battery into the circuit when the juice quits but it also has failed.

And then it hits me. I remember. I remember there is a manual switch. With a flood of relief I snap it into place and like a light in a room long dark, Yeager's voice bursts into the silent pod.

"Al, I'm right on top of him and I'm positive that he can't see out of it . . . he isn't receiving my transmissions." The smooth, honey-soft voice of Chuck Yeager has altered. It is a rapid, urgent call. "Bill, do you receive me? Rock your wings if you can read me."

It takes me a second to answer. "Okay, Chuck . . . I can hear you. I've got this thing *gening* now and I can hear you."

The radio is still and then in the old drawl, "Well, Buddy, you wanted to be a pilot . . . pilot!" He gives me my position. "You're just south of the lake, Bill . . . hold the heading you've got. I'll bring you in."

Quietly and steadily Yeager begins to "talk" me down. I follow the adjustments as he reads them, he will lead me in as if he were in my ship. If he should misjudge, I have no power with which to correct my position. Chuck has got to be right. I follow his voice down. The windshield is a cold, white wall. As I begin the blind spiral down, I attempt to light off the jet engine. No answer. Again I try it.

An instrument landing is something I cannot practice in the Skyrocket. This is new, a matter of sweating it out, waiting to see the outcome. Any experience I have had with instrument landings has been in a passenger airplane where I was assisted by three other men and special instrumentation. The Skyrocket has no such advantages.

"Bill, get your gear and flaps down. We're approaching the lake." I follow Chuck's voice.

"Two degrees left; hold it. One degree left, a little high." He lines me up with the lake-bed runway.

Once more I attempt to light off the jet. She lights! The right set of conditions, the correct air-speed throttle combination is found and she goes.

"I saw a puff of smoke. Did you get an air start?" He continues to give me headings to hold. With the jet engine going the pressurization returns and the cockpit windshield begins to melt clean. I can see the runway 900 feet forward and below. Chuck has me right where I want to be. I don't tell him I can see. He is going such a beautiful job. After the tension I allow myself the joke.

"Two degrees; hold it. One degree left, a little high. Open your dive brakes." He continues to call out the landing as he moves under me to check the gear. on his way in he sees my old red helmet shining in the sunlight and he is not amused by the gag.

"Okay, Navy, you got it figured. You're on your own. Let's see you screw this up by yourself." He moves away fast and lets me complete the landing unassisted and she touches ground.

I lean back into the backrest, throw open the canopy, and let the hot desert air in. They are coming fast across the lake now, Al Carder and the rest of the crew.

Al Carder is visibly shaken by the experience, but the last bit of conversation between Yeager and myself just before I touched down no doubt helped to restore his composure. The prospect of the Skyrocket landing blind and dead stick would be enough to put him into a state of collapse.

As Al approached the cold Skyrocket I made no move to leave the ship; I kept my hands in my lap. When they brought the stand up to the side for me, I acted occupied in checking the cockpit. When I could no longer stay in the ship without embarrassment, I unsteadily backed down the ladder. I grinned self-consciously at the project coordinator who stood below ready to take my helmet. An amazing thing. Once more the experimental ship rested lightly on the field. She had brought me back again.

The engineers and mechanics were all over her.

"It looks like a compressor stall."

"Well, the jet's no good at the altitude that the rocket system will take it to. She'll have to stay down below 35,000, I guess."

What I wanted now was to get away from the plane, to dive into the cool big Pacific. I didn't want to talk to anybody. But there was the long postflight conference to which the engineers looked forward so keenly; there would be questions from all of them about their parts of the ship. Eight engineers with important questions. Another hour or two and I could unwind unobserved. Back at the hangar there was one man I did want to talk to—Chuck Yeager.

Before I joined the group in the postflight room I called his office in the Air Force hangar.

"Chuck, I want to thank you for bringing me in this morning."

Yeager seemed surprised. "Why any time at all, any time at all. The only time I was really worried was when you didn't answer . . . glad to help you out."

Again, somewhat uncomfortably, I tried to express my gratitude.

Outside the office in the hangar George Mabry was calling, "Postflight in five minutes."

CHAPTER XVIII

Without further incident the dual power-plant Skyrocket successfully completed the two remaining consecutive launches required by the new contract. She was delivered in less than a month's time to the NACA hangar next door for extensive research work. The committee could be assured that their "launchable" jet-rocket experimental airplane would satisfactorily enter, for a greatly extended period of time, into the transonic area where so much was still to be defined. As with all the versions of the Skyrocket ordered for NACA, our job was to tell the government agency just how far they could prudently go in their investigations. We had fenced off the area for them. One of the big restrictions was that they would have to stay away from altitudes above 35,000 feet with the jet engine. This taboo would keep her Mach number down around 1.1. They wouldn't be able to make any records with the ship but they would get four times as much routine testing out of her per flight than with the original "ground-take-off" version.

Now there waited to be proved the last and most radical Skyrocket—the all-rocket one. While she still wore her big Navy insignia she was in a spot to hang up altitude and speed records. Feeling ran high among the crew the day she was slowly trucked into the hangar after her creeping-paced journey through the desert.

She was pulled in beside the original Skyrocket where she would be prepared for the big morning. Next to her sister ship she looked identical in line, but cleaner. No air-intake gills were cut out of her sides and under her belly, where the ship alongside had an exhaust port, she was unmarred and polished. With the canopy clamped shut she was glass-sleek; only the frail, swept wings and flowing stabilizer interrupted the immaculate line.

The subtle difference made the ship a stranger. This was the dead-stick variety, the one that would reach way out where no ship had reached before. This was the one that was all for speed, all for performance.

The all-rocket plane was expected to do big things, and the possibility of this discovery was shared by every man who had a wrench on her or helped to plot her exploratory sky path. Here was an airplane that was capable of flying higher and faster than any airplane had ever flown. They were anxious to get it in the air, and the problems involved in the complicated flight were enthusiastically attacked.

The new plumbing was the initial problem. It had been devised to accommodate the big increase in rocket fuel. It hadn't been proven yet and Al Carder, who in the past had always been skeptical of the old rocket engine, was not going to take any chance with the new, more intricate one. So far the company hadn't lost a plane in the Phase Two Skyrocket program. Al meant to keep it that way. Our rival project in the Air Force hangar had had three ships blow up under them already. Al was determined to wind our program up clean. The new rocket system went through a thorough series of ground tests that lasted two weeks.

The day was set. One morning, after a routine flight in the original Skyrocket, Al informed me that the all-rocket launch was scheduled to go in two weeks. I had been expecting the news any day but still the sudden verification that the time was up caused the familiar wave to move up into my chest.

Now there was training to be done and the preparation for the flight kept me from thinking about the morning it would happen. I planned my defense. It was almost a matter of conditioning, a corner of my mind was devoted to the new ship 24 hours a day, releasing new possibilities for emergencies or better answers for old ones.

On the days that the crew had the Skyrocket beneath the jacked-up superfortress, I went over again the flight ritual with Jansen, rehearsing our drop plan. The flight required the protection of the pressure suit. I hadn't had it on since Dayton. Each afternoon I sat in the cockpit in all the gear, breathing under pressure in the confining, tight helmet that touched the top of the canopy. It was difficult to move my head.

At first the business of pressure breathing and trying to perform the synchronization of the flight steps I was to follow did not go easily. Pressure breathing alone required a great deal of concentration until it once more became nearly automatic. During flight it would have to be a reflex. I could not allow myself to be distracted from the rapid sequences of movements necessary to control the airplane for a second. In that second the fate of the flight could be determined. I had to be able to talk and pressure-breathe at the same time, meet emergencies, and control the ship. I practiced talking as I went through the laborious process of reverse breathing and moving the switches in proper sequence.

The daily half-hour in the cockpit, bound in the uncomfortable pressure gear, left me irritable and tired—particularly if I had not been fast enough. I worked the tension out of my muscles and nerves under the searing July desert sun in the base pool. And after 20 laps back and forth through the chlorine-saturated, eye-stinging water, I laid on the steaming edge of the pool and returned to the flight plan.

I was asking for it this time. If I busted my fanny I had asked for it. This final series of flights would take me out on the end of a long, long, fragile limb—into an unexplored area, where, up there in that water-color-blue, serene sky the invaded air can tear an airplane to pieces, where it can burst a man's guts. The engineers had measured the area with their slip-sticks and they were optimistic, but the optimism of engineers did not have a contagious effect on me. I could not fool myself. We were to jump half a Mach number, close to 1000 miles per hour. I went into these flights with doubt, but it was my own decision. Even with the pile of doubts weighing against me as it drew near I would do it because there was a chance that I would find something out there, and the promise of this possible discovery had proven a stronger lure than the lure of security.

The plane I would fly was originally designed as a transonic experimental tool. Each time that she had been pushed a little bit farther than first intended, she had measured up beyond even her designers' expectations. But now she had been given a big assignment: she was to reach for Mach numbers and altitudes no plane had ever attempted to reach. What happens to an airplane at such speed? What's out there? There was once a sound barrier that stopped the impertinent aircraft that tried to pass. What other barriers lay waiting?

Without any sustained power if she got into trouble there was no way out but down. If the lake was not beneath her she had no chance. There was also the very real possibility of "flutter" at the projected speeds—the insidious phenomenon that gives no warning—you hear it, feel it, and one of your control surfaces has snapped off; an aileron, part of the tail section, picked off by the mysterious, mocking power that so far ruled the dark area we were headed for.

She had a whole new set of insides, she carried her own potential for trouble—mechanical failure—the machine perversely resisting its function as set forth so assiduously and painstakingly by its creators. one small cog slips, an infinitesimal interruption or obstruction, and it refuses to complete the proper cycle.

These were the things I thought about in the afternoons by the pool. The engineers consulted me very little now. The flight plan was established. There had been two big decisions in formulating the map of this deep look into the supersonic—how high, how fast. As anxious as the men were to learn what was out there, they were not overly ambitious for the Skyrocket's first journey. There had been no disagreement on these questions. After the drop I would climb up to 40,000, level off, accelerate to Mach 1.5 (1100 mph) on all four tubes; when she was empty, turn her around and glide silently back home where there was only one chance at the lake bed. If the flight was successful the Skyrocket would pass Yeager's X-1 by a .10 of a Mach number, or 76 miles faster.

This afternoon and one more night and the cushion of time would be all used.

The last-minute briefing was attended to. Every man's function in the important flight was rehearsed and verified. The two-hour preflight meeting around the long metal table in the conference room, its blackboards crowded with diagrams and figures, was over. Everyone knew his job well. The pieces of the whole fitted together faultlessly.

It moved in fast now, like heavy summer storm clouds—the awareness. Four o'clock and the offices were empty; there was nothing more to be done. On the desk in front of me lay the flight plan. Two times two is four, four times four is sixteen—I knew what it read without looking at it.

Who were the enemies that I was prepared to meet, wound up tight to meet? I was more concerned about these enemies tomorrow than I ever had been about flying out against the Japs. I hadn't been alone then.

Three enemies. The Skyrocket, the unknown area, and myself. Only one of them I had the power to control completely and I had to use that control well. My mind had to be prepared for any emergency and not be distracted by that emergency. But before the face of something I had no knowledge of, could I trust myself? I had planned as far as I could foresee, but beyond that I had to rely on my judgment at the moment that the unforeseen was met.

Time, labor, hope, the key to a door aviation stands before, a 4,000,000-dollar airplane, were the investments I was responsible for. The sound in the smoke-ladened room was the hum of an electric clock. Four-thirty. A half-hour to kill before I could allow myself the comfort of a drink. Five o'clock was the hour I had set as being a respectable one for a man to be seen escaping into the officers' bar.

With all the unevenness of the ledger I still had no regret about taking the launch program; it was just the weight of waiting for the moment that was uncomfortable. For several months I had been able to avoid the sensation, 15 more hours wasn't much of a price to pay.

On the table at the place where Yeager was sitting during the meeting was a copy of *Time Magazine*. I picked it up. A big picture of Douglas MacArthur returned from Japan. A half-hour with the magazine and now I could go over to the club.

Through the bright heat into the air-conditioned, metallic-smelling dark of the club and I joined my fellow flyers at the bar. Nobody talked about his project. There was no one at the long bar with whom I could discuss tomorrow's flight, or rather the sensation of waiting for the flight. Here no one else was involved or concerned. There was no kidding like there had been at Saipan before a raid when everyone shared the same fear; when Hal Bellew would lift his glass to his chest in imitation of the captain's frequent parting words, *"Gentlemen, I don't think you'll have a bit of trouble, not a bit."* "Buzz" had been dead a long time. Miller's Reluctant Raiders once as real as this moment no longer existed. And tonight and tomorrow and the flight that confronted me would follow the squadron and its purpose in time.

The mission tomorrow was a solitary one. It was lonely in the bar.

From one cave to another through the heat between the officers' bar and the mess hall. At a table in the far corner sat George Mabry and Long John Peat. I carried my tray of roast beef, asparagus, and salad over to their table. They said little. They were ideal dinner companions tonight. George answered briefly the few questions I put to him about the flight and I floated back to the plans in my mind. John Peat, long and thin, the electrical engineer, who lived near me at the beach, told me about the lobster he picked out of the ocean last week end: "I got me a big bull last Saturday." John was a good diver.

"How about the movie tonight, Bill?" Mabry suggested, "It's pretty good, I hear. It's that Dreiser thing, *An American Tragedy*, only they call it *A Place in the Sun*."

"Sounds all right." I wanted to take another look at the Skyrocket first though. As long as somebody had a wrench on her there was a possibility of cancellation. "I'll meet you inside, I think I'll go down to the squadron first."

George looked at me curiously for a moment. "Sure, okay, Bill. We'll see you inside."

Al Carder was in the hangar watching the night crew tighten the last bolt; he assured me that the flight looked definite. There was nothing to do but wait.

Perhaps I had better sit at my desk and go over the flight again. No. I'd tried that before and it only made me fidgety. My office was empty. Mabry's idea was the best. The movie. I could forget about the flight from time to time in the movie and the place was full of people.

While Montgomery Cliff made love to Elizabeth Taylor I stopped watching the film and returned to the flight. I went through the technique of getting all the rockets lit. Okay. The scene was over and I watched the action in front of me once more. Ten minutes and I returned to the flight. I'm trying to hold Mach .8. Keep her nose down. Now here's where I start leveling off, use the stabilizer. . . . In a way, the distraction of the movie was good discipline; I forced my mind to keep the pattern. When I had finished going through the whole pattern, I went over it again, interrupting the steps by returning to the movie.

Montgomery Cliff went to the gas chamber and Elizabeth Taylor looked unscathed and extraordinarily beautiful. The movie was over.

I was tired. I couldn't drink before a flight. There was nothing to do but go to bed. I should sleep well; the heat, the big dinner, and the long, intense movie. Eleven o'clock. I turned the alarm for five. That would give me plenty of time to get into the pressure suit and be around the hangar for any last-minute decisions.

I awoke. The room was still and dark and for the first time I had slept through the Skyrocket's whistle. Sleep hung on me as I sat on the side of the bed and I thought of the people who make a living by getting up at eight o'clock. The nine-thirty majority. Today that kind of life looked good to me. I had little enthusiasm sitting here on the side of the bed, blinking against the naked little lamp. Perhaps, sleeping now somewhere, there was one or two of the nine-thirty boys who wished he were me this morning, who also had no enthusiasm for the job ahead of him.

I moved down the sparsely lit hall to the bathroom. In order to be more comfortable in the helmet I had to shave closely. The face in the mirror did not look like the face of a man about to perform an adventurous feat; it looked hopelessly like my own face. If I was to handle this flight to the best of my ability the capillaries would have to be dilated, the nerve responses ready to spring, right on the edge, not too far because at the same time it had to be easy. The army of alerted nerves had to be held in control until they were needed. It was hard to generate enthusiasm when the base was asleep, the whole world was asleep.

I returned to the face in the soap-splattered glass above the washstands.

Okay. Here's what you've always wanted. It isn't mundane. It's movement, it's freedom, and you've got it. You're to be envied. Why you're lucky, you're really going . . . you're not bound by nine-thirty-to-five. Those guys sleeping would give their two bedrooms and a den and two weeks of fishing every year to be shaving at five-thirty for a rocket flight to Mach I.5. You can always sleep!

Keep talking, you're doing fine. The only sound that broke the dead quiet of the sleeping base was the high, sustained, thin, banshee wail of the Skyrocket being primed for flight under the spread of the superfortress. Before I went over to breakfast, before I checked the wind or found Carder down at the hangar, I went out on the field to look at my plane where she was being fueled at the far end of the runway under the two-story-tall propellant-storage tanks. Half her weight today would be fuel. One of the white figures moving around the stark-white plane lashed under the huge, dark spread of the B-29 came toward me in the dawn light.

"It looks like we got a stable batch this time." The oxygen wasn't boiling badly this morning, the fueling would go faster. "You ought to be able to take off in a couple of hours." This end of the operation was holding up. We didn't need the dawn for take-off on the launch flights, we were not concerned with ground winds; it was the wind at altitude that was important to us today. Take-off had been scheduled for eight o'clock.

The sun was up full before I turned from the operation and headed for the officers' mess and breakfast. Already it was oppressively hot. The vibrating air-conditioning system was going full blast in the half-empty dining room. I was halfway through my eggs when George Jansen appeared with a cup of coffee and three doughnuts. He pulled back a chair.

"Howdy, George. Has the wind picked up any?"

"No. It's holding around 15 knots." He picked up part of the Los Angeles Times.

"I hate to see it this high so early." The front page doesn't hold my interest and briefly I glance at the full page of news pictures on page three.

Jansen looked across the sports section at me. "You been on the field?" I nodded. "How's the weather?"

"I haven't been down to the station yet. You want some more coffee?"

"No." He finished the doughnuts and got to his feet. "You finished? Let's go check the weather."

We took George's new Chevie down to the weather station. The weather, the winds aloft, would decide if we could drop and where. We continued on down to the hangar with the information. Al Carder was waiting at the door.

"For God's sake, where you two been anyway? We've got to check the weather." Carder was more noticeably tense this morning.

George interrupted him, "We've all ready got it, Al. Winds aloft have picked up—but they're out of the north."

"It's shifted, damn it! Now we're done out of the nice gradient we had yesterday . . . Better go on in and get Mabry to replot your track."

The news of the weather change didn't disturb Marby's

consistently even mood. He took the new information and rapidly filled four pages with calculations.

"Carry him out an extra 10,000 yards," he told George. "A little north of the original launch spot."

"Gad! You guys don't want much." George didn't agree. "You want 10,000 yards or 1000 yards? You sure have more faith in the weatherman than I have. Bridgeman will probably end up over Catalina . . . I hate to see him get so far from the lake bed." He ended his argument and added, "I'll split it with you . . . 5000 yards!" He waited for Mabry's answer.

The aerodynamicist was not persuaded. "Well, George," he looked down at his figures, "if you crowd him on this side, he'll have to make it up coming back."

The pilot gave up and turned to me. "I don't care; it's up to Bridge."

I went along with the aerodynamicist. Since his arrival on the base I had learned to trust Mabry. He was concerned equally with performance and safety. The pilot was concerned with safety alone. Besides I knew how far the Skyrocket would glide if the rockets failed. She could make it from where the aerodynamicist wanted to put us.

"Let's stick with Mabry. I'd rather now crowd it on this side."

"Okay!" The big pilot tossed his hand, "It's your red wagon. Let's go!"

It was time to get into the elaborate costume that was designed to protect me on the flight. Major Stum, the pressure-suit specialist, stood solicitously by as I climbed awkwardly into the long white underwear that went under the suit. He helped me with the legs of the tight uniform. It was the major's job to make sure all the lacings and zippers are properly closed. One tiny leak—in the event of a cabin-pressure failure at extreme altitudes—and my body would blow up like a balloon.

For 20 minutes I stood while the specialist fussed with the lacings. The adjustments and small movements and the standing were getting on my nerves. "That ought to do it, don't you think, Doc?" The legs were still unzipped and the top of the suit hung limply over my fanny. "We can get the rest of this monkey suit on in the plane."

An ungallant-looking explorer, I proceeded out of the hangar on to the broiling, white concrete, the top of the OD-colored suit hanging like a banana peeling. My long thin legs appeared even thinner in the lower part of the costume and were further accentuated by the large fur-lined boots on my feet. As I walked, the oxygen bottle bounced on my hip and in my hand I carried the dismantled white helmet, trailing its lines. Behind me Stum followed with the chute.

A green Douglas car was waiting. In it were Ted Just. Mabry's new assistant aerodynamicist and Jorgensen, the rocket-engine engineer form El Segundo. Jorgensen nodded good morning under his breath. A few men came out of the hangar as we climbed into the car.

Lucky me! I repeated the phrase to myself like a slap on the back and I reviewed for the one-hundredth time the steps. *Lucky me!* How did that Perry Como song go? "*Lucky, lucky, lucky me, I'm a lucky son of a gun . . .*" Persistently, like a record playing over and over again, the jogging, rhythmic Italian-derived song played in my head. "*Lucky, lucky, lucky me . . .*" We pulled up to the control tower and I took my flight papers in to the Air Force for clearance.

I am lucky to be doing this; it is a great adventure. I am in an enviable position.

Two F-86's were warming up on the flight apron as we passed by—my fighter coverage, Yeager and Everest.

On an average, engineers were taciturn: Jorgensen and Just were no exception. They had little to say and I welcomed their silence this morning as we moved toward the fueling scene. It was an hour before flight and the mechanics were in last-minute attendance around the mother plane and her hybrid charge. They wished me good morning, and in more number than usual they came forward to give me a hand up the ladder. Ralph Wells, stripped to the waist, his chest a black brown, handed me my parachute and grinned as he heard me singing out loud, "*Lucky, lucky, lucky me.*" He laughed and shook his head.

The fish-bow nose of the 29 pointed down the neat white concert squares of the flight apron toward the east into the sun. It was over-hot in the oval metal cockpit—empty, except for the Skyrocket bubbling off white steam like a tea kettle aft of us in the bomb bay, hanging low over the ground, fat and heavy with three tons of fuel. A round and sleek torpedo.

"Okay, Bill, let's get the rest of this gear on." The major began to lace me into the casing. He worked nervously over me, tightening and adjusting a hundred items. "Turn your head." He was having difficulty with the pulley arrangement that held the helmet in place. "This way a little, now." I snapped my head around irritably. It took so long to get the thing on. In the confinement of the suit and the helmet and the heat it was hard to be patient.

"Hell, Doc, you've been fumbling with that thing for five minutes. Get it on, will you?"

Through the hatchway the voices of the crew rolled up to us from under the ship. "She's carrying 5486 pounds of explosives this trip—enough to blow the whole base up."

They abruptly stopped talking as they came aboard and saw me sitting uncomfortably in the space suit, the major still fussing with the lacings. George followed them up the ladder with Vern Poupitch behind him.

"Wind's out of the east; we can go any time now. You ready?"

I nod. Jansen takes command of his ship. The major crawls down the ladder and the hatch is closed.

Out of the desert heat the B-29 carries its weird cargo and specialized crew into the cold, big sky. Forty-five minutes pass. I hear George checking the wind direction and speed at 30,000 over my earphones. While the rest of the crew continue to breathe out of their masks, I remove mine, hold my breath, and put the glass face piece into the pressure helmet. All of my body is covered now except my hands and I have begun to receive the oxygen into my lungs by pressure, I have started the reverse-breathing procedure. The struggling operation alarms the two men sitting opposite me.

Thirty-five thousand feet. Jansen turns his head and motions to me. It is time. Unsteadily I get to my feet; the line tenders rise with me. We make our way back to the Skyrocket in her drafty compartment.

The canopy is closed and I am sealed off in the Skyrocket. I have ten items to perform at once; they are the listed alphabetically on my clipboard: (a) Plug into the Skyrocket by means of the outlet hanging from the suit; (b) secure the harness and belt; (c) secure canopy latch—okay; (d) the fan has to be turned on to keep the windshield from fogging; (f) turn cabin emergency to off; (g) make the cockpit check; (h) set the stabilizer to 1.5 degrees, nose down; (i) set oxygen system; (j) activate dive brakes. Twenty minutes now and George will call the five-minute alert. So far she is all set. Her gigantic energy lies around me dormant. She is an inanimate object now, and cold as a tomb. There is no life or sound in her but my own, the pulsing of blood into my heart and the great wheezing of my lungs filling and emptying the oxygen into the helmet.

"What altitude you got, George?"

"Coming up on 30,000 feet." The sound of his voice is intensified in the barrel of a helmet.

I can feel the big plane make its turn. My head is held tightly by the enormous pressure inside the helmet. After 20 minutes the force against my temples, eyes, and ears is almost unbearable. The oxygen-outlet valve is moved up to full throttle to meet conditions all the way up to 80,000 feet. Every five seconds I let the air into my mouth, 1001, 1002, 1003, 1004, 1005. Blow it out. The climb and run will take only three or four minutes. After it is over I can take this damned thing off.

Four minutes. It is called! On my knee pad is the card listing the nine steps I follow at the four-minute warning. Although I know the list backward, I glance down at it anyway. *Pressurize the rocket system.* The dead plane will begin to stir slightly now for the enormous effort that is required of her minutes from now. The first gentle stirring of the birth trauma. She flutters. The 12 pressure dial and gauge eyelids wave up as the lever beside my leg releases a little of the restless, pent-up liquid oxygen into the fuel system with a soft, explosive whoosh-h-h. They settle in the green.

Why do I want to do this thing? "Three minutes to go, Bill." *There must be a 1000 guys who would do it. It is a huge joke that it is me, an old airline pilot! One false move and I'll blow myself all over the sky. Why aren't I on some warm beach with my ass planted in the sand?* There is no room in my mind for such idle speculation.

In a few seconds I'll need a great amount of concentration. Through the window of the face-plate I review the instrument panel in the half light.

A red flag waves! Hold it. The pressure on Number One system is dropping low in the green. *Oh my God no . . . not when we're this close.*

After all this preparation I must inform Carder of the snag. "Al, we're losing pressure in Number One system." I quickly report the failure to the men standing by on the lake, waiting for the Skyrocket to let go with all her rocket tubes and three tons of fuel. The dial, that drops a fraction then holds, then drops a fraction more, will cause the flight to be canceled.

Today is not the day. The time is not right. The system is not functioning properly—now the flight must be aborted. Next week I'll have it to face all over again.

On the ground they know the flight will be canceled but the engineers are unwilling to give up without a word. "How fast is it dropping? What's the rate of drop?"

The questions are senseless and it is with annoyance and sarcasm that I deliberately call out the rapid and futile drop of the needle: "1800, 1600, 1400, . . . do you want to drop? . . . holding steady at 1400. you want to drop?" The pressure must be between 2500 and 1800 pounds per square inch in order for the system to function efficiently.

Carder breaks it up, finally land abruptly. "Knock it off. Bring it back."

No contest. "Okay. Preparing to jettison."

Everest flying chase beside the Superfortress hears the warning and repeats. "Getting ready to jettison."

And from the ground the message is again repeated, "Getting ready to jettison." Three tons of explosives are bled into the sky—1000 dollars' worth of fuel. The superfortress leaves the area—the Skyrocket still heavy in her bomb bay—and returns to the base. No hits. No runs. No errors.

We tried it again two weeks later. At the two-minute warning a scanner in the tail section of the superfortress reported a white vapor oozing out of the turbine pump exhaust port. Carder called the show off. And so it went flight after flight for three tense, frustrating months. The winter passed and still the all-rocket experiment, the big promise, was not ready to leave the mother ship.

Twice a month it happened: the ship was readied for flight, hauled to altitude, the flight-test engineers standing attentively by 35,000 feet below us, squinting into the desert sun. But always during the last five minutes before the drop something slipped out of order—we brought it back. Each time was to be the time. Before each unsuccessful flight I went through the enervating process of screwing myself down to the ordeal that never happened. Six times in a row I repeated the ritual of getting into the pressure suit, handing my orders to the Air Force control tower, and then waiting in the freezing superfortress for the altitude where I left the rest of the crew and crawled back to the Skyrocket.

Trouble usually showed up at the four-minute warning when I pushed back the lever that pressurized the rocket system. One of the 12 round eyes that came alive among the mass of dials in front of me would waver, its needle would slip out of the green, the pressure would drop, and automatically without any conversation with the engineers below I would announce that we were aborting. Three tons of liquid oxygen and alcohol were shed into the sky, informing the base below that the big Douglas flight didn't make it again.

Most of the trouble, we discovered, was caused by extreme low temperatures, minus 50 degrees, at altitude where the rocket system was expected to perform. The warm sea-level air caught in the system on the ground would condense and freeze during the 45-minute grind to altitude, blocking the lines and fouling up the check valves. A faulty reading or a sudden drop of the needle on one of the pressure gauges would register on the panel. Patiently the bugs were worked out of the intricate, highly sensitive engine. The line-freezing problem was combated before we left the ground by blowing dry gas through the systems to get rid of any moisture that might have settled there during the night. All control valves were removed from any low spot on the lines where moisture would tend to collect. Painstakingly the engineers worked the trouble out of the system as the trouble was discovered.

If the flights weren't aborted at the last minute before the "count down," they were stopped on the ground. Al would catch something out of order and cancel the flight—the wind, cloud coverage, the B-29's engines. Carder had the final word; his word remained firm. The plane wasn't going to drop until conditions were perfect. The strain of the enormous responsibility that weighed upon the project coordinator showed those mornings of flight; he chewed aspirins like jelly beans as he paced up and down the lake bed waiting for word from his crew up in the sky for another try.

After the third abort my two celebrated chase pilots, Yeager and Everest up to shepherd the big event were already bored with the delays. Yeager answered when I called over to the Air Force hangar for the chase planes on the fourth try. "You think you're going to get it done?" he drawled, but he was up for the flight. It was the last time. After the fourth failure Yeager and Everest didn't show up again when we put in the call for chase planes. There was no point in getting up at dawn to watch the Skyrocket jettison her fuel flight after flight. The Air Force sent in the second string to ride herd on the big Douglas project that never came off.

Our troubles were no secret. No one connected with the Skyrocket program escaped the wisecracks and kidding that the rest of the base aimed at the sagging project. At first we met the onslaught with mild amusement, but as the flights continued to meet with failure the repartee began to hit home.

The merriment boys hit their peak the morning we found a carefully lettered sign, a foot tall, tacked to the hangar wall: *Old Skyrockets Never Die—They Just Jettison Away.* Nobody laughed much.

It became a frustrating chore for me to prepare myself for the flight and I approached them with waning zeal. The thing was never going to drop. It was a dangerous attitude. An experimental test pilot has to be right on the edge, at the peak of his performance; and the delay was sapping this capacity. It became more and more necessary to simulate the important physical and mental state that was mandatory for a successful flight.

Added to my growing irritability a half-doubt began to gnaw

at me. Perhaps I was being too careful; perhaps, subconsciously, I didn't want it to drop at all. So it was a little low in the green, maybe it would not have any effect on the flight. There was always a temptation to drop anyway. No. It has been established by the engineers concerned with the power plant that the ship is in danger if the pressures drop below the green margin. I was becoming extremely touchy about my last-minute decisions to abort. Carder seemed aware of the conflict and he went out of his way to reassure me, to let me know that he approved of my judgment. "You're right, Bill. Don't do it until it's right," persistently he repeated. Despite his confidence I became grateful for the recording devices. The reasons of abort were all there; there could be no room for doubt. Although no one ever questioned my decision, there it was in black and white and on the film. The pressures failed. There it was for anyone to check.

Toward the end of the barren three months I began to argue with Carder when he called off a flight on the ground. There were times, I convinced myself, that I could handle the situation that he considered dangerous. His answer would be unequivocal: "Don't do it until it's right."

His engineers, edgy with waiting, became increasingly impatient and they began to press him more. "Come on, Al. It's a far chance. God, we'll never get it in the air." Carder remained firm. In a testing program the project coordinator has the last word.

Arguments were sprouting like leaks in an old water hose. Although the men in the Douglas' flight-test offices were often impatient and sorely tried by the constant and frustrating failures, they were merely letting off steam in arguments with the project coordinator and each other: not one of them would take a chance on the lives of the ten men in the flight crew in order to hurry up the program. Primarily they were concerned with safety, just as Carder was.

Tension in his own group wasn't all Al Carder faced. The Santa Monica office was becoming alarmed. The contract extension we had received from the Navy called for three successive drops and light-offs in the all-rocket D-558-II. Three months had gone by and we hadn't made any progress toward that goal. There was a firm budget for the project and the contract money was dwindling fast. Soon the Navy was going to be on the company's back for some action. It was a bad situation all the way around. Still Carder conducted the program his way. He hadn't lost a plane and he wasn't going to, no matter how much pressure was put upon him.

After the reports of the fifth abort passed over his desk, Hoskinson emerged from the head office at Santa Monica to make one of his infrequent trips to the Fight Test Center. He came up to see first hand why the D-558-II program was falling on its face.

"What's the matter? You didn't drop *again*?" Hoskinson was accustomed to programs running into delays and snares. No testing program was ever known to move flawlessly. But this program was giving him the most trouble of any he had had in a long time. Perhaps something wasn't coming over his desk and he was anxious to find out if everything was running properly or, if not, where the program was coming apart.

During his visit every phase of the Skyrocket project was under scrutiny. The records, the film, the charts, were pulled out for his inspection and an informal inquiry took place. It was all there. The chief of the testing division couldn't find any holes. The inquiry revealed a lot of bad luck. An unsatisfactory answer! Something was wrong somewhere. Perhaps the program was too cautious.

"Let's get this thing on the road," he warned. "You know, you can to *too* careful. It's good to be conservative, but you can carry it *too* far." It wasn't hard for Carder to understand Hoskinson's point of view. The testing of airplanes has never been known as a safe bet. That's the business. So you lose a pilot—it happens every day.

Besides it was a time of emergency, it was wartime, the information was badly needed. Already at Edwards during the last nine months the Air Force had lost 62 pilots testing aircraft that were earmarked for Korea. They were losing pilots over there too.

Still the Skyrocket was a tremendous investment and Carder's approach was wise—if it paid off. Hoskinson wanted to make sure that it did—and soon.

A flight came up the morning after Hoskinson arrived. He was very much on hand to watch it unroll for the sixth time. It was the same flight plan we had had on the last five attempts.

The tedious procedure was repeated again. This time the weather stopped us. It was overcast. The head of flight testing was impatient with this latest delay and he saw no reason why we couldn't drop through the soup. The company, the Navy, were on his back and we balked at a little overcast. George and I were in Carder's office with the report. "What the hell, you can get through that, can't you?" he demanded.

I wasn't into the suit yet. "How about ice?" I reminded him.

"You'll be going fast enough to shake that off . . ." he was convinced.

The coffee I held was cold. "I wouldn't bet on it." This was one time that Carder wouldn't need to convince me. George backed me up.

"I wouldn't bet on it either. It's pretty risky stuff."

Again we didn't fly.

Two weeks later Hoskinson reappeared for the sixth take-off of the reluctant experiment. This time he got to see the show proceed all the way up to the scheduled altitude of 35,000 feet. Forty-eight minutes of climbing and one of the chase planes reported a fire warning and bowed out. in a weary voice Carder called, "Well, check and see how soon we can get another chase plane."

"Ten minutes." Ten minutes meant 20 minutes.

"Al, by the time the chase get up we'll lose a hell of a lot of propellant. Everything's holding up. I can make it with one." For the first time in six trips the systems were behaving. We were so close. But long ago on the ground Al had decided that the flight would have two chase planes, come hell or high water.

"Forget it, Bill. Hang on, wait for the chase."

"But Al . . ."

"You heard me!"

Forty-eight gallons of liquid oxygen had already boiled away on the grind to altitude and this delay would cause a greater loss. It had been figured that the 48 gallons would shorten the speed run by 25 seconds—a loss of a quarter of a Mach number, or 165 mph in the total speed in the run.

Fifteen minutes later the chase plane that was on its way to replace its stricken sister reported that his engine was surging and he was heading back down. That did it.

"Okay, Bill, bring it back," Carder ordered resignedly. Once more I tried to talk him into letting me go.

"Bring it back, I said." Carder was firm.

The flight was canceled and the disheartening call to jettison was given.

The B-29 carried the Skyrocket back home again for the sixth time and taxied slowly into the NACA parking apron next to the Douglas hangar. The entourage of engineers had come in from the lake bed and were waiting solemnly to meet us.

Hoskinson said nothing about the abort this time as he walked with me back to the hangar. He was quiet. The rest of the crew moved on into Carder's office, but Hoskinson stayed behind in the hangar, beside the lockers, and watched as I unwrapped myself from the suit. I had the top half undone when Hoskinson put his hand on my shoulder, "You're losing a little weight, aren't you? Nothing's that serious."

I was unprepared and had no reply. Hoskinson slapped me on the arm and forced a jovial tone. ""That's the way it is in testing. Just keep at it until it works. Don't worry about it." He turned and walked off quickly down to Carder's office.

NACA's representatives tactfully kept an official eye on us and our run of bad luck. They were ready on every level to receive the airplane. And it was obvious that the committee wouldn't be opposed to the idea of making their own records in her. When and if they did, the glory would be NACA's and not the Navy's. And if we weren't successful soon nobody expected the Navy to go along with us much longer. The Navy Bureau of Aeronautics wasn't going to pour money down a rathole. The conclusion would be that Douglas just didn't have it and that NACA might as well take over sooner than had been expected.

There was one record that the Douglas project could point to— Carder's show had never lost a Skyrocket; the slate was as clean as a new sheet of paper.

To make up for the terrific loss in time caused by the aborts the mechanics worked in around-the-clock shifts, the flight-test engineers sat at their metal desks late into the night, smoothing the way for the reluctant Skyrocket. No matter how weary and disappointed the crew of mechanics became, they prepared their ship pains-takingly as always, they performed their duties exactingly, as if every time she was rolled from the hangar it was for a triumph. And with determination that each time would be the lucky time, the plotters of the experiment, confident that they had searched out every possibility for failure, stationed themselves optimistically out on the baked, dead lake to wait for the results.

And I was the performer who never was allowed to perform. It was rather an ironic joke that I couldn't have dropped when I was at my peak, when I was ready. Now when the day came the flight would catch me worn thin by the three months of aborts. The pressure suit fitted more loosely than before and had to be laced in tighter, just as the reality of the flight plan began to fit more loosely. I approached the flights with resignation.

Three months ago when we embarked on the ambitious program that would prove the Skyrocket to be the fastest plane in the world Al Carder, waiting out on the barren lake bed for the news of our first attempt at the big adventure, paced restlessly up and down, and as he paced he picked up burned-out cartridges that lay scattered on the parched, gray floor from gunnery practice in the last war. He carefully saved these shells in a large box that he kept inside the hangar. We were coming up on the seventh attempt to send the Skyrocket blasting through the sky and the big trunklike box was half full.

CHAPTER XIX

Test Flight Number 24 Navy D-558-II. April 5, 1951. Two years with the Skyrocket, two springs in the desert. This morning would be the seventh time that we'd try to ram our way into the unknown—beyond the sound barrier. Only we moved toward the flight like streetcar conductors making the same tedious run.

A sight that once seemed an enormity to me now seemed ordinary. The Skyrocket half borne from the superfortress did not appear out of order, and the equipment I wore no longer seemed a curious costume to me or the rest of the crew. It looked as if we would be able to take off this morning. The wind was holding steady, the sky was clear, the 29's engines were functioning. Once more I had to manufacture the tension that I would need for the flight ahead.

George's volunteer crew dressed in Air Force surplus had learned to handle their oxygen masks well, the uncertainty they first displayed was gone. In three months they were veterans of an unfulfilled mission. The line tenders on the long, cold climb were like men riding a subway—they looked out the window, at me, at the pilots, and back out the window.

On the long path up I review the flight to assure myself that it is still securely locked in my mind, still ready to be put into effect if this time I drop. The navigator's altimeter above my head to the right reads 25,000 feet. In the drafty forward compartment of the vibrating, roaring bomber boring her way up through the minus-50-degree-below-zero sky the cold penetrates the cloth of the pressure suit that is tightly bound to my legs. I slap my thighs and fold my arms over my chest. The exertion of the movement has forced me to let the air in faster from the helmet. The water should be beginning to warm up at Hermosa now.

I cannot allow myself to sit here leisurely thinking of the week end ahead of me. There is the flight. Twenty minutes from now I may need all the help i can get. I force myself to go over the emergency procedures and my mind wanders back to the week end.

Twenty-eight thousand feet! Here's where I get off. This is my street. I get to my feet—thump Jansen on the shoulder to let him know I'm vacating his ship fro the seventh time. George bends around and without inspiration lifts his hand in a ribald gesture and shouts over the roar, rattling through the compartment, "*Gentlemen,*" and in a precise imitation of Hal Bellew he recites, "*I don't think you'll have a bit of trouble. Not a bit.*"

How the hell did he get a hold of that? It is with great amusement that George watches my face as he repeats the familiar and faraway imitation of "Buzz" Miller's nostalgic salutation before a difficult strike. But the line tenders are beside me ready to convoy me back to the Skyrocket, and I turn away without asking where he heard the line. As I do Jansen drops the rest of it: "*Go get 'em, Tiger.*"

Today we are going to drop. I know it. I am ready for it. My hands run over the familiar knobs, levers, and buttons. I follow the

26 steps necessary for a cockpit check. Test the fire warning circuit . . . circuit breakers down . . . set the oxygen system . . . call the chase planes . . . check with Carder . . . check with Jansen. I move the switch that will set the stabilizer to 1.5 degrees, nose down, and I open and close my dive brakes. Performing the familiar tasks that set things in order, I prepare the plane for the flight.

"*Five minutes.*" Change over oxygen to the Skyrocket's limited supply. Apply full pressure into the helmet. I'm under water now, breathing laboriously. Instrumentation power switch on. Okay. I release the valve that pressurizes the cabin for 35,000 feet.

"*Four minutes.*" Here is where we can meet trouble if there is to be any. Turn rocket master switch to on. Pressurize rocket system.

The rocket pressure gauges are all in the green. The 12 dials are in an even line and appear to be holding. Catalyst temperature okay. *Maybe this is it!* This is as far as we have ever come. I am expectant and alert and the tension automatically increases and without any effort now I am on the edge.

"Fifty seconds!"

The stream of practice steps continues to flow ahead without interruption, building in momentum, and I hurry along before them. Prime the rocket system, twist the knobs, turn the levers, read the dials, 12 of them—the pulse of the pressures wrapped up aft to me in the bullet fuselage. This must e it. This is the time!

In the twilight of the B-29's belly the black faces on the pressure gauges command my attention. The white, quivering needles are holding and I watch them intently as a fakir with a cobra weaving in front of his flute.

Then the white sliver on the middle gauge slips out of line! Number Three system pressure is weakening and as the needle drops a plug has been pulled and I am suddenly drained. Again we must abort!

"No drop. This is an abort." That's that. I yank the circuit breakers up, shut off the valve beside me that puts the rocket system back to sleep, and begin to secure the plane. As I do I hear, with disbelief, George starting his ten-second count-down as if he had not heard my order to cancel the flight.

"Ten, nine . . . ," slowly he calls off the seconds.

I shout through my throat-mike, "Don't drop me, George." But his voice doesn't stop and the count continues in my ears as I frantically repeat, "Aren't you receiving me? Don't drop me; the pressure on Number Three system has failed." No response.

". . . eight, seven," the steady count moves on unperturbed. I can't break through. George has his thumb on the key. He does not hear my frantic protestings. Now as I futilely shout into the helmet in the hope that he takes his thumb off the mike key between seconds, I work furiously to reinstate the ship for flight.

It is an accelerated, precise scramble. With both fists I pound the board of circuit breaker buttons down into their holes, move the stick to neutral.

The hollow voice of the pilot drones on, ticking off the seconds, ". . . five, four . . ." And still I try to get through, to break the count.

"Don't drop." There is no doubt. No getting out now. He is going to let me go.

Am I forgetting anything; God, am I forgetting anything? I force myself to retrace the steps I performed to inactivate the Skyrocket— although I know there is not enough time, before I am dropped, to thoroughly retrace the steps, to see if I have opened all the right doors that a minute ago I closed. Swiftly I start at the beginning to go over the movements that will bring her back to life. There are some big decisions to be made in three seconds . . . whether or not to hit the first rocket switch and take a chance on her blowing all over the sky or whether to jettison the load of fuel that will allow me a longer chance at gliding home. To jettison the fuel is bad: if only one tank empties she will lose her balance. *Make up your mind, quick.*

"Three . . . two . . . one . . . *drop!*"

Time's up. The bright light of the world bursts over my eyes as I plunge through the trap door from the protective, dark gut of the sheltering bomber and the traffic is moving. I'm thrown into the middle of the sky-sea without a life belt. It's a living, moving world, where the Skyrocket must be alive. She is dropping fast with her heavy load—15,650 pounds of pure rocket, silent as a bird dropped by a hunter, straight down with no control of her own yet.

A living ting! I think of my father. I remember what he said the day he came down to see me off to Pensacola, when he offered me the armament of his 30 years in the air. He told me about airplanes.

"You can't think of an airplane solely as a piece of machinery, Bill; she isn't. She's a living thing. Her world's the sky and when you get her up there she wants to fly, she wants to live. Thousands of man-hours have created an intricate nervous system that makes her want to fly, that compels her to; the man who controls her can keep her from her function, the pilot's the villain. Now if the pilot doesn't panic, if he trusts her and presses all the right buttons, she'll fly!"

The airman—my father, whom I barely knew, who had spent his life in a plane—finished his offering to me, "Go ahead. Go ahead and be a pilot . . . only remember someday it's going to get real deep . . . maybe you won't meet it for a long time, but just keep flying and it'll happen." It was pretty deep right now, so deep so fast that it was almost a joke.

I reach for the first rocket switch! Six seconds pass before the explosion, before the rocket blasts on with a giant reassertion. She lives! And hopefully and thankfully I click on the rest of the tubes as fast as possible. The force slams in . . . Number Two, *slam* . . . Number Three, *slam* . . . Number Four . . . she is accelerating with all the power in the world blasting her on. She's a living thing! A big hunk of energy that wants to go somewhere. Twenty-five seconds and 3000 feet down from where George spewed me helplessly into the sky, she begins to shallow out. The rockets have lit miraculously enough, but I don't expect them to last long with the pressure low in Number Three. But as long as they are burning I will follow the flight pattern.

Tentatively and timidly I point the long bayonet nose upward. It quivers. Too much! She's on the edge of stall according to the vibrating pole that I use as a stall indicator. If I feel around too long for the correct angle she'll burn up her fuel before I reach the pushover altitude of 45,000 feet—the altitude, planned to keep her Mach number down to 1.5, where I will begin the speed run.

Forty-five degrees. We are around the corner, sucked up through a hole in the sky, accelerating fantastically, and it requires a great deal of attention to hold her at her climbing speed that will eventually run into Mach .85, the number I will hold on the Machmeter until the indicated air speed falls to stalling speed. In the thin, sheer air, shooting for the top, the air speed falls off now as the Mach .85 holds steadily on the Machmeter. My eyes move back and forth between the indicated air speed and Machmeter. When the indicated air speed drops to 230, I hold the speed on the gauge and let the Mach number move up on its own. And as it does the thrust grabs hold positive and powerfully. This is complete freedom and detachment. This is the world and I'm the only living thing in it, running away from pain, boredom, desire, and fear.

And then I remember, as if they were people I left a long time ago, the crew. No more than 35 seconds have passed since George dropped me. There is a second to call now that the steps are successfully and wondrously following the pattern. It seems an enormously long time since I have opened my mouth to speak.

"Goddam it, George, I *told* you not to drop me." The words are ridiculously inadequate and without purpose.

Pete Everest, up for the first time in months, laughs somewhere in the sky in his F-86 and his is the first voice I hear, "You got keen friends, Bridgeman . . ."

Then Carder's shaky voice: "How's he doing, Pete?"

"He's accelerating away from me in a climb. Looks like he's doing all right . . . all four rockets appear to have lit off."

The patient is rallying. Carder is relieved, but he will have to wait approximately ten minutes before he will get any news from me. I am busy. He doesn't call to me.

The radio is silent and the altimeter hand is a whirring pinwheel as I hang on to the Skyrocket on her way out of this world. Mach 1 . . . she doesn't react as she does at a lower altitude and the sky is still as she runs away from the speed of sound, a rocket ripping through space, carrying a pilot that is audaciously put there to control the trip. She feels like she is never going to quit, like she is going clear out the top.

I follow the plan that I have carried in my head these last three months. She is to pick up five tenths of a Mach number, almost a third faster than she has ever demonstrated. Up until this minute I have crossed into the shallow end of the supersonic region and then backed out quick. Now I am all the way in and I will be here until the fuel burns up. I can barely read my altitude with the altimeter

100-foot hand a revolving blur obscuring the 1000-foot and 10,000-foot hands.

I move the stick forward to control the angle of climb. The control stick moves loosely forward without effort. It's as if the cables have been cut. There is no response! She won't be controlled at this speed by ordinary means; the elevators are useless, completely ineffective. I have anticipated this reaction at sustained supersonic speed, but the helpless feeling of holding a stick in your hands that can be moved back and forth forcibly with no effect at all on the ship is a sickening surprise at 800 miles a hour.

It has been by feel that I have flown an airplane. By putting the right amount of pressure on the stick I've produced a desired amount of G. It has become a matter of conditioning. It is like being part of the ship—one of its reflexes. By feel I have prevented my plane from stalling out—it comes through my fingers, I can sense it. Now all this conditioning is no good to me; the feel isn't there. In order to direct her a more rigid control is needed to stand up to the terrific forces at supersonic speed. I must fly her with the stabilizer that I move electrically by means of a small switch. I must fly by a switch, trust a switch that gives you no feel, no warning. If I move it too far I can instantly put enough G on the plane to black myself out. Subsonically, movement of the control column brings a gentle response—there is a big displacement and little action. But not here. The little switch I fly by has a subtle displacement and a gigantic reaction.

A ghost control takes over the silent ship. It is a matter now of moving a tiny switch and reading the 86 dials and lights before me that register the functions, the automatic warnings, temperatures, and myriad reactions imposed upon the Skyrocket as she is shoved off the edge of the cliff.

The rocket-cylinder seconds are running out. Twenty seconds remain for the push over the top. I watch the fire warning devices, and I listen. If I detect the buzz of flutter on the controls immediately I will cut off the rockets.

We are at the top, 45,000 feet, or close to it.

Beneath the blurring altimeter needle I try to figure the altitude. *Z.zz-zut, zut, zut,* I move the electric switch to direct the plane over into her run at three tenths of a G, and as she begins the long arc over the top I am lifted up from my seat and my body grows lighter by the second as I approach zero G. A white, blazing bullet in the bright blue around her, the Skyrocket shoots through the lonely, silent sky, accelerating over the rim of the pushover, blasting toward the shallow dive. All the black dials before me are shifting, changing, and whirling. I fly by only one now—the accelerometer that is measuring the degree of G I am putting on the ship. The G hand holds steady on .3 and briefly I move my eyes from the gauge to see the Machmeter dial moving up 1.2 . . . 1.25 . . . *what the hell is this?* The action is unreal, incomprehensible. A helpless feeling; my body, light as a balloon, oscillates from side to side with the ship. I grab the stick to dampen the gyration, but the ailerons have little effect and the ominous rocking continues.

Before fear has a chance to set in solidly the Skyrocket is in the sloping dive and steady once again. The Mach needle reaches toward 1.3 and I hang on and wait for the rockets to quit . . . 1.32 . . . 1.38 . . . 1.4 . . . plowie . . . she decelerates in the brick wall as one rocket cuts off and slam, slam, slam, the other tubes follow, pulling me violently into the instrument panel. One by one I hear them sputter off as I lay jammed tight against the wall of whirling dials, and then she is silent and powerless once more, pointing her way across the sky following the path she was directed along.

My recovery has to be quick; every second is an important one. The steps must be followed, to delay can be awkward. I pick myself off of the panel and move her into a 3-G climbing turn, as scheduled on my map, toward the south end of the lake, using four degrees of horizontal stabilizer until I reach a set air speed. There is no time to experience any relief at completing the important mission of the day's flight. Ahead of me waits the dead-stick landing and on the way home I am to pick up added data—slide-slips and constant-speed runs. I have planned to pick them up in a box pattern over the lake as I glide down.

Data! Oh God, no! None of the flight has been recorded. Under pressure of the unexpected drop I have neglected to turn on the data switch. The flight has brought home no information for the men who wait on the ground. It is as if she hadn't dropped again.

The radio speaks. "Fifteen thousand." Mabry prompts me. "Dump the cockpit."

Fifteen thousand feet and I pull the plug. In an instant the cockpit pressure equalizes to that surrounding the airplane; it is like an explosive decompression, as it was in the tank at Wright-Patterson Aero Medical Laboratory. A heavy blow in the chest that forces a loud gasp deep out of my insides and at the same time the pod is filled with a white fog that evaporates at once.

Now it is safe to take away the face-plate. After 20 minutes of confinement in the big helmet, the pressure squeezing my head in a tight grip, I have the delicious relief of a man coming up to the surface after being under water too long. I drink in a long gulp of air and savor the experience of breathing normally. There is no time to just sit and breathe luxuriously the pure air. Already Mabry is checking the steps to be taken in preparation for the dead-stick, 175-mile-an-hour landing three minutes away from me.

The air splits by the canopy like a river around a rock in its path. It whistles mournfully at the seams that seal the cockpit, and there is not another sound in the world. Silently the hushed rocket eats through 7000 feet in a gradual descent toward the position I have, months before, plotted on the map that is now clipped to my knee. The spot marked is three miles out from the lake and 7000 feet above it. This is where I will move out on the downwind leg of my landing. There is no alternative now. Only one way. Down.

Okay, junior. There it is! Below me is the bean-shaped lake bed, the sanctuary that I aim for. Between me and the rest of the world lie 7000 feet of booby traps where a slight miscalculation can be embarrassingly fatal. I talk to myself. The sound of my voice helps to break the tension. *You're three miles out from the lake bed. You're at 310 miles per hour. Slow it up, get the gear down.* A detached "other" mind begins to direct the show.

The chase pilot is beside me and he calls, "Gear shows. Appears to locked down." Reluctantly I head away from home on the long downwind leg of my approach. It must e just the right length—not too far, not to close. The altitude is gradually being used up and she is dropping closer to the ground. There is an uncomfortable tightness in my chest as I leave behind me the only island I can safely land on.

Perhaps I am going too far. *Don't be a kid.* My judgment remains firm despite the little panicky wave. *Simmer down. You're doing all right.* Behind me the lake has melted away in the flat, nubby-textured desert bottom. I can no longer see it.

Okay. This is far enough, stupid. Where are you going to land— Palmdale? Steadily she is using up the protective altitude and the color of the spring desert is now clearly defined: the cactus stands out like warning figures waving their arms. It is with some relief that I move her into the turn for the base leg. By the way she reacts to the wind that she is now nosed into I can gauge the distance home. It gives little resistance. The wind is weak today. My turn is a wide one.

"Don't forget the data switch on the landing, Bill," Mabry interrupts me. The radio links me with the control tower, the chase planes, and the little knot of men on the lake bed. All other radio traffic on the base and in the sky was halted when Douglas' 558-II left the 29. Every plane in the area will have to wait until she is back on the ground before receiving their landing or take-off instructions. Everest reserves any advice on how to handle the dead-stick landing. He sits quietly by off my right wing, waiting.

Forty-five hundred feet. One mile straight ahead sprawls the big, safe, empty lake. I am committed. I've got to be right the first time. I cannot change my mind now and go around again. How big an S turn will put me on? Damn little wind. *Make up your mind quick. Take it out a little, bright boy. Widen it up!* Eight hundred feet below the scrubby hard bottom rushes by in a blur. There is the runway. I "S" back on to it. *Not bad, not bad. Looks pretty damn good, Bridge.* Two hundred feet and I am over the edge of the lake, looking ahead at the mile marker coming at me. Peter keeps me company; he is right at my side. He moves in and reads off the distance that separates the silent rocket shell from the runway.

"A good attitude, Bill. You got about ten feet. Let her down a little more. Now a little more, on down . . .five feet . . . one. Hold what you got. That's a boy!" And he proclaims the reassuring fact, "You got seven long miles of runway ahead of you, boy."

A great, big beautiful margin. She touches the bumpy, hard surface at 175 miles an hour. She's down! I have made all the right decisions and adjustments and I got the right answer. There is no time to congratulate myself. I've got to guide this thing along the lake bed. Far ahead of me, dragging rows of dust behind them, the fire trucks and ambulance turn in to meet me. And, as always, instead of continuing along a straight path, I point the Skyrocket's needle-nose directly at them. They veer wildly from their course, scattering like chickens in a barnyard. The sight of the scurrying fire trucks is enormously funny.

"Thanks, Pete."

"My pleasure," Everest sweeps out the words. He skims across the deck over the bewildered group of trucks, points up, and heads north to the Air Force runway. Radio traffic resumes. Life begins again around me.

"The D-558-II is on the lake bed," the control tower announces and at once the radio crackles with calls.

"Nine-ten to control tower requests landing instructions . . ."

"Control tower to 558, the fire chief would like you to release the trucks as soon as you can. We've got a project ready to go on the north side of the lake that needs them."

Mabry manages to break through the jam-up of calls; "Bill, cut the data switch off."

Three miles of runway behind her. She is rolling at 20 miles an hour to a stop and I open the canopy. The hot, clean desert air washes over my face and the white flash-bulb brightness of the lake bed bursts into my eyes. Now she is motionless. It is over. Everything is done; the chain of steps is completed. There is no emergency to anticipate, no race to keep the steps moving. I have nothing to remember. Remembering and anticipating are no longer tools needed to stay alive and to keep my ship in its original state. The muscles in my legs and arms begin to slack, the thing that has gripped me begins to let go a little but it will take a day to get rid of the whole armament.

The eighth time—a mistake—and she did it. The tension was put to use at last. Sitting alone, motionless, slumped in the cockpit with the placid, now-comforting desert holding me on all sides, it is a rich and full moment.

The moment was soon over. Around the burned-out rocket shell that was now the last mutation of the Skyrocket, the trucks and cars converged. The men ran toward me. Two were on the platform to receive my gear and lift me out of the tight cockpit. It was impossible to leave the ship unassisted. I was like a medieval man in armor that had to be hoisted from his horse. Tommy Briggs helped extricate my head from the helmet. The skin around my neck burned from the rubber-glove, tight hood that served as a lining for the rest of the helmet. My ears stung with the release of pressure. Now they lifted me out. I wore a calmly detached air.

At the bottom Carder waited excitedly. "What happened, for God's sake?"

I explained the communication difficulty and the subsequent drop in the most matter-of-fact voice I was able to summon. Ted Just and George Mabry joined the circle. The project coordinator turned to them briefly.

"We're sure as hell going to get that straightened out," he warned. His face was florid and he fixed his attention on me as if I might suddenly disappear. There was urgency in his questions.

"God, you dropped a long way before the rockets lit off . . . was there any malfunction there? Did you run into trouble getting them fired?"

My job was over. I'd brought in the ship. I'd met and solved the problems the test presented and I wanted to get away from the airplane and the post-mortem. I was hungry, hot, and tired. But the flight-test engineers' problems had just begun and they urgently wanted to know what those problems were. The only practical justification for the 15 minutes I had just returned from were the answers that I would give these men. And although I would repeat for them what happened—and they would look at the film, today nothing but miles of blank lines on the oscillograph—only I could go back to the reality of the flight. They were an audience watching stoic players on a film with no sound. No one could hear the noise of my breath forcing into the helmet or feel the awful doubt the oscillating movement of the plane released. The reality of the flight existed with me alone.

"The rocket system worked all right, Al. The reason they were so late in lighting was because it took a little while to get organized after George let me go. I had the whole thing shut down for the day as he started counting."

We moved toward the car, away from the spent Skyrocket glittering in the heat and surrounded by the corps of pleased engineers who were smiling and talking among themselves with the relief and reserved pride of men greeting a son returned unharmed from a battlefront. They pointed to the spots where the paint had been worn away by the high speed she had just reached. In little groups they dispersed for the cars, as they saw us preparing to leave. The rocket engineers would ride with us and they followed over to Carder's car.

Mabry walked along one side of me, Carder on the other. The assistant commented again, "You really dropped a long way before they lit. Like a bomb you dropped. What Mach number did you hit?"

"Around 1.4, I guess, after I got it bent over. I don't remember." I wanted to tell George about the roll, ". . . but you know it felt funny in the climb, it seemed to want to roll laterally and the ailerons didn't want to control it. Didn't seem effective! Then the rudder seemed to oscillate. But it wasn't so much an oscillation as it kind of hunted back and forth. It's peculiar. You're controlling the ship all right with all this business, but you don't know what action is doing the controlling—you're making so many adjustments. It was like she was flying me!"

A doctor passively listening to symptoms, George offered no opinion or reaction and he asked the obvious question I knew he would ask next.

"Hmmmm-mm. Any sudden trim change?"

The question irritated me. If there had been any trim change I would have told him. "No, no . . . if I could tell you exactly I would. It's . . . it's eerie."

In the car the rocket engineers listened with only a little interest. When I had finished, Jorgensen was ready with his question.

"When did the pressure nose-dive on you, Bill?"

"Just before the ten-second count."

He leaned further into the back seat; "What did it drop to?"

"Went down to 1800 pounds."

"Boy, when it starts down it really unwinds. Did you get a good clean light-off?"

I nodded.

"Well, I'll be darned." Then he turned to Bob Osborne sitting next to him: "I hope the oscillograph worked. I'm anxious to see those records."

I didn't bother to tell Jorgensen now that there was no record. That fact would be discovered soon enough.

The Skyrocket's success, at last, had a pronounced effect on the engineers. Already they were anxious to go deeper and soon; they were optimistic now and my complaint about her strange behavior caused them no alarm. They attributed the Skyrocket's gentle complaint to a high Mach-number effect. There was no other plane to compare symptoms with, the Skyrocket was all by herself in an unknown area. There were bound to be some new reactions on the part of the explorer. As long as she was controllable and was able to bring back the data, the test engineers would be satisfied.

Nobody slept on the way back to the hangar and breakfast. Conversation was animated and punctuated with limp jokes that were met with appreciative laughter. The Skyrocket program was moving again and big days lay ahead. The men who planned her future had potentially the most phenomenal performing airplane in existence. They were sure she could beat the world's fastest plane, the X-1, by half a Mach number. The new contract called for two more successful drops and light-offs in a row. And that was all—not much time to conclusively prove that she could do it.

The car pulled to a stop outside of the hangar and the men waited, the doors open in the shade, while I went inside to get rid of the pressure-suit casing.

Jansen was standing in front of his locker putting away his gear. He was caught off guard. I waited to see what he would say. George was obviously suffering but the "General" did not apologize. Instead he protested, "Why, hell, if I hadn't of dropped you we'd never have gotten rid of you . . . we'd all be old men."

The crazy bastard was running true to form, always on the offensive no matter what happened.

"Brother!" I needled him, ". . . I don't think you'll have a bit of trouble. Now there's the misstatement of the year. Where'd you get a hold of that line anyway? You reading my mail or something?"

"Oh that," George warmed up a little. "I just happened to slop up a couple of martinis with an old sailor friend of yours . . . guy called Hal Bellew."

"My God!"

"Yeah. How about that? I ran into this character last week end at Johnny Wilson's *Ready Room* uptown. We have a couple of drinks and eventually, after kicking it around a while, I find out he's an old fly-buddy of Bridgeman's." Jansen, recovered, moved into the pilot's room. "He gave me a number for you to call next time you're in town. It's here someplace in my desk."

It would be good to see Hal again. Together we could celebrate the first lap of my journey. There was something to celebrate; after all, I had met the enemy tentatively and I no longer had to guess what it was going to be like. There was a reality on which to base my defense. The reality was vividly in my mind. I could shut my eyes and I was back in the Skyrocket, trying to keep the steady rhythm of supplying my lungs with oxygen. And I could feel the creeping fear all over again when she began her strange, gentle rolling. She still had a long way to go. This was just the beginning. I looked forward eagerly to the week end and my old buddy Hal Bellew. But right now the engineers waited outside in the heat with more questions.

CHAPTER XX

Unceremoniously the Rocket was returned to her berth. She had finally done it and her appearance in the late morning, moving slowly across the Air Force runway, announced to the NACA hangar next door that at last she had flown—a fact that no doubt caused the expectant advisory committee to diplomatically reshuffle their plans at a time when it began to look possible that the Navy might give up and let them take over the airplane.

NACA had been fairly confident they were going to get her soon. Now they would not be so optimistic.

Two weeks passed before McNemar and the crew had her back in shape—with a whole new skin of paint. The high Mach number had worn her thin in spots and 15 layers of lacquer were needed to make her coat sleek enough to add an extra one hundredth of a Mach number to her total speed.

With only two more flights left to demonstrate her potential, the flight plotting was focused on performance—more speed. Next trip I was to push her over at 40,000 feet—5000 feet higher than the first time. The increase in altitude would give us the higher Mach numbers the engineers were so anxious to get. I okayed their plan; theoretically it was conservative enough.

But I was uncertain. She waited for me alone, a dead-white machine lying in the shadows of the dark hangar, the darker figures of the crew crawling over her day and night. I had felt the first quiverings of protest in her—the roll. She was no longer the same ship I had learned to know; she was unfriendly, an intimate friend turned psychopath—a stranger wearing the familiar face I have known, but with another mind. I had the feeling she would turn on me.

Safe on the ground, rehearsing the next flight, the instruments sleeping on the panel, the instant I wrapped my fingers around the corkwheel she burst into life. There was no longer the need to project myself into what it would be like. I knew. I was back up there with the subtle quiverings she had warned me with. But then perhaps I was overanxious, the tension of the program; the "quigie-board artists" had assured me the roll is nothing to be concerned about. An effect of high Mach number.

April 5, 1951. I am prepared for this flight. On the slow climb up the crew is more aware. The stunt has worked: they are alert and I can feel their eyes on me as if they are looking for some reaction. Well, they won't get any. In ten years of playing the role of pilot I have learned the part well.

George shouts over the deafening roar of the bomber straining and boring its way through the sky upward. "Okay, Bridge, time to get into the bomb." He raises his hand in the friendly, ribald gesture that undoubtedly is to bless all of the Skyrocket's launches. Don Pruitt and McNemar move over to give me a hand. Pruitt shouts,

"Leave us not light the fuse on that thing till you're in the open." I am too busy thinking of the flight now to give them a bright retort.

This time there is no communication problem. A big red warning light has been installed on the control panel of the bomber. If something is out of order in the Skyrocket I press a button and the light flashes on.

Inside the half-light of the freezing Skyrocket I wait for the moment when she is freed. I review the flight plan. *Climb to 39,000, push over into the big arc that will take me, at its rim, to 45,000.* I hold my hands between my legs, avoiding the chilled metals of the cockpit. I will not put them on the icy wheel until George counts down to three seconds before "drop," so that my hands will not be stiff with cold when it comes time to use them. I have given up the warmth of gloves, they get in the way of the knobs and dull my sense of touch.

George's farewell works again. He is on the count-down and the rocket-system pressures are firm. I rub my hands together to keep them warm. Everything is in order. This time I will not drop as far—I am prepared.

Mathematically she is figured to accomplish this feat easily. All I can do is perform my part properly: push the right buttons and make the right adjustments and the mathematical formula will prove itself in a successful flight. There is, of course, always the chance that this morning may be my last flight, but it is a possibility I am willing to face if it is a result of the unforeseen or if it is because, even, of a slight engineering miscalculation. To die because of my own stupidity, to be tripped by my own inadequacy, is the big fear that hangs over me. Do I know everything well? Have I planned against every conceivable emergency?

"Three . . . two . . ." My hands grip the corkwheel . . . one second and I'll be in it again!

"One . . . *drop!*"

I hit the four switches. The cavities of my stomach and guts are pushed up into my chest as I fall fast, straight down the blazing bright shaft of light. No more than six seconds and the rocket tubes light off. Four violent explosions and she is on fire again, blasting into life. Six thousand pounds of thrust "right now" at the click of the four small metal switches. Into the climb, on the edge of stall, keeping it steep to hold the Mach number down below the drag rise as long as possible. Every bit of perception I have is pinpointed on the indicated air speed and the Machmeter. Let her nose down. It's vibrating like a harpstring out there . . . God, now she's picking up more speed . . . pull it up again.

Now is the time! I hold the indicated air speed steady and let her Mach number move forward fast, past the critical .91. In a matter of seconds she has accelerated into the supersonic side, into the quiet zone. Spewing a 45-foot river of rainbow red, blue, and yellow fire, the Rocket shoots effortlessly up the steep climb path. The altimeter spins as she eats up over a quarter of a mile a second.

It begins again. The roll. From side to side she starts the insidious rolling motion and I have trouble with my pressure breathing. The gentle protest alerts every nerve in my body, ready to combat whatever danger is coming. I move the ailerons to straighten her out. They have no effect and the rolling motion at 800 miles an hour becomes stronger as the ship accelerates. At my feet the rudder pedals jerk convulsively in and out with an independent power. With all the weight of my body pressing down through my legs I cannot quiet them; the gigantic force that has grabbed the rudder won't be controlled and it pushes my rump back and forth into the seat with angry force. I am 4000 feet past the pushover altitude. She's got the bit in her teeth. I read the decreasing figures that stand alone on the rocket-second counter—121. The numbers click off and the dial turns them back into the panel. Only 121 rocket-seconds to go, a quarter of a minute before the fuel is burned off. I can just hang on until the figures are used up and the run is over. Just a quarter of a minute. Follow the plan, move the wheel forward gently to .7 G into the arc that will end in the final speed spring across the face of the sky.

I begin the pushover. The roll is becoming more urgent. But I perversely wait for the rocket-seconds to disappear instead of killing her power. When the second counter spins to "o" it will be over. Watching the seconds click away is a game that tends to make the Skyrocket's rolling, weird complaint endurable. Surely I can hang on without altering the flight plan until the rocket-seconds are used up.

The seconds click away and the rolling becomes worse. The ship is growing more and more out of control, revolting wildly against the strenuous ride I am imposing upon her. The ship I fly is an empty barrel in an enraged sea.

"Oh, God . . . ," the word is a whining complaint. I look at the rocket-second counter. It is only down to 100. It takes such a long time to burn away. A ton of fuel a minute but still now it seems an interminably long time before the tanks empty. Mach 1.32. Almost at the top of the arc and the roll is still wilder. The game is no longer sensible. I cannot play a game with myself until the wings snap off. I must make a decision. Obviously the roll is becoming progressively more serious.

"Oh, hell." I have said it out loud and the frustrated groan brings Carder's voice into the chaotic, singular world of the cockpit. The periodic cursing and the jogging vapor trail I am dragging through the air have moved him to break the silence.

"How you doing, Bill?"

"Be quiet. I'm busy." Again the radio is silent and once more I am alone locked in an erratic plane, ripping up the sky at 1000 miles per hour, who won't answer to her controls. I am no longer a part of my plane. She is a threatening, sinister stranger whom I must outwit. My weapons are the controls that are still available to me. By manipulating them in a certain way I have worked my way into this chaos, I can still use them to correct the situation. She doesn't want to fly under these conditions. It is a big step. I abandon the flight plan. To hell with it. I cut off the rockets; she skids over the top at 45,500 feet, pressing me tightly against the bank of instruments, the gauges spinning furiously registering the sudden enormity.

As soon as I can recover I move the buzzing little trim tab that will slam her into a bank and turn her back to the stable, bleeding off what's left of the rocket propellants into the clear morning air. I don't fly by feel any more; I fly by experienced calculation. The roll fades away and she is again something I can understand. Chuck catches up with me and guides me home.

Nobody had predicted the "roll." It is an uneasy feeling to know that the Skyrocket can fool a whole corps of diligent engineers.

From the ground they had seen the long sheet of rocket fuel melting into the sky. Carder wanted to know at once what fouled up.

"What went wrong with the rocket engine?" He asked me as once more I was extricated, in one piece, from the Skyrocket. Mabry, Just, and Jorgensen stood in a line behind him, taking priority over the other engineers. Under my feet I could feel the ground, hot and hard, and nothing seemed very important except that another flight was over and I was standing easy once more in the sun.

"Nothing went wrong with the rockets . . . I *cut* them off." The brash news drew the line in closer.

"Why did you have to cut them?" Carder anxiously put the question for the group.

I looked into the faces of the men who waited curiously for my answer. "Because I couldn't control the ship." This was the most serious offense a test pilot could charge against an airplane, an answer the flight-testing crew did not want to hear. Another big problem to delay the program, one they hadn't figured on. The Skyrocket had a surprise reaction all of her own at sustained supersonic speeds.

The fact that they had not predicted the research airplane's unruly behavior caused the aerodynamicists no embarrassment. The "lateral-oscillation" report, brought back from the front lines of the new flight area, was met with interest as to why she behaved so erratically—along with the frustration of further delay while the mystery was solved. Actually it was not the flight-test engineer's problem. The incident was attributed to design. It was the El Segundo designing staff's problem, not the flight-test crew's.

At nine o'clock the following morning a planeful of Douglas designing brass, summoned from the El Segundo plant, arrived with confident smiles and slip-sticks. They were dressed comfortably for the desert in vivid cotton shirts and lightweight slacks. They carried with them the holiday mood of businessmen stepping off a plane at the Palm Springs Airport. It was as if they welcomed the brief release from their neon-lighted desks at the beach-city factory. These men were the designers of the Navy's highest performing aircraft. They were received anxiously by the grim-faced flight-test engineers of the research program who sought their expert advice. No time was wasted. The visitors were hustled into the long conference room where we assembled to hold the post-mortem on the Skyrocket's unpredicted behavior of the day before. As the situation was laid before the designers in the form of miles of oscillography charts, volumes of flight reports, and blackboards filled with diagrams, the holiday aura disappeared from our visitors. They quickly screwed themselves down to the big problem.

A brief period for lunch and the meeting progressed on into the late afternoon. No sure answer came out of the session as to why the rudder oscillated back and forth with the peculiar motion of a shutter banging rapidly against a house in a wind storm. There was the possibility that the gigantic blast and shock patterns that came out of the rocket tubes caused pressures strong enough to disturb the rudder above them. It was an unknown area and there was no past knowledge on which to base an answer for the Skyrocket's protestings—as yet no frame of reference existed. That was our purpose out in the draining heat of the Mojave: to establish that frame.

Although the cause was not thoroughly understood, the symptom could be controlled. Out of the confab came the quick-fix answer: Lock the rudder with a plunger device that could be removed for landings. It seemed a logical solution. The thorough examination of the Skyrocket's revolt left me reasonably optimistic. The consulting doctors had all agreed on the remedy and intuitively it was, I felt, the right one.

The next flight had to be a success. Negotiations for further flights, beyond the three successful ones we had contracted to demonstrate, were in process with the Navy. We had to look good on Flight Number Three.

It took a month to install the corrective measure that presumably would bring the plane back into line. During this period the flight-test boys dreamed up a big jump for me in the last contracted flight. Ten thousand feet higher at the pushover at a speed of Mach 1.51 .. . and then let her go.

Summer was crowding again and the desert bowl was an

unrelenting furnace once more. The purple and yellows and pinks of the spring were melted away by the sun and the brown-gray of the summer reappeared. The third exploration.

Flight Number 26, the third drop, might well be the last time that Douglas would be able to prove what their ship could do, if the Navy, under pressure from NACA, who was strongly petitioning for delivery, denied our request for further flights.

We left off the griddle-hot, white runway and head for the test ground, 35,000 feet up above the desert bowl to the big, cold flight laboratory. It is going to be all right. Every detail has been checked, the charts studied, and the corrective measures taken. I have agreed with the decisions.

Twenty minutes up. It is bitterly cold and I don't look forward to the flight. Because of the complexities of the tightly laced suit I am supplied with Dixie cups in the event I need a receptacle on the journey to altitude. With annoyance I find I have to use the dainty facility. It is dropped out between the 29 and the Skyrocket. Immediately Everest, who is shepherding the drop end of the flight, reports the falling object to the crew on the lake bed; "A small white object has just left the belly of the 29."

Before Carder can swallow another aspirin, Jansen calls down: "Relax. That was just Bridgeman's preflight Dixie cup.'

Jansen manages to squeeze more altitude out of the 29. Level with my mouth I can see, by rolling my eyes down in their sockets, an opaque patch of frost forming from the warm, moist air out of my lungs as it blows against the cold glass face-plate. There is no defrosting device in the lens. Carefully I blow the air out into the bottom of the helmet in order to delay the growth of frost that is building under my mouth. At the rate it is rising I figure I can still drop without any vision problem. After the speed run is over I can dump the helmet altogether at a lower altitude.

George begins the count down at 34,000. I forget about the inherent blindness in the face-plate. When the tubes light off I am able to get a sharper climbing altitude than I had before, but I run into the same problem of keeping the scheduled climbing Mach number of .85. In the actual drop I pick up a few seconds. I am more proficient at the mechanics of the light-off and the pull-up. The reward is more rocket-seconds for the speed run at the top. Locking the rudder works.

The roll is still with me but it is sluggish and can be damped out almost entirely by the returned effectiveness of the ailerons. The rudder pedals float only slightly. Into the supersonic area I return to the uneasy business of flying the ship with the electric switch that trims the horizontal stabilizer. At 55,000 I push her over at the lower load factor of .6 G at nearly twice the speed of sound. Blessedly she takes it like milk, barreling across the sky in her sprint, wide open until her fuel runs out.

Back down at low altitude, I notice briefly with a fleeting qualm that the glass face-plate that I have dropped on the floor is more than half covered with thick frost.

She came back home with a recorded Mach number of 1.72 and an altitude of 63,000 feet—four tenths of a Mach over the last flight. She had beaten the Air Force's X-1 by 200 miles per hour. The Skyrocket was now the fastest airplane in the world.

Our contract was completed. NACA wanted their plane. We had demonstrated that she would drop the light off successfully and they were ready to take over. But the Douglas crew after two years of grooming the Skyrocket for this moment did not want to give her up yet. She could do better. Just a few more flights and we could do it. Mach 2 was the goal.

Further flights for maximum speed and altitude were granted by the Naval Bureau of Aeronautics. We received the TWX to go ahead and the committee swallowed hard and politely stood back while we continued our flights for more speed.

With a new jolt of enthusiasm the engineers, convinced that the ship was now controllable, went to work on getting the last one hundredth of a Mach number out of her. Fuel and altitude were the determining factors. The higher we could sent her, the faster her fuel would take her. Through experience I had learned to save fuel in the pullout and climb, but we were losing propellant during the 72-minute free ride in the 29. By the time we got to the drop altitude

48 gallons of the liquid oxygen had boiled off.

Jorgensenand Osborne sharpened their pencils. They came up with an answer that would give us higher Mach numbers on the fourth drop. An intricate plumbing apparatus was installed in the 29 to replace the stuff that boiled away during the ride up. In three weeks the tubes and tanks were installed in the bomber. Added to Jorgensen and Osborne's top-off device, the aerodynamicists altered the flight plan to pick up more speed in the pushover. The plotters lessened the pushover load to a slim .3 G from the original conservative .7 G. We expected big gains. The Skyrocket was going to try for Mach 2.

The fourth attempt. Flight Plan 27, June 11, 1951. Waiting in the darkness of the Skyrocket for the moment of drop, I can hear Carder calling to the tower, "Better send up the second chase, the B-29's at 34,000." With uneasiness I learn that the chase plane hasn't left the field yet. George is getting more out of her this trip. Last flight he dropped me at 34,000 but today he is still climbing. Thirty-four thousand feet and the margin of frost inside my face-plate is growing faster than the increase in time and altitude. The rapid increase in the rate of growth creeping up to my eyes disturbs me now. It will take 15 more minutes for the chase to get up and George is still climbing. During the three-minute rocket flight the ice won't grow much, but in 15 minutes it can cover the lens.

It is an unfair surprise. I had thought about every snare but this one; I thought I had it all figured. Perhaps if George doesn't climb any higher, if he starts outbound on his approach bearing now, the curtain will remain below my eyes. It is a chance. I decide not to alarm Carder about the frost, so much preparation has gone into the flight. If we head out now, if George stops his climb, I am almost certain I can make it. Five minutes go by and it is up to my lower eyelids.

"I think we ought to go out now, Buddy."

"For God's sake, what's your hurry? I can still get another couple of thousand out of her . . . "

"Look, George, start your turn, will you? I've got a framis in the weeb box." I garble the words to Carder won't stop the flight.

"I don't know what the hell you're talking about but okay, it's your show," George complains.

I blow the warm air from my mouth down to the bottom of the helmet to delay the growth of frost, but the contortion isn't helping any now. Thirty-six thousand. One thin layer crawls over the lens but it is still possible to see out. The opaque, heavy layers still remain below my eyes where I have blown my breath downward as George begins the count-down.

". . . four, three, two, one, *drop!*"

I am gone and without any trouble climb up to the scheduled 60,000 feet—the blood-boiling area. I forget about the translucent lens. This time the apprehension is predominantly due to the extreme new altitudes I am hitting. The roll is under control. In the event that there is a canopy failure I am not convinced that the suit will work. As long as I have to remain in the danger zone from 30,000 feet up I am worried. Even if the damned suit does work in an emergency, the deeper I climb into the thin air, the longer I have to operate under emergency conditions coming back from the low-pressure area. The prospect of controlling the ship in an inflated pressure suit, trying to breathe in the glass bowl at nearly twice the speed of sound for a nasty ten minutes down to the safe altitude region of 15,000 feet, is not pleasant. So far the suit has not been proven under actual emergency flight conditions.

I glance at the dials low on the panel. At the bottom of the face-place another layer of veiling is growing fast, obscuring the instruments. I have taken too big a chance. There is no time to think about it now. It is time to start the pushover. With the load factor close to a negative G I strain against the leather webbing, my body near the floating point. Just as advertised she accelerates faster as the six-second run begins, and once more I hang on in awe as she carries me into Mach 1.79. Again I find myself returned to the uneasy state of being ego-drained before the face of a thing I cannot explain.

"What Mach number did you hit, Bill?" Mabry was the first one to ask as I left the cockpit.

"Close to 1.80. Something like that." The spectators groaned. In order to find out what the Machmeter read during the flight they would have to wait until the film came out of the processing room but they complained anyway.

"Don't you know?"

"Not exactly. I'm pretty busy up there." Tommy Briggs pulled the zipper that released me from the binding suit. It helped.

"What was the indicated air speed?"

"I don't know."

"Don't you ever look at anything up there?"

"Hell, yes. I look at the accelerometer." I moved toward the car and the animated group of inquirers followed me like fight trainers after a bout.

It would be two days before the data was reduced and the Skyrocket's exact performance was made available. The instrument readings cannot e considered accurate although they are indicative.

Al Carder, his face red with the heat, sat beside me on the way back.

"Al, we're going to have to do something about the faceplate. It was practically frosted over when I dropped. The long time it's taking us to get the extra altitude in the 29 is making it worse. It was all right before we began getting these extra thousand feet out of the 29—it only frosted halfway up, but now we're going to have to rig up something to wipe the moisture off the inside."

"God, do you think it would ever get so bad the thing would frost completely over before you could get low enough to take it out?"

I remembered the frost layer ten minutes ago, a fraction of an inch below my retina. It was a private joke and inwardly I was amused at Carder's question. "Possibly," I told him.

"The only thing I can think of is a windshield-wiper device."

We both laughed.

C H A P T E R   X X I

Two days later the news came out of the aerodynamicists' office. The chance in load factor, the increased altitude, and the newly installed top-off system had picked up .07 of a Mach number. Still she hadn't hit Mach 2 as we had hoped; at 64,500 feet she reached a top speed of 1.79. Her performance, however, was encouraging; she was making good progress and was giving us no trouble. We just hadn't hit the right combination of conditions to push her through Mach 2. One more try and the engineers were sure we could do it.

Our reluctance to hand over the plane to NACA had them in a state of great frustration, and at every possible opportunity they were letting their impatience be known. Under their intense needling, the

Navy liaison officer would in turn needle us to deliver the Skyrocket to the anxious agency. With promises of only one more flight the project engineers were able to assuage the harassed emissary.

NACA in Washington also was in constant touch with the Navy and through our capitol representative the Navy Bureau of Aeronautics sent us inquiring dispatches:

WHEN ARE YOU GOING TO TURN THE PLANE OVER TO NACA?

The last dispatch was met with another request for one more flight. The big goal was very close. The Navy promptly granted another flight. NACA diplomatically accepted the fact that their hangar at the Flight Test Center would be empty of the Skyrocket for a little while longer.

Another chance at Mach 2. Everything had to go into the next flight for maximum speed. There was no way to save more fuel for the speed run; every fuel-saving refinement had already been put into effect. It was possible that she could carry more fuel, of course, if some of her data-recording apparatus were removed, but such tactics, merely to break records, would defeat her important purpose: the gathering of complete and precise data on an area into which only she was capable of going. There was only one alternative: decrease the load factor at the pushover to .2, just a shade this side of negative G. That would bring the added acceleration.

Summer had set in solidly and oppressively before the flight plan was formulated and the Santa Monica engineers had combatted the frosting problem by designing—actually—a tiny, manually operated windshield wiper for my helmet. It was toward the end of June. At the beginning of the pushover I would be 5000 feet higher than any plane had ever flown.

Sleep wasn't hard to find before the flight. I wanted to get it over with and I looked forward to the morning with a kind of perverse eagerness. The Rocket could have no surprises for me at this late date—I was used to her. She had given me trouble but it had been ironed out all right. Tomorrow would be the payoff.

Far into the dark area she was behaving admirably. Two flights deep and high into unknown territory had made her first and she had taken the rides. There was no reason to suspect that tomorrow she wouldn't behave as well. The flight plan was in no way more radical than the others before it. Just more altitude and a lower load factor at the pushover point. As long as the charts and figures and equations had been well studied by the slip-stick artists it would be all right. The only other enemies were the old ones—my own inadequacy and the unknown.

This, perhaps, was the last one. It was possible that the Navy would send the dispatch ordering the transfer of the Skyrocket after today's flight. Today, if I walked away from her, it might be for the last time—I could walk away, forever, from the awful reactions she could impose upon me in a thousandth of a Mach number, the constant vigilance and then the ego-defeating surprise of the gigantic reward she paid me.

In the cover of dawn the twin Air Force hangars loomed out sphinxlike from the flat desert floor. The base slept. And the pitch-whistle shriek of the plane I was to fly floated over the coming morning. A flashlight moved along the gravel and the headlights reached ahead of the oncoming cars toward the back of the Douglas hangar. In the air was the smell of sage and dryness and high-test gasoline.

"Bill, you'd better to in and talk to Yeager," Carder advised me as we drove past the Air Force hangar. "You probably want to tell him what's going on today since he couldn't make the preflight yesterday."

We pulled up alongside the hangar offices. I found Yeager upstairs in the locker room. "Can I see you for a minute?"

He looked up from his locker. "Hi, Bill. Sure, be right with you." He took out his flight jacket and gear and moved into the hall to meet me. "Come on in the office." The room was smaller than the one Jansen and I shared. I had never been in it before. Most of the conversations Yeager and I had had, had been in the Douglas hangar. Now that the program was moving he paid my office frequent visits. Outside of Pete Everest, who was flying the X-1 now, I as the only other pilot on the base he could compare notes with; his erstwhile plane and mine were the only ones flying supersonic. It was a small fraternity. And now the Skyrocket was Number One.

"I understand you're really going to twist your tail today." He said it from under his eyebrows.

"Yeah, I think we ought to have better luck today."

"You figure you'll get a little more out of her at higher altitude?"

"That's what the geniuses say."

"A-huh . . where you going to push it over?"

"64,000."

Yeager cocked his head thoughtfully. "Hmmm-mmm. Take it easy up there, Bridge." He squinted his eyes a little. "You're getting up where it counts."

"Yeah, I know what you mean." This would be the last time though. Today I was going to get it over with. "Naturally we'll run out a little shorter than usual. You'll pick me up a little closer to the lake, don't you think?"

"Yeah."

"Okay. See you after the drop."

"Have yourself a good one, Buddy."

There she was, a celebrity now, the crew, members of a midnight cult, priming her for the big flight in their cumbersome, hooded uniforms.

I was at the height of conditioning as I approached the fueling scene, half out of the pressure suit, followed by the specialist Stum. I was determined to get everything out of her this time, to get it over with. There was nothing to fear. The roll had been conquered and no structural damage had resulted from it. She sat snug in the belly of the mother ship, gleaming iridescent white with her new skin of lacquer. Today was the culmination of three years' work.

The fueling was completed. The engineers came up one by one to offer some last-minute word, the equivalent of "Good luck." "See you after the flight" . . . "We'll discuss it afterward"—optimistic references to the future. Stum finished fussing with the helmet and thumped the top of it with his hand. The 29 fired up her engines, taxied out, and we were airborne.

I am no longer embarrassed by my need for the Dixie cup. It has become an established part of the flight. When it drops out, Everest, familiar with the sight, calls, "Dixie cup away."

Thirty-five thousand feet. I acknowledge Jansen's salute. Twenty minutes later my hands are gripping the wheel.

"Two . . . one." The shaft of light, a sensation I am accustomed to meeting. Today the pullout is smooth, without any loss of rocket-seconds. How practiced I have become! How easily I control the power pouring from the four tubes. The tension I have felt waiting in the bomber has left me and the action of performing the job well acts as an exaggerated salve. Even the constant adjustment in the climb is an effortless series of practiced movements. How well she responds.

At the top I will push her over sharply and let her go. I am really going to put it to her . . . with the added acceleration at the pushover, she should do it.

Piercing up through the minus-80-degree sheer air, I hit 64,000 feet in a matter of seconds—the top of the hill. Now! She eats up 3000 feet while my hand moves the wheel. Over the top, right down into it. No gradual rocket-second devouring arc, but over the top like a roller coaster. Straight down in front of me I push the wheel and the limitless blue brilliancy ahead slides away and out of the sliver windows the curve of the horizon moves up in its place.

And quietly she begins to "roll." The thing that had me on the edge of my parachute three long flights ago I take as a matter of course. And now, .25 G, just the other side of zero G where you beat gravity, where a pencil on the cockpit floor will float in mid-air. I glue the white needle to .25 on the accelerometer. Let's see what you can do with this, baby! She accelerates into the supersonic zone at one third of a mile a second.

The roll! I can't ignore it. It sets in more firmly as she plunges deeper into the pushover. Well, let it, damn it. We're going this trip. She can take it. Without changing the condition she protests against, I grip the wheel. Nothing is going to jar her loose from the .25 holding steady on the accelerometer. There is nothing she can show me that is going to stop me. Hunched over the wheel, I hang on.

Harder she rolls, harder and faster. The flat horizon line flips wildly through the squinting slit windows. I fight the crazy gyration with the ailerons. They are no weapons. They are feathers in a wind storm. Still, they are the only weapons I have. The flipping is so fast that I cannot get in phase against it with the ailerons. She has turned on me! I am making it worse with the ailerons and panic floods up into my chest and throat. I am almost sick with it as I fight a force so great now that my frantic flailings against it are pathetically puny.

There has got to be a way to bring order out of this. I release my hands from the aileron control and try to get out of phase with the roll that snaps me violently back and forth in its teeth, flipping me over on my side level with the horizon, then instantly back in the other direction. A dog beating a cat against the ground. I do not fight it now, but wait to allow the crazy accelerated, windshield-wiper-like, flipping of the Rocket to neutralize so I can jump in and hold my strength against it. Now. I missed it. *I'll get it this time. I'll get it now.*

The action has a meager effect on the force that has grabbed us, but it is positive. It is a glimmer of control and I am somewhat retrieved from total despair. The wheel is a ridiculous toy against the thing that has hold of the ship. *Why don't they give me something to fight with, for God's sake?* A toy in my hands to fight the whole Goddammed sky that has turned on me. One hundred and eighty pounds against a new world full of enraged energy. The frail weapons of my arms ache with the futile exertion put upon them.

I turn my back on the ridiculously matched contest long enough to glance at the Machmeter. It is building fast: 1.79, 1.80, 1.81, 1.82, 1.83, 1.84, 1.85.

That is the answer! That is the reason. No-man's-land. She's going. It is a justification.

I am aware of the face-plate that separates my eyes from the panel before me. Coatings of steam from my breath rapidly appear and disappear on the glass and the terrible sound of my lungs gasping and heaving air in and out vibrates like wind in a barrel through my ears. Despite all the activity I am aware of the terrible, animal-frightened sound.

Into this isolated, hopelessly vulnerable world that is myself and the Skyrocket comes another kind of faraway unreality—the voice of Al Carder, high and thin, crackling through my helmet.

"Has he started to descend yet, Chuck?" From his position on the floor 13 miles down, the project coordinator has been able to follow my white vapor trail in the climb. Then the Skyrocket reaches air too thin to condense.

I am swallowed up by the sky. It is an easy matter to get lost in the sky.

Yeager's voice, lost from me somewhere out there, "No. He was still climbing when his vapor trail disappeared and he left me."

"Any idea of his position, Chuck?"

"Last time I saw him he was heading east over Barstow."

It is like hearing voices of people standing over you when you are half-conscious. You are unable to answer. I would like to say something memorably glib, but I cannot.

My hands and face are wet with perspiration. Rivulets of stinging sweat drop into my eyes. How curious that a man can sweat in minus 80-degree-below-zero temperature.

If a horse is throwing you, you can let yourself be thrown. You can get away from the beast. But not this thing. I am part of it. Until she wears out the tantrum, I have no alternative but to go where she takes me.

Still doggedly I hold the needle on .25 G. The horizon of gyrating, half-blue, half-brown, is gone now and in its place is solid brown earth in a half-circle spin, spinning half around and respinning back again. A corkscrew at Mach .187 down toward the ground. Beyond the thickening fog of my face-plate there is no sky. It is all flat, hard earth that I head for.

I am losing the battle. To hang on longer is stupidity. A decision must be made. Cut off her energy! That will surely stop this horror. Behind me I feel for the switch that will turn off the 6000 pounds of thrust. I click it forward.

She shudders and decelerates into the wall, but the wild ride continues as if no change had been made. It doesn't alter her furious action. It is with terrible surprise I realize that the loss of power has no effect upon her condition.

The lake is 40 miles behind me and getting further and further away as the Skyrocket carries me far from my only port. To enter a turn back to the lake is impossible. I cannot force her into a bank. She won't leave her path! And now over my eyes the frost on my face-plate has thickened into a heavy white curtain and I can no longer see the gyrating, whirling bottom below me.

My cramped cockpit world has moved into my helmet. All that exists now is the white frost on the face-plate, the violent thrashing of the plane, and the feel of the wheel under my fingers. In the silent ship the terrible, convulsive breathing is my only companion.

A blind man in an out-of-control Rocket plunging, through low-pressure areas that can burst my body like a balloon, toward the ground at a speed twice as fast as a bullet in flight.

Altitude. It is the only road left to me, the only way I can go now. It is the margin, the delayer. In altitude there is some security. Time to think. With all the strength I am able to summon I pull back on the wheel and inflict a radical directional change on the downward-screaming ship. Bent upward into the big, safe sky—the tremendous force of the tight pull-up sucking me down into the pressure suit, my lower jaw grabbed wide open like a man screaming for his life—I know that I am moving away from the awful brown that I was headed into. It's soft blue before me now.

And now like a black night diluted slowly by the incipient water-color dawn, the gyrating falls away. I feel it fade away. It has stopped. All of the violence and horror is gone. The Rocket has changed back into a silent, gentle, featherlike missile, whooshing straight up in a steep climb.

She is controllable but I cannot see. The windshield wiper! I remember with a flood of thankful discovery the windshield wiper that had been installed after the last flight at Al Carder's insistence. Thank God for Carder and the ridiculous little rubber level that I move manually to clear away the frost.

Without power and bent into the steep climb, she will start shuddering into the first warnings of stall. The indicated air speed is the dial that commands my regained sight. It is sinking fast. *Fly her now, Bridgeman; she's all yours again.* Once more I am a pilot. I drop the nose a bit to pick up speed. Now I roll her over, drop the long nose, pulling positive G, and pull her on through. The Skyrocket is turned back in the direction of home. My ship again.

The chase pilots have lost me. Right now I am incapable of worrying about getting the rest of the way home. At this moment I am overwhelmed with relief that the Skyrocket is once more something I can understand and that she is heading in the right direction.

The last few minutes have left my body still in a state of emergency despite the abrupt cessation of the nightmare. My legs and arms shake uncontrollably.

Some time during the pushover I re-enter the altitude where my vapor trail forms again. Carder has seen it. From the ground it appears like an erratic corkscrew furrowed by my wild path. The jumble over the radio starts as Carder sees it with alarm.

"Chuck, can you see the vapor trail again? Can you get over there?"

Weakly I hear the sound of help coming and I wonder absently how I am going to explain this one to Carder. And why did I hang on so tenaciously to that .25 G? As I sit here trembling, guiding the empty Rocket sapped as dry of energy as I am, I remember the moments just passed.

Holy God! Not once did I think of the escape lever. Is it possible that I would have let her take me right into a 40-foot hole in the ground?

"Yeah, Al, I can see it. I'll be on him in a couple of minutes."

"That's a crazy-looking trail he's dragging. How does he look, Chuck?"

Chuck is coming. The now-obedient Skyrocket decelerates out of the supersonic zone down through the critical .9, emitting her usual shudder. The once-awesome shudder makes me smile weakly.

"Hold on. I haven't found him yet." The warm, competent, Southern softness of Yeager's steady voice is soothing as the first inhalation of fine sour-mash whisky. "Now I've got him. He's pretty far away but he seems to be all in one piece."

"Bill," Carder calls to me now, "How are you doing?"

There is it! I can see the lake bed far below me and ahead. Just a few more minutes. "Shut up, will you?"

Beside me Chuck Yeager's silver F-86 slides in close and cozy.

"Hi, hotshot." A friend to see me home. I lift my hand to him. He is silent as he follows my glide path down. He knows. It is all I can do to follow the precise maneuverings necessary to get the still-hot little ship onto the lake bed. Even without power she'll land nearly a third again as fast as the F-86.

After a respectable length of time Chuck says, "I thought you were going to Arizona for a while there, Buddy."

With a great deal of effort I was able to answer. "I thought so too."

CHAPTER XXII

❚❚ Why the hell did you hang on so long to that .2 G? Why didn't you let go?"

"It beats the hell out of me, George. I can't figure that one out myself." From the beginning I had found it easy to talk to Mabry, a serious, shy man and a brilliant aerodynamicist. George knew the answers. He had become my teacher.

"What did you do, pull up finally?"

"Yes. How did you know?"

"When your vapor trail began again at the end of the dive, I saw the sun reflect suddenly off your wings. I figured you had pulled out." George was ready with the diagnosis. "It looks like a function of negative G. We'll have to go back to the higher load factor next time."

"She damped out all right as soon as I pulled the nose up." It seemed simple now. But nobody had predicted the revolt that had been inherent in her, since the first drop, all these months. Now I was uneasily certain that this area I explored was unknowable— even to the men who measured it with their slip-sticks and years of study. "George, I can tell you that I never want another ride like the last one."

Reports of the Skyrocket's unexpected lateral instability hastily brought the planeload of designers back up from El Segundo to make another investigation. They were inclined to accept my description of the hairy flight as an exaggeration. Test pilots were often temperamental. Then they saw the records!

Two days later they came up with the verdict: "The lateral-directional instability of the airplane at a low load factor is an effect of the displacement of the principal axis of inertia." Change in distribution of the airplane's weight, and hence inertia, which took place when the ship was altered, and the low angel of attack in the .2G pushover were the items that caused the oscillation.

Her secret was uncovered. The thing that I had subconsciously anticipated from the first rocket-powered drop had manifested itself: she had finally turned on me. The force she nibbled at and protested against had shallowed her. I had never known the kind of fear I felt on the last flight. She had scared the hell out of me, but running headlong into the soup and successfully escaping made the villain known. No longer was she hiding anything from me. The defense was a simple one, I had to fly in a narrow band of sky in order to make the run for more speed. If I lifted her above the band I would lose speed and if I dropped below it, I dropped into the storm of the last flight.

The rapid pushover was no longer feasible as a means of added acceleration; I had to return to the more gradual nose-over into the run. I would have to depend solely on an increase in altitude and careful manipulation in the band of sky now allowed to me, to squeeze any more speed out of her.

NACA was breathing heavier than ever down our necks for their airplane. Unctuously they were assured that it would require only a few more flights to prove we had solved our "lateral-oscillation" problem, and then they could have the Skyrocket. After all, we had to prove what the ship would do before they could safely begin their extensive and long-range investigations.

Again the Bureau of Aeronautics granted their official approval to continue, for the time being anyway, the flights for maximum speed and altitude.

Urgently the program continued, one flight to the next, never knowing when it would be our last chance.

A month of planning and investigation went into the last try for Mach 2. There was no air of excitement the morning of flight, it was more of a mutually shared anxiety. No one allowed himself enthusiasm; too many things could happen to prevent the new record or even the flight itself.

The sixth flight and once more I have 45 minutes to think before I walk through the freezing, raw fuselage back to the Skyrocket. I know this plane that hangs heavy, ready to be born. I have experience. I know exactly how I will handle her. The challenge that she has offered me, that now I am confident I can meet, is so big that it crowds out the memory of the beating she gave me during the last flight. If fear is a form of respect, then I live with it. It is a familiar sensation; the hollow, undulating emptiness before every flight is the thing I first met in combat, a thing I expect. I can subjugate the reaction with the activity of preparation or even the movies. In this way I have learned to delay the growth that always forms and crawls up from my bowels. Not until it is needed, not until I am too distracted controlling the Skyrocket to control the growth, does it move in independently. Then it is beneficial, it is the big dose of adrenalin that makes every reaction defined and brilliantly clear.

She will behave this time in her flight 'way beyond the sound barrier. Altitude and treading a narrow band of sky at 68,000 will have to be the way she gets in any deeper. Over the top at .5 G. Only I will nibble at it; I will treat her very tenderly. When she begins to roll I will pull up the nose, then drop it again to pick up speed.

We are at 34,000 feet. My cue. Ten cold minutes preparing the ship for flight. The trap door springs and releases the captive Skyrocket swollen with explosive propellants. She blasts into flight.

Thirty seconds and I am supersonic. Sixty-eight thousand feet and this is it. Over the rim. Easy. The electrically controlled stabilizer flies her now. It takes over for me. At .6 G I push over just enough to get my speed. I am on the ragged edge of the storm between .6 G and .8 G. It is working! Everything is going according to my plan. It is so easy this time. Surely I cannot be breaking my last record without having to pay for it. The Machmeter is moving up, fluttering toward the Number 2 . . . the rockets sputter and the fuel is gone. That's all she wrote.

Late that afternoon the official speed attained by the Skyrocket reduced from the data and film came out of the aerodynamicists' office. Mach 1.88. A little less than one tenth of a Mach number under Mach 2—1258 miles per hour.

George Mabry read me the news. "Looks like we broke our last record. You picked up three-one-hundredths but she didn't hit 2. What do you think?"

This morning before the data was reduced it looked like I was closer to Mach 2. I wasn't sure that I hadn't reached it. At altitude the instruments read slightly off. Only the data gives you the real story. I shook my head. "I guess that's it. We should get another five-one-hundredths of a Mach number, but not a whole one tenth."

"It looks that way."

I knew now we weren't going to make it. Too many things stood in the way. We would need still more flights, probably a structural modification, before we could reach up to Mach 2. Our time was running out.

There was the altitude flight to get in before the Navy sent the inevitable dispatch to release the plane to NACA. The day after the speed record was set, a high-level meeting was called in Hoskinson's office to discuss the flight for maximum altitude.

Pettingall, chief aerodynamicist in the Testing Division at Santa Monica, his assistant Andy Mahoff, Hoskinson, and I sat around the long table. On the blackboard were the huge parabolas that were, supposedly, to infallibly map the way to 100,000 feet—the ambitious height the theorists aspired to. I sat and stared in astonishment at the projectilelike track that was a steep, white, chalk-line hump across the blackboard. Above the hump, at intervals, was marked the altitude figure, the indicated air speed, and the number of rocket-seconds that remained for the completion of the climb. At the top of the track the indicated air speed read 90 miles per hour. The Skyrocket stalls at 160 miles per hour. The engineers were quick to explain that because of the tremendous amount of thrust she will have built up she would not stall. The Skyrocket was, according to their proposal, to be like a projectile, a bullet aimed at the sky. Only she wasn't a projectile. She was an airplane with wings and a tail! My impulse was to argue with the theorists, but I listened, trying to be convinced of what they were saying. I listened to the matter-of-fact droning of the voices discussing the fantastic flight. A lot of slip-stick, wishful thinking.

"Bill, if you hold a 50-degree angle after the pull-up," Pettingall retraced the flight path with a stubby piece of chalk, "the thrust will get you there."

I didn't comment. When they had finished kicking it around, I had decided to follow their plan although I had little faith in it. I would follow their plan as long as it could be put into practice, but I would have my own plan to substitute.

"Okay. I'll do it. But it's my flight and, if it's all right with you, I'll use my own judgment as to whether or not to continue your plan."

It was agreed. The flight would be truly experimental. There would be no hard set of rules to follow. I organized my own flight plan as a substitute for the way the theorists wanted the altitude hop to be handled.

The projectile theory was this: I was to pick up 1.2 G's at Mach 1.12 in the climb and then constantly increase the angle of attack. Almost straight up.

My own plan was to hold the best climbing Mach number and keep on climbing at the angle it gave me until the rockets quit, then pull the wheel back on my chest and wait for her to mush out.

Back at Edwards, Carder was elated over the flight for maximum altitude scheduled for the coming week end, more excited than I had ever seen him. The idea of hitting extreme new altitudes in the Skyrocket appealed to his imagination far more than the speed runs. His enthusiasm spread through the rest of the group. Carder hadn't been in on the conference and he wasn't entirely familiar with the principles upon which the flight was being based. But he didn't seem too worried. Carder left the flight up to me; his only comment was, "For God's sake, use your head. don't get in so deep you can't get out."

The rest of the group of flight-test engineers gave no advice. They stood expectantly back to watch the show and speculate on the outcome. There seemed to be a difference in opinion among the three sectors of theorists as to what to expect on the journey into the stratosphere. The Testing Division at Santa Monica held a slightly different idea of how to handle the flight than did hte aerodynamicists, who designed the plane, at the El Segundo plant. Even the flight-testing crew at Edwards, who had no real say in the coming flight, held slightly diverse ideas. No one could say for sure. I still remained a matter of exploration.

Amid all the opinions and conjectures I attempted to remain detached. I listened to all the possibilities and formulas, but it was my own experience in the airplane that I relied upon solely this time—something I would never have dared to do two years ago. Unless I received an order to do otherwise, I would follow my own light in this matter. If I strenuously disagreed with the order I could challenge it. It was my neck.

One of the possibilities that intrigued the flight-test crew standing by in the desert for the week-end flight was how she would behave if she got into a spin in the extreme altitude. I listened uncomfortably to the talk.

"If she goes into a spin, George, what do you think? Will she fall forward or backward?"

"She should fall forward. Chances of the controls being effective in air that thin are slim. It would be impossible to damp it out." And so it went.

The speed runs were more carefully controlled, bitten off a hunk at a time. The achievement had been gradual, enthusiasm suppressed. This flight was different. We were going to try for maximum results the first time, and the plan for the flight three days away was wide open. I felt very much alone.

The three days were busy. Special bottles were supplied to the pressure suit in order to accommodate the longer journey. The suit mechanism was carefully adjusted to bear down harder to meet conditions at 15 miles up. An angle-of-attack instrument was added to the crowded control panel. And inside the inert Skyrocket, receiving a new layer of lacquer for her next performance, I sat hunched over the stick practicing the movements I would be making every second of the flight. When I had finished my afternoon's rehearsal before the morning of flight, Ponder, the painter who was meticulously applying her last coat of lacquer, complained as I backed down the ladder, "Try to leave some paint on it this time, will you?"

It was four o'clock and not noticeably cooler than it had been at high noon. The pool would be full of kids and the laughter of the officers' wives. By five the sun would be behind the mountain on the west end of the valley and I could take a walk. I wanted to move my body and I wanted quiet.

Through the shallow waves of heat that rose from the concrete runway I walked toward the flight that waited for me tomorrow morning. It was as it had been two years ago when I first saw the Skyrocket, the way it was before my first flight in her, only now I lacked the faith that accompanies inexperience. Suppose I should follow the theorists' plan, about which I had reservations, too far? I would be unable to retreat. It would require all of my meager resources to execute this flight successfully.

Two years ago when I came out into the desert to fly the Skyrocket, I held an exalted belief in the engineers. They had a mysterious knowledge; they could tell me what to expect from the ship before it was demonstrated. My faith was great. But in unexplored areas no one could known for sure. They had not always predicted accurately. No longer did I have the final authority to look to for security. The responsibility for my neck now, I knew, rested on my own judgment. Independent of the theories, I had to depend on myself.

At the edge of the runway that dissolved into the sterile, sun-seared desert I turned and headed back to the dark of my room to lie in the cool of the air-conditioning until it was time for dinner. The room was a cell and the flight plan posted in Carder's empty office hung in my mind like a sentence.

At seven that evening I moved through the heat, dimensional like fog, thick enough to cup in my hand. It clung to my clothes. It was too hot to eat. I ate lightly with George Mabry and Ted Just. We discussed the flight a little and after dinner I went down to the hangar to visit the Skyrocket one more time before the flight.

The crew had completed preparing her for tomorrow. The cockpit was sealed with tape and a guard stood watch over her. There was nothing more to do. It was nine o'clock. Too early to sleep. I gathered up a week's supply of dirty socks and carried them into the communal washroom where, with deliberation, in one of the small, round, chipped bowls I washed out the six pair.

August 15, 1951. It was eight in the morning when I walked into Al's office. The flight was called for ten.

"You all set?" Al asked perfunctorily.

"Uh-huh."

"Well, just use your head, that's all," Carder anxiously swallowed the last dregs of coffee from the paper cup on his desk. "Incidentally, we got an order from Heineman's office this morning . . . after the rockets quit don't keep on going up. Push over immediately."

A last-minute decision toward conservatism. It was all right with me. "Immediately?" I wanted to be sure.

"Immediately."

"They're a bunch of sports, aren't they?"

Carder shook his head. "They can't swear to the stability of the plane at the high angle Santa Monica has proposed. At the altitude you'll reach they won't take responsibility for the safety of the plane if you don't nose her over when the rockets give out."

Perhaps we would be allowed another flight for altitude. On the next one I wouldn't push over; I'd pull the stick back and keep going. I could afford to be conservative the first time. I'd follow the design offices' advice.

Carder asked, "What do you think?"

"If that's what the man says, that's what he says."

There was no horseplay this morning, no labored wisecrack. My associates were vaguely ill at ease when they greeted me. I suppose it was because I was more preoccupied than usual. The crew picked up the mood. They waited for me to open any conversation and they were more attentive than usual. Before I could ask for anything it was right there. I was grateful for the silence. Horseplay takes time and effort; it breaks the chain of thought. There had been other mornings when I had restrained myself from cutting a well-meant joke with, "Shut up." It was sometimes awkward and taxing to be obliged to make the effort of a retort.

The hoses had been withdrawn from the Skyrocket and the last lacing had been adjusted on the "corset." Everything was in order. George received his okay to take off and the big bomber began to jog along the runway.

This flight will be discovery. I will know a thing I have never known before. Mixed with the clinical thoughts of how to handle the ship and the familiar counterpoint of the fear syndrome, today there is expectancy. Adventure. Before, the flights have been carefully controlled. Today I am going to let her go as far as she will. It is up to her.

Time! It will begin in ten seconds. A new road. The chase plane at this end checks in and stands by. Silence connects me now to the two chase planes, the men who wait on the ground, the mechanics in the hangar—clustered around loud-speakers as if for the last game of the World Series—the control tower, and Jansen who holds the pickle in his hand ready to count off the ten remaining seconds of security that I have snug in the womb of the mother ship. Now!

"Four . . . three . . . two . . . one," I hold the cold wheel in my bare hands and lean forward, Drop!"

Four buttons down. One, two, three, four, and four gigantic blow-torches rumble into life. Mathematical at the beginning. A formula of numbers. Breathe air on the count of 1001, blow it out at 1005. Around the corner, feel it, at 1.2 G's. Going up. The numbers on the dials, .85 on the Machmeter. Hold it ! Everest's voice in the F-86 counting, "One is good, two is good, three is . . . good." The report from the chase plane fades into distance. It is faraway and barely audible now, . . . "He's got all four!"

The needle on the indicated air speed falls off as the number .85 holds on the Machmeter. Change the numbers on the dials now. The needles slide up and down and around--.85 becomes Mach 1, she bumps into the quiet area and the high-drag rise of the shock waves. The larger altimeter hand winds up to 42,000, 43,000, reeling off the altitude. No pushover. Straight up. All the way, bending back a little more, a little more. The only world I am aware of is the world of dial eyes in front of me. The perpendicular light on the newly installed angle-of-attack instrument creeps up steadily as I move the stabilizer trim switch. Zut . . . zut. Zut . . . zut, pointing her nose higher, a little bit higher.

I follow the plan of the aerodynamicists in the Testing Division at Santa Monica. It looks like it is going to work after all. Five dials. A constant check as they all speak at once. Indicated air speed, Mach needle, angle-of-attack light, the rocket-seconds that remain, and the reeling off of the altimeter hand. Reeling off 57,000, 58,000, it rapidly reels back every 1000 feet I climb through.

In the thin air, actually, she does not want to fly but miraculously she does; she is held by a fantastic power that takes over. A ball atop a slim stick, she maintains an uncanny balance in the unresisting, weak air. She is going up at such speed that in reality she is close to stall. We are buoyed on a pivot that keeps us in balance. Although I am acutely aware of this circumstance, I am not alarmed by it. I am reluctant to believe she will not continue to fly.

Fifty-nine thousand, 60,000, reeling off 61,000. I have left the world. There is only the ship to identify myself with, her vibrations are my own, I feel them as intensely as those of my body. Here is a kind of unreality mixed with reality that I cannot explain to myself. I have an awareness that I have never experienced before, but it does not seem to project beyond this moment. Every cell, fluid, muscle of my body, is acutely awake. Perception is enormously exaggerated— black is blacker, white is whiter. Silence is more acute. It is the tender edge of the unknowable. And with this adrenalin-inflicted state floats the feeling of detachment.

It is an incompatible set of emotions I experience. Fear seems to be independent, a ghost sitting on my shoulder. And although it is most surely there, I am anesthetized to its warnings. I am without anxiety. I am powerless to anticipate what will happen the next moment. Time is now. Nothing but this experience is significant now. The rocket pressures are meaningless, the world of figures and equations that a second or two ago held such urgency have no reality in the face of this reality. I have the unshakable feeling that no matter what the instruments read, it will have no effect on the power that is making this ship fly. An independent, supernatural kind of power she has. She is alive with her own unknowable and unmovable power. I have complete faith, a faith that wraps me like a warm blanket now, that she will not be interrupted in this freedom.

Sixty-two thousand, 63,000 feet reeling off, reeling off the climb. The left wing is dropping! I respond automatically with no alarm, a robot racking in aileron against the dipping wing. I watch the eyes in front of me. The instruments stand out brighter—64,000 feet on the altimeter, reeling away . . . the Mach number . . . the rocket-seconds left to spend. Gently the wayward wing eases down again. Aileron full throw against it. No response this time. No effect. The wing keeps on going down. I kick the rudder against it but, of course, the rudder is locked. Seventy thousand feet. Check the Mach number: 1.4. I know I must bring her nose down. I am reluctant to reduce the altitude but I must; she will surely roll otherwise. Now slowly the aileron control comes back and I can once more return the ship to the nose-high attitude. Zut, zut, the pole-nose moves up. Seventy-five thousand feet. Again the wing dips. I ease the pole down once more and bring the wing level. It is a matter of easing her along the steep path tenderly. Give a little and grab a little. Seventy-six thousand feet registers on the dial and the rockets sputter off.

From hours of rehearsal my hand automatically hits the stabilizer switch for the pushover. It is with elation I feel the great force that shoves her over the top at .5 G. Even without the rockets she still has enough power to climb higher. Next time I will convert this energy to more altitude. In the arc she picks up a couple of thousand feet. The altimeter stops its steady reeling and swings sickly around 80,000 feet. The altitude is too extreme for the instrument to function.

Eighty thousand feet. It is intensely bright outside; the contrast of the dark shadows in the cockpit is extreme and strange. It is so dark lower in the cockpit that I cannot read the instruments sunk low on the panel. The dials on top, in the light, are vividly apparent. There seems to be no reflection; it is all black or white, apparent or nonapparent. No half-tones. It is a pure, immaculate world here.

She levels off silently. I roll to the right and there it is. Out of the tiny window slits there is the earth, wiped clean of civilization, a vast relief map with papier-mâché mountains and mirrored lakes and seas. The desert is not the same desert I have seen for two years; it is a pale brown hole bordered by dwarf mountains that run into other dwarf mountain chains that plait into other chains down to the Gulf of California and the Republic of Mexico. The coastline is sharply drawn with little vacant bays and inlets, a lacy edge to the big brown pieces of earth that dissolve into grays and the glimmer of lake puddles cupped in mountaintops and back to brown, gray, and finally the enormous black-blue of the Pacific. A globe-world in a planetarium, the earth curves to the south.

It is as if I am the only living thing connected to this totally strange, uninhabited planet 15 miles below me. The plane that carries me and I are one and alone.

There is a world down there and it must be revisited. There is the turn back to the place where the field is a pinpoint on the globe under me. The only way back from the springboard I am on has to be from memory, automatic. This, now, is the payoff for my preflight conditioning, for the drills, for the memorizing of steps back. Without this conditioning I am sure at this moment that I would not be able to return quickly enough from the euphoric state that holds me.

Following the steps mechanically, I am able to enter the turn. I am on my descent and slowly I return to what I knew before. Again I hear myself laboring for oxygen inside the helmet, and the world under me comes gradually into focus as something identifiable with life. At 15,000 it is comfortingly familiar. I take the face-place out of the helmet and breathe air again, deeply, and I am back, fully returned to time and dimension and the brief span that is allowed me.

C H A P T E R   X X I I I

The Skyrocket's steep ascent into the low-pressure area, where nothing from the earth had ever ventured, had been tracked by NACA's radar equipment. When I returned the empty Rocket to the lake, dead-stick, for the seventh time, Al Carder was pretty sure where the ship had been. The official word would come out of the photo lab later in the afternoon but the radar gave a close reading.

Carder was the first one to greet me. He was grinning and he did a thing he had not done in the two years I had been flying his ship. He put his hand out warmly and delivered a succinct speech.

"Congratulations, Bill." He was pleased. "Thanks to you, I don't have to apologize when the brass drifts through the hangar. I can say,

'Yes. This aircraft has been to Mach 1.88 and close to 80,000 feet.' It'll be a long, long time before any plane can top that!"

The rest of the group smiled happily. They wore the quiet air of relief that comes after months of work and tension. They hadn't much left for celebration.

I turned away from the engineers to watch the Skyrocket being towed lifelessly across the lake. *Baby, I beat you again!* I felt a big release. The kind of release that would make me sleep for 24 hours. The pressure had been removed; no matter how many more flights we could talk the Navy into, we wouldn't go much beyond the speed and altitude marks of the past week. The big job was completed.

Back in the hangar, the mechanics who had heard the flight over the loud-speaker were proud of their ship. Eddie Ayers was the first to say anything. "Hey, Bridge," he called, "you been after it a long time . . . I guess you really made it today. Congratulations." One by one the others came up to me.

That was all. The day settled into routine while we waited for the film. By three o'clock it came out 79,000 feet, about what we figured. I was as tired as I have ever been in my life, but after I received the official news I drove out of the desert, down to my apartment on Hermosa Beach. Three hours later I was calling the girl who waited to hear from me and then I fell asleep without dinner. It was eight o'clock the following morning when I woke up.

Saturday came up one of those rare, sparkling California days with a steady, cool breeze coming in over the surf. On the beach the incredibly pretty brown girls and the Saturday-dedicated guys lay stretched out in the warmth of the morning. It was a clean, soothing kind of warmth with the sun far away, touching you through sea-breeze-cleaned air. The desert and the Skyrocket and the big experimental flights into the future seemed far away for another week end.

Patty Godsave, a soft girl with a soft, low voice, dug her elbow into the sand and propped her head up on her hand. "Bill, you seem to be so darned relaxed this week end. What's happened anyway?"

I wanted to tell everybody that I had done it, but the results of yesterday's flight were secret. It would be a year before the actual speed and altitude figures were released.

"Oh, you think so? Well, maybe I am a little." The tension of the last six months must have showed more than I thought. "We've been working toward something for two years and yesterday I think we made it." The week end was a secret celebration.

Monday morning I stopped by the Santa Monica office to see if a flight had been scheduled out at the lake.

Bob Brush was the first one to see me come in. "Well, nice of you to get up this morning." It was around ten o'clock.

"Oh, well, I thought I better get down here to give Don junior a hand. As a matter of fact I've been over at the hangar since seven." The remark unleashed the usual banter, with everybody joining in. There was always time to kill in the pilots' office while the men wait for airplanes to fly or study or outsmart.

When things calmed down I walked over to my desk and put in a call to the Flight Test Center. Carder gave me the news. "We got the TWX this morning, Bill. The Navy has ordered us to transfer the ship."

"That isn't it, is it?"

"Not necessarily. It will depend on what Santa Monica decides."

Johnny Martin was not in his office. He would have the word. While I waited for the chief test pilot to show up, I went through a sizable pile of mail. With some amazement I opened two letters addressed to me written by young ladies I had never met. One from Germany, one from Virginia. At the bottom of the pile were a couple of requests for pictures from some junior spaceman. I was embarrassed the please.

After the office had settled back to the financial page or a flight report, Bob Brush came over to my desk and shook my hand. "It was a hell of a long, nasty program and it ended up the way we all hoped it would. You did a great job, Bill." The others began to sidle over one at a time, Larry Peyton, Russ Thaw, Bob Rahn, and the rest. All the old-timers. They asked about the flight. Soon I was into stories about the Skyrocket. As I talked the audience grew. I noticed that the younger and newer pilots were the last ones to join the circle, but nevertheless it was a proud hour.

I was on my way back from lunch when Johnny Martin caught up with me in front of the 30th Street entrance. "Hey, Bill, wait a minute. I want to talk to you." He waved me over to a bus bench.

"We got a TWX from the Navy this morning. They want us to turn the ship over to NACA as of Wednesday morning."

"Yeah, I just talked to the lake. Al told me."

"What's she got left? What do you think she'll do, Bill?"

"I think she's got more altitude. Maybe a couple thousand feet if I pull the stick back and let her go instead of pushing over. There seemed to be a lot of energy in the pushover that could be converted to climb."

"A couple more thousand feet, huh? What about Mach number?"

"Maybe five-one-hundredths of a Mach number. We can probably get her up to 1.93 . . ."

Johnny didn't wait for me to go on. "Look, before we have a mishap, let's knock it off." He was telling me that the program was over, that the company didn't want to risk a pilot or the plane on a better record. In the background I could hear him saying, "The old man is very satisfied with the results of the program, he called me into his office this morning . . . we've had good luck so far, we've made big records . . ." Quietly, on a bench in front of the plant, the street already empty after the lunch hour, the two years were ended. The same as it was on Saipan when the order abruptly came to return home. The enemy you prepared for was removed. You stood with a barrel in your hand, ready to put it in place, when it suddenly was no longer necessary to complete the action. The movement had stopped. It was all over.

A couple of days passed before the reaction moved in solidly, before the unwinding process could set itself in motion. Johnny's announcement lifted a great weight, but it wasn't comfortable. It was like a big hang-over, a period of inertia. Gradually I began to see that I had been wound far tighter than I had been aware of these past six months, this past year. Something had happened to me during the program, something so gradual I never noticed it. Removing the object that brought about the alteration made it apparent. Now there was time to think about it and to analyze.

The week ends after flights had always been frantic. I allowed myself lots of drinking, lots of playing, before I went back to the isolation and concentration of planning and defending myself against the next flight. Now there was no next flight. Until Johnny talked to me on the bench I had done no long-range planning about anything other than the Skyrocket. She inadvertently ran my life. If a situation required patience or even the time to understand it, I turned my back. No complications. It had to be all fun and games. There just wasn't time for anything else.

My mind and body were regimented to meet emergencies. If someone touched my shoulder I was ready to spring; if the Skyrocket dipped her wing I was ready. I was finely conditioned to fight, but now there was nothing to fight and the muscles just didn't relax suddenly. It was going to take time. I tried to plan life without the Skyrocket, to put something in her place. I reached for something and nothing was there. The house was bare—like a woman gone. It was an uneasy period of frustration.

A goal had been reached, but there was no reward waiting. The reward had been already paid me while I painfully made my way toward the goal. To reach it was empty.

The end of the first week without the Skyrocket I flew out to Muroc to pick up my gear. It was the last day of school. Some of the crew who had been with her four years were cleaning out their desks. They would go back to Santa Monica for reassignment to new programs. Others were staying to work on the A4D and the F4D, which would soon be coming into the hangar.

In her dark lair, unattended, the white airplane stood dressed and immaculately intact, ready to be delivered next door. No crew worked over her preparing her for flight today. A mechanic hooked her to the back of a jeep. He slapped her high, graceful tail: "She's been a nice old lady."

"Yeah. She was." We were alone in the hangar.

The mechanic climbed into the jeep and then leaned down. "Would you like to go with me?"

"No. You do the honors."

Serenely, the beautiful white ship glided behind the jeep across the flight apron toward the group of men, standing outside the open NACA hangar door, who waited to receive their new airplane. I would never have another flight in her.

Two weeks later the news of the big altitude gain was released. Again, as it had been a month ago when the speed record was broken, I uneasily saw my face on the front page beside a bold, black headline.

> A Navy Skyrocket, piloted by Test Pilot Bill Bridgeman, broke its own and all existing altitude records . . . the exact altitude reached by the supersonic airplane was not revealed. Bridgeman's flight topped the officially recognized record of 72,394 feet established in 1935 by a man-carrying balloon. The Navy announced that this latest flight by Bridgeman successfully concludes the first phase of a research and development program three years old. The plane will be turned over to the National Advisory Committee on Aeronautics for the next phase of a planned research program . . .

Momentarily the publicity was enjoyable, sort of a private joke seeing my face on the front page of my morning paper. But it was the Skyrocket who had done it. Any satisfaction I got out of the records was the fact that I hadn't kept the Skyrocket from fulfilling her potential, that I had been able to handle her.

At first the attention brought on by all the fanfare was a welcome distraction. Something was going on. It helped the hangover. I found I was some kind of a celebrity. I found myself at the head table being introduced to a roomful of brass, in front of TV cameras, on radio shows; automobile companies were asking me to endorse their product; and there were writers—newspaper, magazine, and free-lance writers—who made appointments with me. Articles began appearing with a man-from-Mars slant. people I hardly knew asked me to attend cocktail parties: "This is the fastest man in the world" . . . like a new vase stuck in a corner. The people I met regarded me as unusual, an oddity: *"How does it feel?"* I could not tell them how it *feels* and they would excuse themselves and go get another drink. To avoid any further disappointment I eventually invented a set of answers that seemed to be more the sort of thing the inquirers wanted to hear. A stock one was, "It feels like you've got a bull by the horns." They seemed to like that.

I found that nobody wanted to hear that it was clean and very bright at 80,000 feet, so I told them, "Above 72,000 feet it is very dark blue with flashes of red and multicolored strips. The earth is a smudge."

Chuck Yeager was a frequent companion at symposiums. Invariably bored, we ate our way through chicken and shriveled peas at speakers' tables across the country, where we suffered through several hours of important speeches and escaped together into the night as soon as we could.

One particular evening Chuck was introduced as "the man who first poked a hole through the sound barrier." Chuck bowed and made his usual stock speech. Then I was introduced as the highest and fastest man . . .

"There was really nothing to it—I just found one of Chuck's holes and went on through." Chuck was very cool the rest of the evening.

Still the wave I was riding wasn't big enough to wash away the aimless, lost restlessness that ate at me. I began to think that maybe it was because I missed flying. All I needed was a good wringing out and I would be all right. I had been away from an airplane for some time.

When I returned from New York and Washington where I had delivered speeches to branches of the Institute of Aeronautical Sciences, I drove over to El Segundo to fly one of Brownie's AD's. It didn't help. The little fighter, awkward and noisy compared to the Skyrocket, felt like a truck. Where was the speed? In a steep dive she shook and groaned at 400 mph. I pulled G's and split S's until I was worn out, but the exercise in the AD only exaggerated the vacancy in me. I would never get my hands on another airplane like the Skyrocket.

Three weeks, four weeks passed by with no assignment. The

company was giving me a vacation of sorts. Every morning I reported upstairs to the flight-test office, read my mail, and about noon slipped out to go surfing at Malibu's Paradise Cove.

Then one morning Johnny called me into his office. "Bill, we would like you to take a look at the X-3. Maybe you would like to test her. She's in the final stages now over in Hangar Three. Go over and take a look at the mock-up. See what you think."

The X-3. I had heard vaguely about an experimental ship that was mysteriously taking form behind locked doors. This was it. Only a couple of pilots had seen it, Gene May, Johnny Martin, and Benny Howard. Santa Monica plant Chief Engineer Ed Burton had been working on it for nearly ten years with a whole floor full of engineers. According to Johnny she was the first practical supersonic design, capable of flying at sustained speeds only touched briefly by the Skyrocket. A "going" supersonic airplane.

On the ground floor in front of a door marked KEEP OUT. SECRET PROJECT MX656, a company policeman stood guard. Cautiously he scrutinized my pass.

"Okay." He slapped it back into my hand and opened the door.

"God!" Poised menacingly in the center of the room was a full-sized mock-up of the most extraordinary aircraft I had ever seen, a sinister, 45-foot-long, out-of-this-world design that looked incapable of flight. The Skyrocket was an airplane—but not this thing. This was a new breed, all long, narrow body wrapped tightly around twinjet engines bulging out from her sides that tapered into an enormously long projectile nose. Far back out her engine-fat sides protruded thin, straight, stubby mirror-metal wings. The wing span looked no wider than the tail section of a DC-3, but the weird craft was every foot as long.

This ship was designed to handle in the new area the way AD's or jet fighters now handled at subsonic speeds. It was being offered to me to prove the designers' claims There would be nothing like her flying for probably another five or six years. This was *tomorrow*. And although I had felt the old restlessness, I hadn't expected to meet a bigger challenge than the one I had just left. I was not sure. Here was the most unholy-looking machine I had ever seen, a sinister hybrid.

After knowing the Skyrocket for two years, it was a wiser and warier old test pilot who walked toward the sharklike airplane. The Skyrocket was a beauty and a "going" concern when I took her over and now, looking doubtfully at the X-3, I thought of first flight—the thing every pilot dreads in testing. What would it be like the morning I had to prove for the engineers whether or not she was capable of flight? Out in the cold, barren lake this winter—a sterile bird sitting on a dead planet, waiting for me. It would be first flight in a thing that didn't even look like an airplane, that had never been off the ground—it was a far greater risk.

There also was the tremendous responsibility of doing a competent job. Ten years of labor, and something more, faith given by 500 engineers, designers, draftsmen, and aerodynamicists, had gone into the strange design. She was designed to go through the supersonic high-drag rise like a warm spoon through ice cream; at speeds above 650 mph she was supposed to come into her element. But what happened at speeds below 650? The problem was suddenly reversed. Low speed would be an added enemy this time. Those stubby little wings couldn't possibly support that huge, bulging frame at low speed. No wonder she would need to land at over 250 miles per hour. What tires would support that kind of wear? A blowout at that speed and I would "have had it."

The radical X-3 was scheduled to slip through Mach 1 and 'way beyond at sustained supersonic speed up to the "heat barrier." The Rocket had touched such speeds but for no more than a couple of minutes—not long enough to allow the intense heat she created by her own friction to cause any structural damage. This ship was scheduled to remain at such speeds for a sustained period. She had been provided with a cockpit refrigeration system and materials strong enough to pass through the new barrier—according to the engineers. The last group were not always right. But experimental flights wouldn't be necessary if the answer was already known. The hypothesis must be proved.

I climbed aboard. In order to get into the cockpit, the seat was mechanically lowered to the ground. There was a button that raised the elevator. It buzzed ominously as it very slowly lifted me into the nose. Visibility was extremely poor from her windows, they ere faired-in exaggerations of the Skyrocket's slits. It was impossible to see the ground. The thin, insecure-looking wings were so far in back of me that they were out of sight. It would take some weighing to decide whether or not I wanted to bet my life on the integrity of this ship. Perhaps the security of the past several months was more comfortable than I had supposed.

I was *afraid* to take on this airplane. I was also *afraid* someone else would accept the challenge. And I was *afraid* that I would decide to accept it.

Here it was before me again. Liberty. The chance to reach out, to move on. It wore a fearful face, it was a nasty-looking beast, it promised no security, but it moved forward.

I pressed the button. *Buzz-z-z* and the seat descended to the floor, releasing me from the X-3. I turned my back on the austere experiment and headed out of the building into the light and warmth of noon. The sun was good on my back.

Johnny was waiting for me in his office—I'd see him early tomorrow morning instead. After all, there was no hurry about a decision. She wouldn't fly for almost a year.

And, although I gave myself the rest of the afternoon to choose a future—it was only the same old game. I knew the answer already.